The Australian
Decks & Pergolas
Construction
Manual

by

Allan Staines

Dear Pete and Sheila

This is your "homework" for when you come back to help us with our hovel.

Loadsa luv xxx

the Shearer—Boyd's

Pinedale Press

Other Books by the Same Author:
Take Me Back to the Eighties
 (A Pen and Ink Sketch Book of 19th
 Century Australian Homes & Buildings)
The Australian Owner Builders Manual
The New Zealand Owner Builders Manual
How to be a Successful Owner Builder &
 Renovator
The Australian Renovators Manual
The Australian Roof Building Manual
 (Hiddle & Staines)
Australian House Building the Easy Hebel Way
The Australian House Building Manual

Published by Pinedale Press

Text and illustrations © Allan Staines.
Apart from private study, research or review as permitted under the Copyright Act, no part by means of any process should be reproduced without written permission.

National Library of Australia
Cataloguing-in-publication data

Staines, Allan 1942
National Library of Australia card number and ISBN number 1 875217 10 X

Holder of Copyright
Pinedale Press
2 Lethbridge Court
CALOUNDRA QLD 4551
AUSTRALIA
For Orders, please fax (07) 5491 9219

Ist Edition	April	1995
2nd Edition	March	1996
Reprint	August	1997
Reprint	September	1998
Reprint	March	1999
Reprint	December	1999
Reprint	August	2000
3rd Edition	March	2001
Reprint	October	2001
Reprint	February	2002
Reprint	November	2003
4th Edition	November	2004

Timber Queensland & TDA ACKNOWLEDGEMENT

This manual was prepared in co-operation with Timber Queensland and TDA (The Timber Development Association of N.S.W.).

Source of Tables
The tables for timber members in pergolas and decks have been prepared by Timber Queensland using the 'Timber Solutions' design software and comply with AS1684.2.
The tables for post footing sizes have been prepared by the 'Timber Development Association (NSW) and comply with AS2870.

The Author and Publisher express their appreciation for their advice and for their wholehearted co-operation.

Appreciation to the Artist
Colour and ink renderings by Tina Homer created over structural and base line art designed by the Author.

To Noela Ollenburg for her computer skills in preparing this material.

Disclaimer
The author has attempted to ensure that the information contained in this manual is accurate as at the time it was written but the author and the publisher do not warrant that it is accurate. Persons intending to act on any information contained herein should first check all relevant national, state and local building laws and subordinate legislation, relevant Australian Standards and manufacturer's specifications or requirements. The author and the publisher are not liable for any loss, damage, cost or expense suffered or incurred arising directly or indirectly from the use or reliance on information, drawings, designs, data or other information contained in this manual. It is provided in good faith without express or implied warranty.

Product Related Disclaimer
All products suggested in this manual have been suggested in good faith. The author and the publisher do not endorse any of the products referred to. The author and the publisher will not be liable for any loss, damage, cost or expense suffered or incurred arising directly or indirectly from the use of any product. All persons should make their own independent enquiries of manufacturers to determine whether products are suitable and appropriate.

Contents

CH1 Designing & Estimating
Designing Decks & Pergolas	4
Preparing Plans for Council	6
Terminology & Abbreviations	7
Timbers to Use	8
Estimating the Cost	9

CH2 Deck Designs   10-20

CH3 Deck Construction
Footings & Post Supports	21-23
Post-to-Bearer Connections	24,25
Making Housings in Round Posts	24,25
Attaching Joists to Bearers	26
Attaching Decks to Walls	27
Bracing Decks	29,30
Concealing Bracing	31
Laying Decking (Flooring)	31-34
Waterproof & Tiled Decks	35-37
Building Outdoor Steps	38-40
Hand railing & Construction Details	40-45

CH4 How to Build Decks
How to Build Decks Attached to the House	46-50
How to Build a Freestanding Deck	51-55

CH5 Designing Pergolas
Pergola Design Ideas	56-65

CH6 Pergola Construction
Pergola Construction with or without Roof Cladding	66
Preparing a Plan	67

Pergola Posts, Columns & Footings	68
Post-to-Bearer Connections	68
Beam-to-Post Connections	68
Rafter-to-Beam Connections	68
Attaching Pergolas to the House	69-71
Bracing Pergolas	71,72

CH7 How to Build a Pergola   73-75
Painting & Preserving Decks & Pergolas	76

CH8 Deck & Pergola Tables

Tables 4, 5 & 6
	Deck & Pergola Post Footing Sizes	77,78
Table 7	Post Sizes for Decks or Pergolas	79
Table 8	Deck Bearer Sizes	79-81
Table 9	Deck Joists	82
Table 10	Decking (Deck Flooring) & Fastenings	82

Table 11, 12
	Stair Stringers & Treads	83

Table 13, 14,15
	Handrail Sizes & Spans	85-86
Table 16	Fastenings for Balusters/Infills	87
Table 17	Pergola Beams N1 to N2 (Non.Cycl).	88-89
Table 18	Pergola Beams N3 (Non Cyclonic) to C1 (Cyclonic)	89
Table 19	Pergola Beams N3 (Non Cyclonic) to C1 (Cyclonic)	90
Table 20	Pergola Rafters N1 to N2 (Non. Cycl.)	91
Table 21	Pergola Rafters N3 (Non Cyclonic) to C1 (Cyclonic)	92
Table 22	Pergola Roof Battens	92
Table 23	Pryda Post Anchors	93
Table 24	Pryda Framing Bracket (Joist Hanger) Design Loads	93

Table 25 & 26
	Pryda Bracket Sizes & Selection Chart	94

Explanation of Wind Categories

The design and dimensioning of timber framing, and other members is firstly determined by the wind category allocated to the individual building site.

The wind categories mentioned in tables in this manual are N1 to N4 (Non cyclonic) through to C1 to C2 (Cyclonic).

To determine the wind category for an individual site enquire at either the Local Authority Building Dept, a Local Designer, Architect or Engineer.

1 Designing & Estimating

Designing Decks & Pergolas

Decks and Pergolas serve varying purposes. Some are mainly constructed to provide a place to relax in the shade, while others provide a place in the sun. Decks and Pergolas can be located attached to the house to increase the living and entertainment areas of the house or can be sited away from the house to utilise a steep property or to surround a pool.

Decks should be designed for their intended use and consideration must be given to the following factors:

- a). **Aspect**
- b). **Privacy**
- c). **Views**
- d). **Proximity to Facilities**
- e). **Architectural Integration or Conformity to the House Style**
- f). **Timber** - *Species, Strength & Treatment Type*
- g). **Surface Coatings, Paints & Stains**

Aspect
For maximum use, decks and pergolas need to be sheltered from prevailing winds or wind screens provided. Similar considerations may need to be given to direct sunlight.

Privacy
Privacy can be achieved by constructing screens or planting appropriate trees where necessary.

Views
Take care that the handrail design will not obstruct views. Consider using clear panels such as safety glass.

Proximity to Facilities
Where the deck or patio is to be frequently used for entertaining or barbecuing, it may be practical to be in close proximity to the kitchen.

Architectural Integration or Conformity to the House Style
The deck or pergola and hand railing should be designed to suit the house period and style and not appear like an afterthought or add on.

Timber — Species, Strength and Treatment Type
See Page 8.

Surface Coatings, Paints & Stains
See Page 76.

What Size Deck

Establishing the required deck size is difficult for some folk.

The following suggestions may help in the decision.

Consideration must be made to the fact that decks have to be painted every six to eight years, more frequently if stains are used. However, apart from that, the criteria for size will vary from one situation to the next. If you have a very steep site unusable for any other purpose, you may desire a very large deck over some of the site to regain the use of the site.

Suggested Minimum Areas:
2-4 people with just table & chairs=3000x2400mm
4-6 people with just table & chairs=4000x3000mm
6-8 people with table & chairs & BBQ=4800x3600mm
8-10 people with table & chairs & BBQ=6000x3600mm

To help you decide, make a full size mock up of the proposed deck area by demarcating an area in one of your existing rooms or outdoors with a rope or similar and position some proposed typical items of furniture. Allow space to manoeuvre the chairs. Remember, that the deck is surrounded by handrailing not walls and so will feel more spacious than an enclosed room.

The Common Bearer Positions

When designing decks the handrails must be considered as they can't be just tacked on later. For safety reasons it is best to continue the bearer supporting posts through to handrail height, see more on this in Chapter 3.

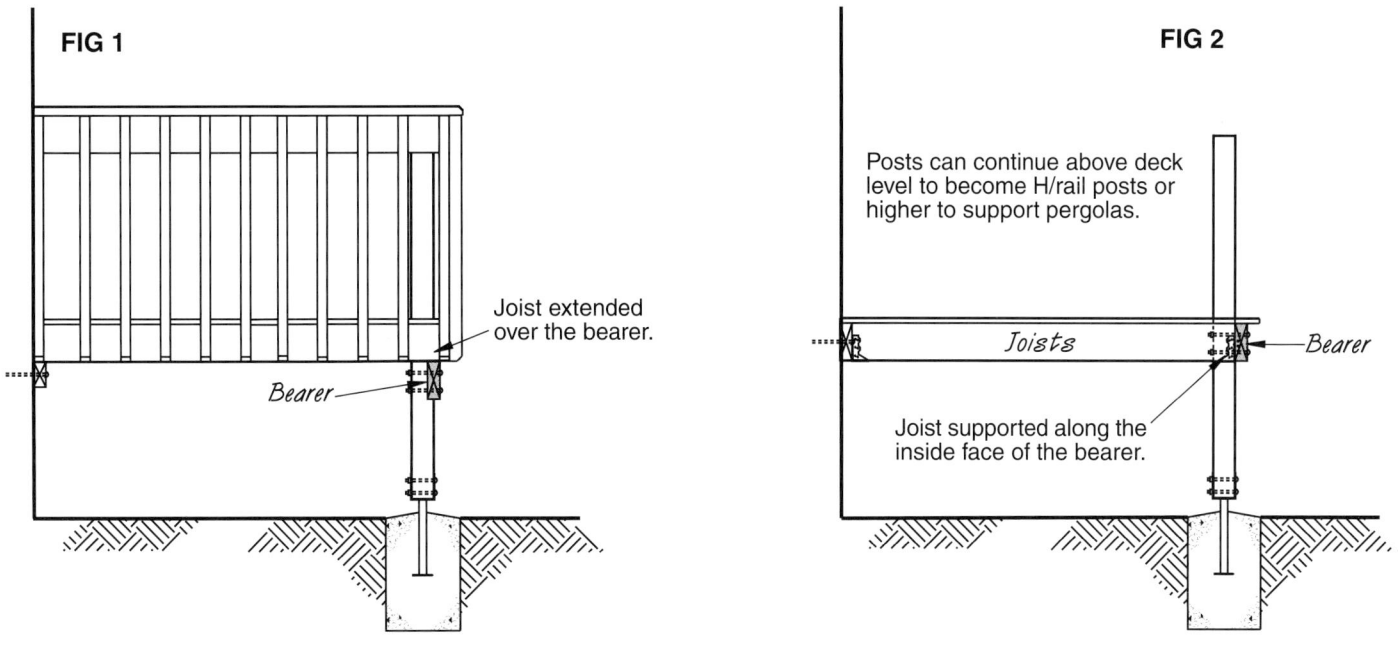

Trees Growing Through Decks

Constructing decks around existing trees or planting trees to grow through a deck especially shade trees can provide great benefits. However, you may consider deciduous trees to allow sunlight penetration during Winter.

When planting a tree, ensure it is sufficiently advanced to penetrate the deck from the outset to ensure it receives sunlight.

When laying the joists, allow sufficient space for the trunk to reach its mature circumference. This may mean that some temporary safety boards should be laid around the opening until the tree is further developed.

Trimmers

Provide trimmers to the opening sides to give a finished appearance as in fig 4.

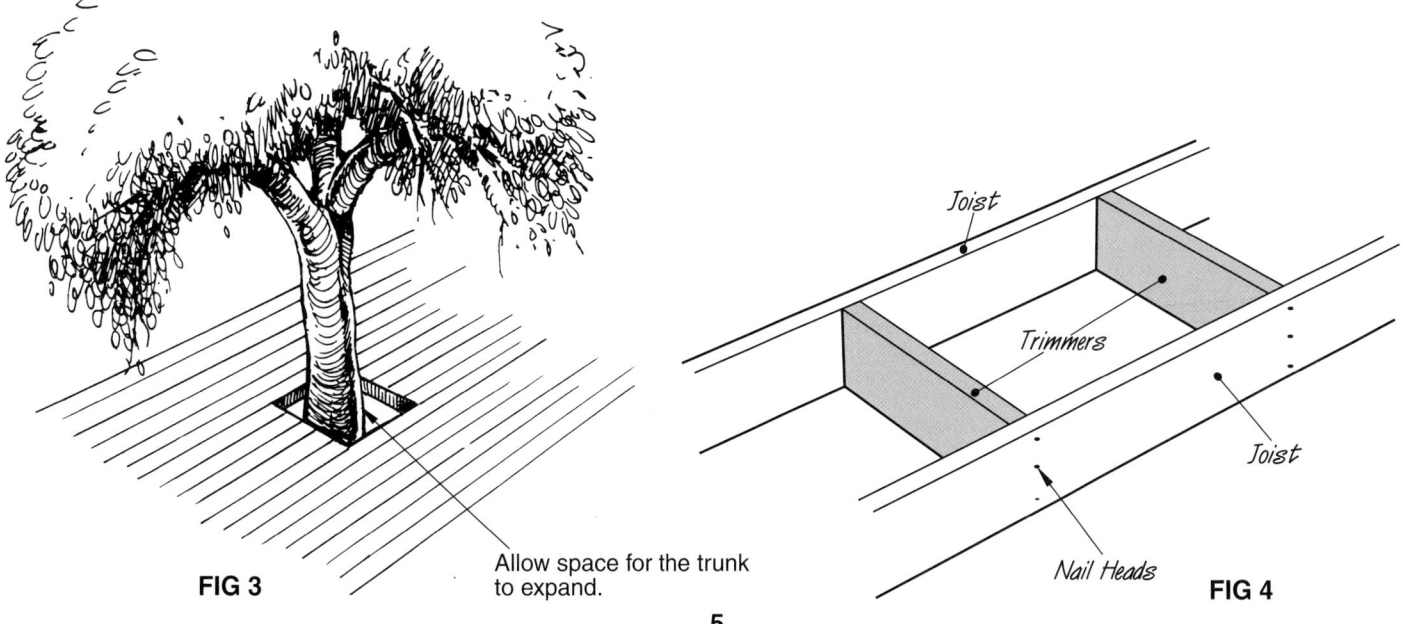

Preparing Plans

Council Approval

Check with the Local Council Building Department or Building Certifier if you require submission of a plan for approval before commencing.

Plans for submission to Council should contain the following:

a). *A Plan View* to scale 1:100 min. with width and length dimensions including post spacing.

b). *Side and End Elevations* to scale 1:100 min. with overall heights and hand rail height dimensioned.

c). *A Cross Section to Scale* 1:50 showing timber specifications and fastening types as in the typical plan below. Also footing dimensions.

d). *A Site Plan* to scale 1:500 min. showing the existing house with the deck delineated with hatching or similar.

Also required are:

Real Property Description, Allotment No., distances to boundaries and proposed means of disposing of storm water if guttering is applied to pergola roofs.

Three sets of the above plans should be submitted.

For your own benefit a plan with sections or details drawn at 1:50 or 1:25 scale will be of great benefit in accurately quantifying and costing the project and will help to avoid measuring and cutting errors.

EXAMPLE PLAN

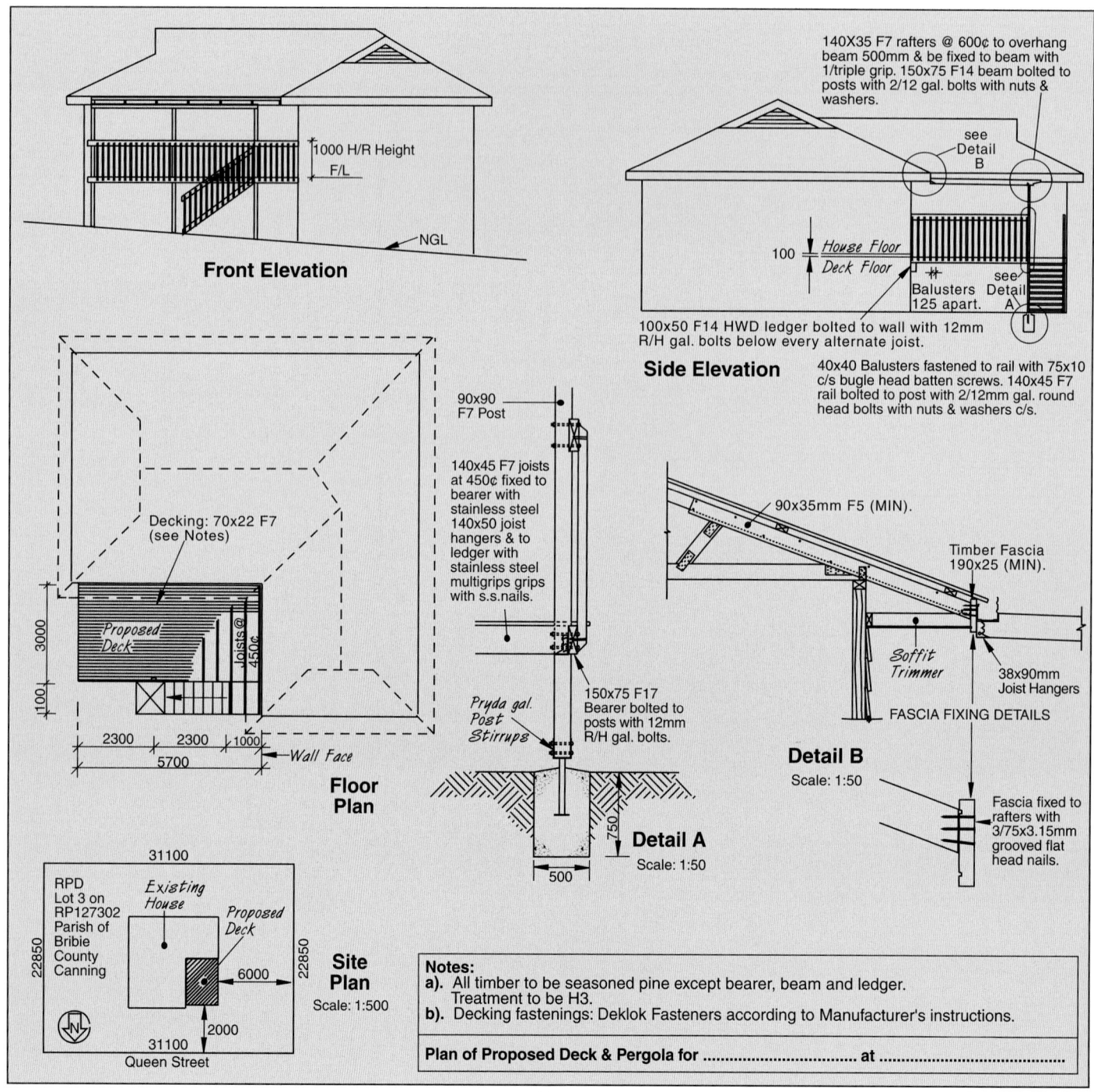

Terminology

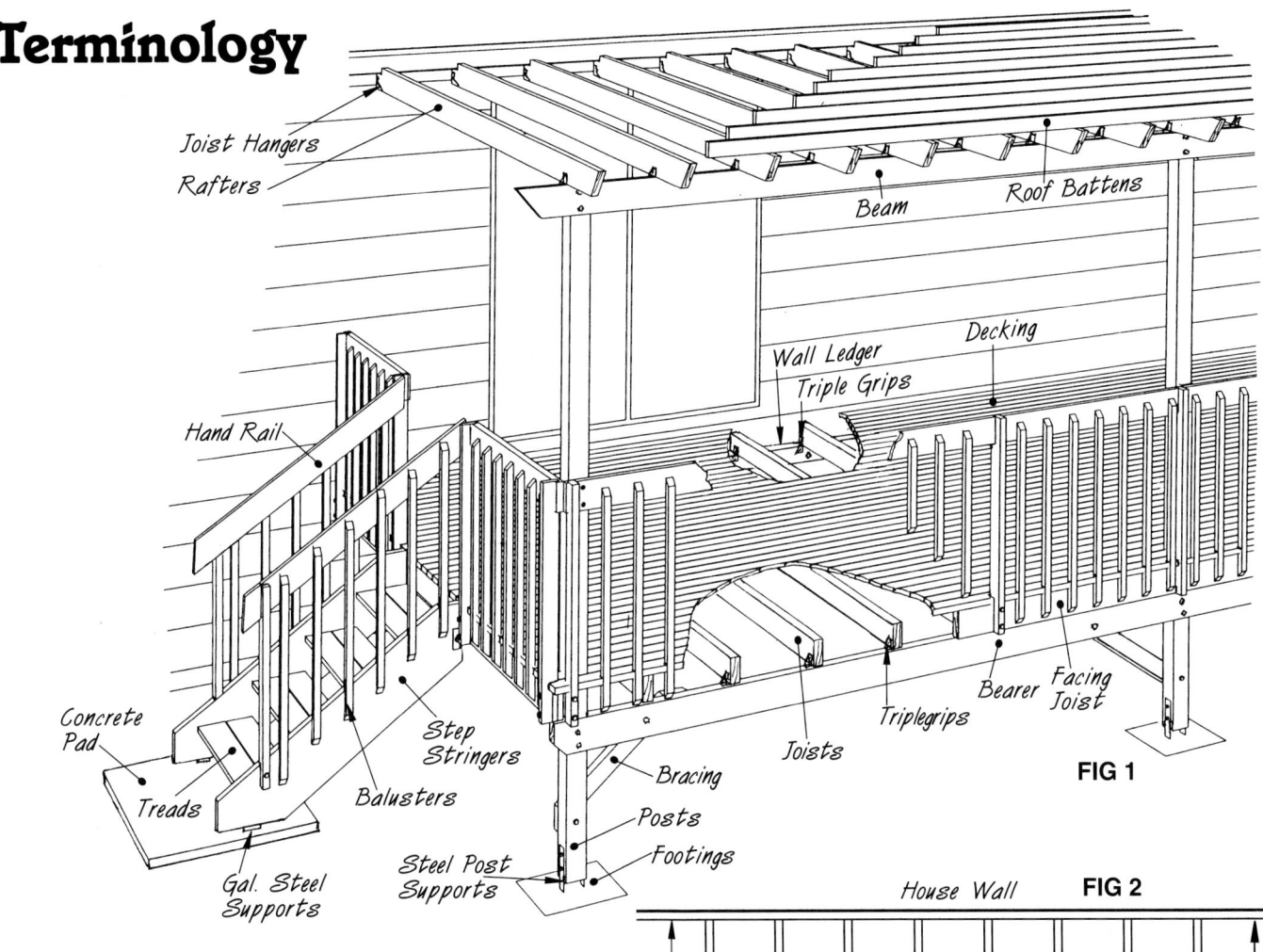

FIG 1

FIG 2

Spans & Spacings

The spans and spacings of bearers and joists determines their cross sectional dimensions see fig 2. The greater the spans and or spacings the deeper the member.

Building Abbreviations

accord.	according	M^2	Square Metre
A.S. (Code)	Australian Standards (Code)	M^3	Cubic Metre
¢, cts, crs	centres	m/s	metres per second
c/s	countersunk	min.	minimum
BCA	Building Code of Australia	mm	millimetre
bk	brick	manuf.	manufacturer
DAR	Dressed All Round	MPa	Mega Pascal Pressure
deg.	degrees	MS	Mild Steel
DPC	Damp Proof Course	NGL	Natural Ground Line
FC	Fibre Cement	N	North
flr	floor	Ø	diameter
F/L	Floor Line	O/H or O/HANG	OVERHANG
gal.	galvanising	R/H	Round Head
G/L	Ground Line	reinf.	reinforcing
H/R	Handrail	RPD	Real Property Description
hex. head	hexigon head	sq.	square
ht	height	SA	Standard Association of Aust.
HWD	Hardwood	SWD	Softwood
HT	Height	spec.	specification
kN	kilo Newtons force	s.s.	stainless steel
kPa	kilo Pascal pressure	WI	Wrought Iron
m	metre		

Timbers to Use

To select the right timber for use outdoors exposed to the weather or in-ground, you must consider the ability of the timber to resist rot and termites. Softwood treated according to the A.S. (Code) and the correct 'H' level for specific end use is suitable and some suppliers give a forty year guarantee. Common softwoods used for this purpose include Radiata, Slash and Hoop Pines.

Hardwoods of 'Durability Class 1' can be used in-ground while both Durability Classes 1 and 2 are suitable for above ground use. Any sapwood on hardwood should be very limited or be preservative treated to H3 or H5 see Table 1.

Cypress is suitable for decks and pergolas, however, for in-ground use, all sapwood must be removed unless only small amounts are present.

Inground Applications

Where possible it is best to attach posts to hot dip galvanised brackets or stirrups above ground. The brackets and stirrups are embedded into concrete in-ground. However, treated round posts are often applied directly inground or embedded in concrete or crusher dust.

The end portion of treated posts embedded in-ground in concrete or crusher dust *should not* be trimmed on-site otherwise the untreated core of the post will then be exposed. Pressure treatments sometimes *don't* penetrate to the central core of the timber. Preservative coatings applied after trimming *do not* provide as good a protection as pressure treatment.

Preservative Treatments Available

Four preservative treatments are commonly available, these are CCA (Copper Chromium Arsenic), ACQ (Ammoniacal Copper Quat), Copper Azole and LOSP (Light Organic Solvent Preservative). LOSP is not suitable for in-ground use.

'H' Treatment Levels

The treatment level in the timber will depend on the intended purpose. *For example,* timber used in- ground will require a higher treatment level than for above ground timber such as hand railing or for where the timber will be given opportunity to dry out quickly after wet weather. The level of treatment is prefaced by the letter 'H' (the initial of the word 'Hazard').

Treated timber marked H3 is suitable for above ground use **only** and H5 for inground. H4 is permissible in some states but is only suitable for moderate Hazard applications or non-structural applications. If in doubt, use H5.

Table 1 provides a description of treatments and end uses.

Dry-After-Treatment or Seasoned After Treatment

Dry-after-treatment or seasoned after treatment for softwoods is preferred as they will be more stable and give less movement on-site. The timber is firstly kiln dried to 10-15% moisture content then put through the vacuum pressure treatment to receive the preservative treatment then kiln dried again to 10-15% moisture content. Request 'Treated and Seasoned'. (This may *not* be available in hardwoods for framing).

IDENTIFIYING TIMBER LABELLING
Timber will be labelled on the end with numbers as per following example. Each group of numbers is for a different purpose:- **099   10   H4**
Treatment Plant No.   Preservation Code No.   Hazard Class No.

User Safety Precautions

The following safety precautions apply when using all preservative treated timbers.
a). Wear gloves
b). Wash hands and face before eating, drinking or smoking
c). When sanding timber, provide good ventilation and wear protective clothing plus dust mask
d). NEVER USE IN FIRES FOR HEATING, COOKING OR B.B.Q.'s.

TABLE 1   USING TREATED SOFTWOOD

END USE	'H' TREATMENT LEVEL
ABOVE GROUND for Posts in stirrups, bearers, joists, ledgers, handrails, step stringers, step treads, bracing timber, deck flooring, pergola beams, joists & battens.	H3 Common species Radiata, Slash Pine & Hoop
Should only be used for non-structural landscaping.	H4
IN GROUND or EMBEDDED IN CONCRETE Posts or stumps	H5
IN MARINE CONDITIONS Posts for decks or jetties	H6

F 'Ratings' or 'MGP' Grades

Specific 'F' ratings found in the Tables are values required for timbers to perform a specific task. The 'F' value is a stress grade designated to a particular piece of timber.

Another form of stress grade is designated as 'MGP'. MGP10 may be used in lieu of F5 and MGP12 in lieu of F7 or F8 softwood. The higher the stress rating the greater the strength. In many situations the higher stress rating may enable the use of smaller sectional sizes.

Seasoning

Seasoning is the term used for timber which has had its moisture content reduced by either kiln or air drying. Moisture control quantity is expressed in percentages e.g. 12% moisture content. Unseasoned and green timber is likely to shrink or suffer distortion (warping, bowing, etc) after installation. *Decking (flooring) is required to be seasoned.*

Estimating the Cost of Decks or Pergolas

NOTE: *The 'Materials List' below covers many situations.*

Before costing, rule a line through any listing which doesn't apply to your project.

LABOUR & MATERIALS	TYPE & QUANTITY	ESTIMATED COST

PRELIMINARY
    Plans
    Council Fees
    Other
		$

FOOTINGS
    Excavations or hole digging allow hourly rate of sub-contracted hole drilling machinery plus travelling time
    Concrete for stirrup holes (Ready-Mix add waiting time)
    Concrete Pump for difficult to access site & travelling time
    Labour to pour concrete and install posts or stirrups
    Other
		$

DECK OR PERGOLA TIMBERS
    Posts, ledgers, wall plates, bearers, beams, joists, deck flooring, rafters, battens, handrailing, step stringers & treads, timber bracing, temporary props or posts, profile (hurdle) timbers
    Other
		$

HARDWARE
    Gal. mild or s.s. steel post stirrups or brackets with gal. or s.s. bolts
    Ant capping if required
    Gal. or s.s. bolts to anchor bearers to posts, wall ledger to wall, handrailing to Deck
    Gal. or s.s. bolts or coach screws to anchor Pergola wall or fascia plate to the wall or fascia
    Gal. or s.s. bolts to anchor Pergola beam to posts
    Dynabolts, Trubolts or Chemset bolts for anchoring Decks, Pergolas or handrailing to masonry walls
    Timber Connectors- joist hangers (framing brackets), triple or multigrips, metal bracing if required, cyclone straps for rafters, joists or battens if required
    Connector nails or Pryda Product nails, other gal. or s.s. nails & screws
    Materials for Waterproof Decks - compressed fibre cement sheets, plastic membrane, Selleys 'Brick & Cement Crack Sealant', fastenings, joint foam beading, Hardies cellular PVC angles
    Paint, primers & top coats, nail hole wood filler
    *Hire of Equipment -*sawing & drilling equipment, nail fasteners, scaffolding
    Labour
    Other
		$

	TOTAL	$

2 Deck Designs

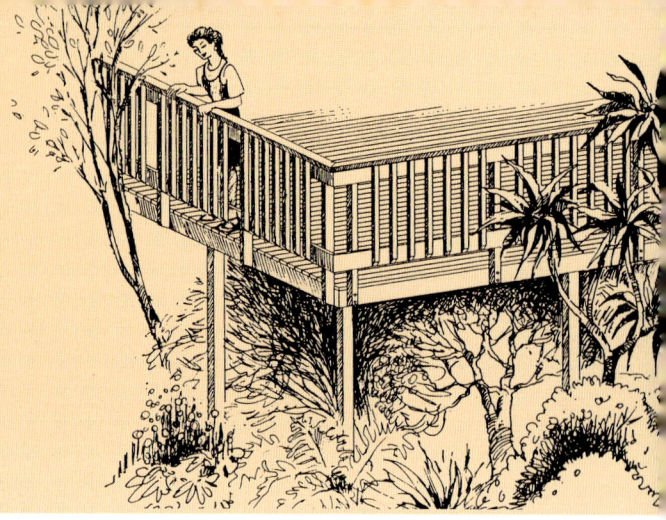

The following deck designs are intended to stimulate ideas and at the same time illustrate how a particular style or design will appear in a chosen setting.
You may find that one idea from one deck can be taken to compliment other features on another.

Corner Post
Bearer
Joist
Joist Hanger

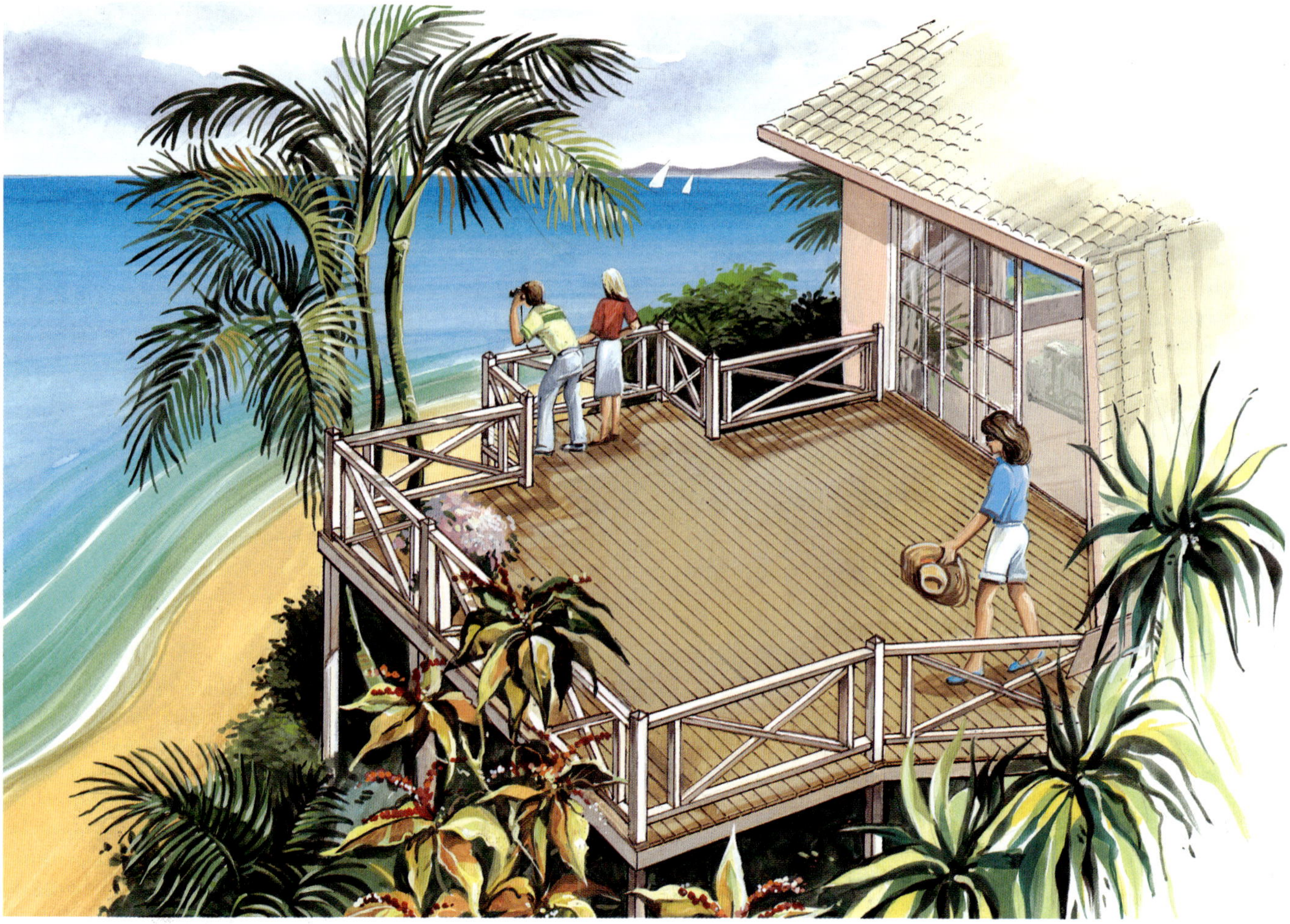

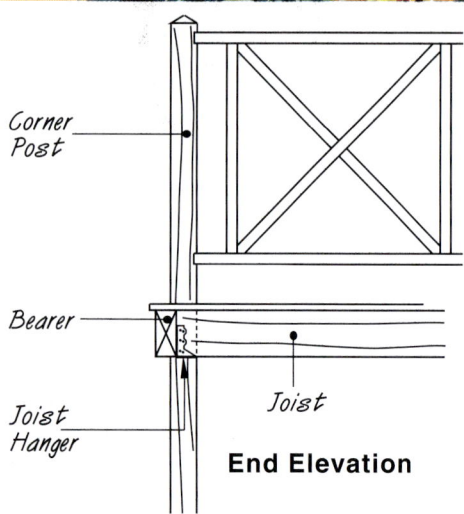

End Elevation

Note: Check Page 41 for BCA handrail requirements also the infil elements must *not* be climbable alternatively safety glass could be applied to prevent climbing.

In this design deck posts support the deck and then extend through to become handrail posts.

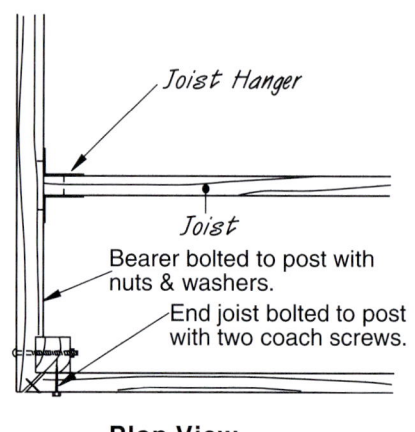

Joist Hanger
Joist
Bearer bolted to post with nuts & washers.
End joist bolted to post with two coach screws.

Plan View

The Freestanding Deck

Note: Check Page 41 for BCA handrail requirements also the infil elements must *not* be climbable alternatively safety glass could be applied to prevent climbing.

Freestanding Decks (those unattached to the house)

These can provide many benefits. Besides creating a totally separate recreation or relaxation area they can utilise a steep unmanageable site, take advantage of privacy, views or breezes or reduce the lawn mowing area of a large garden.

Take care in siting the freestanding deck that maximum use and advantage is made of existing plantings and views. An existing tree may be left in place and the deck constructed around its trunk. It may be necessary to raise the deck only a little to take advantage of a view. When designing to take advantage of a view, use a step ladder to carry out a siting from various heights.

Experiment with Different Shapes

At the planning stage be adventurous with the shape, don't allow tradition to limit your design possibilities. Various angles can set a deck completely apart from the ordinary.

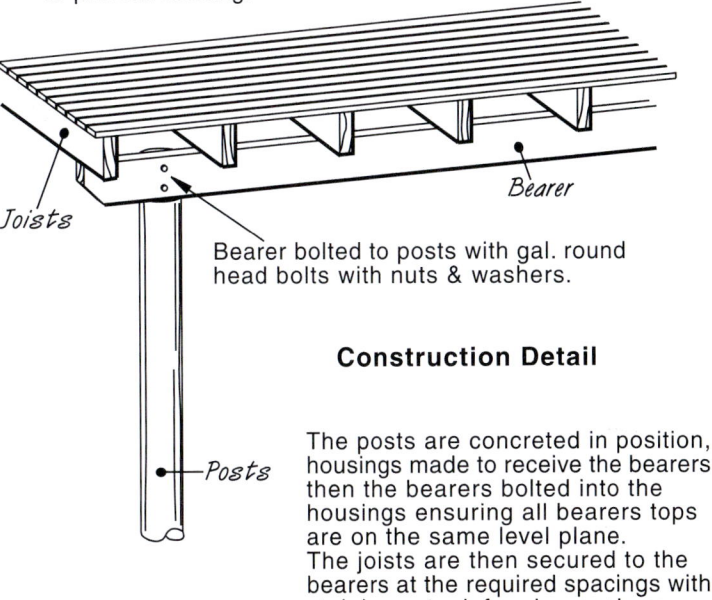

Bearer bolted to posts with gal. round head bolts with nuts & washers.

Construction Detail

The posts are concreted in position, housings made to receive the bearers then the bearers bolted into the housings ensuring all bearers tops are on the same level plane.
The joists are then secured to the bearers at the required spacings with stainless steel. framing anchors.

Decks to Increase Living Areas

Decks attached to the house create additional living space.

These outdoor living areas can be utilised for outdoor entertainment B.B.Q.'ing and meals on hot summer evenings. They offer an entirely different atmosphere to the internal living areas. This can add interest and stimulation.

In many instances these areas can be covered with a waterproof pergola and even the sides can be enclosed with shutters, lattice, canvas roll-out awnings or even glass windows. Whichever the preference, for these areas to become really practical and well utilised, they require privacy, protection from prevailing winds and good access to kitchen facilities.

A well designed outdoor living area can greatly increase the value of a home and can be the deciding factor in a future prospective house buyer's decision making.

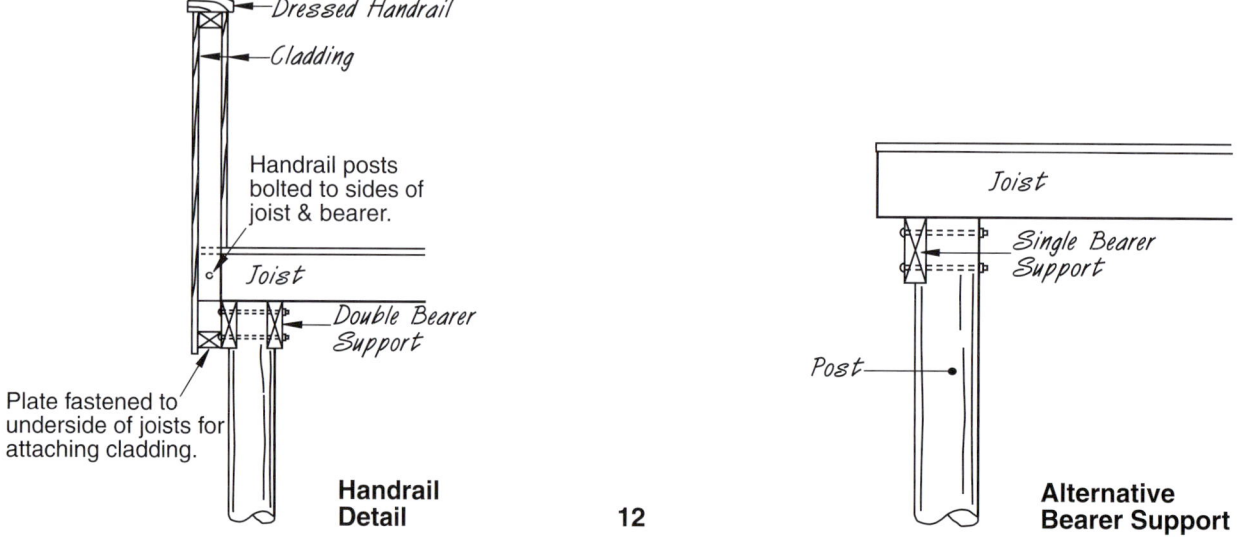

Handrail Detail

Alternative Bearer Support

Multilevel & Polygon Decks

Split or multilevel decks are most practical when sited on the sloping site.
The different levels enable party groups of adults and children or teens to function on a different level should they desire a measure of privacy.
Decks don't have to be square or rectangular. Polygon shapes such as illustrated are a little more costly to construct, but stimulate the imagination, create a distinctively separate relaxation area and can increase the value of the property markedly.

Waterproof & Tiled Decks

Elevated decks can be designed to become a weather protection for vehicles or recreation areas. These decks are often paved with ceramic or terracotta tiles.

HardiPanel™ Compressed panelling used in conjunction with a satisfactory waterproofing system is an ideal method of construction for such a deck, particularly when a tiled surface is required. See Pages 35 to 37 for 'How to Construct Waterproof and tiled Decks'.

The compressed fibre cement sheets are applied over the joists. Check the manufacturer's literature for the various methods of installation.

One method illustrated on Pages 35-37 is for waterproof decks suitable for above living spaces. HardiPanel™ Compressed is commonly applied to decks in either 15 or 18mm thick sheets. The 18mm sheet will enable joist spacings to be increased to 603mm centres.

The sizes/spans given in this publication are *not* suitable for these types of decks. These would have to be provided by an Engineer.

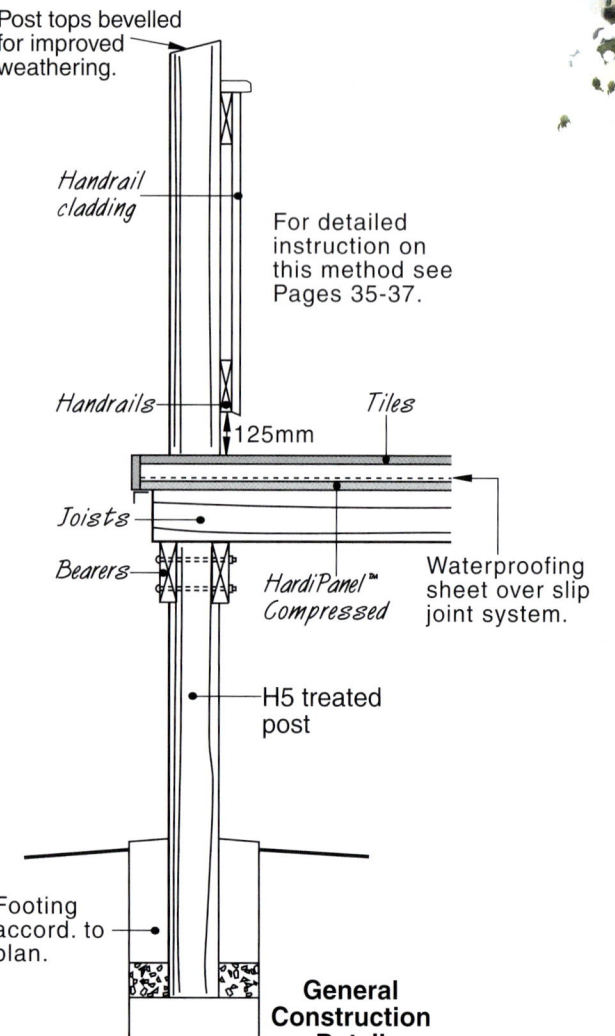

General Construction Detail

Cont.

Tiled decks with enclosed handrail designs as above open up a wide range of combinations and material options for the designer to work with.

The enclosed handrail could utilise battens arranged in a desired pattern such as the herringbone one above or a stuccoed surface could be applied to the traditional paper and wire support.

A handrail capping board should always be applied in these situations to provide weather protection to the framing and cladding.

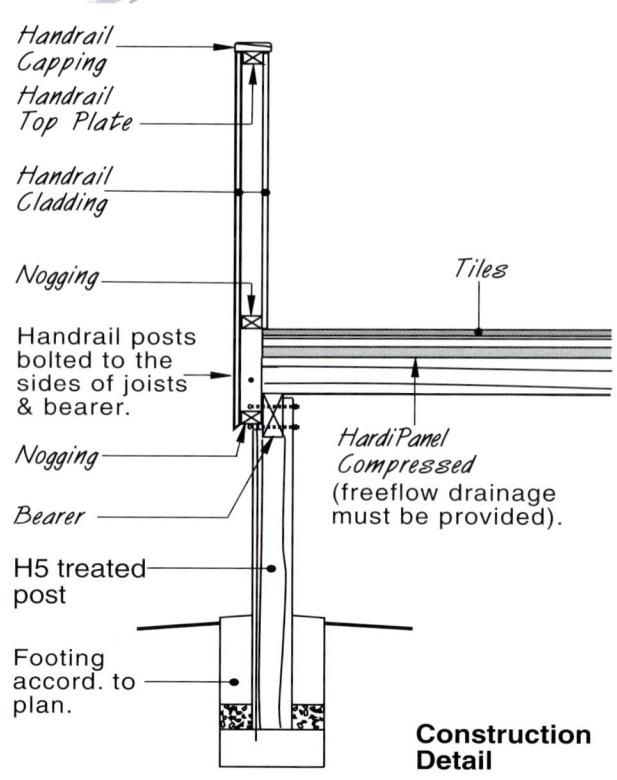

Construction Detail

Pool Decks

The pool deck can be designed to be simply a border to the pool or it can incorporate a full outdoor entertainment area with seating, wind protection and B.B.Q. facilities.

Where chlorinated or salt water will frequently splash on the deck. Ensure all fasteners are stainless steel and that deck coatings or paint finishes are appropriate.

Note: Local Councils require pools to have a safety fence.

Decks on Steep Sites

Decks are an ideal method of utilising a steep site however, where the outer posts are required to be too long or where they are located over a spring or watercourse, the deck could be cantilevered or the supports angled back to the house or to another row of posts as in fig 3. The support system for the latter should be designed by an Structural Engineer.

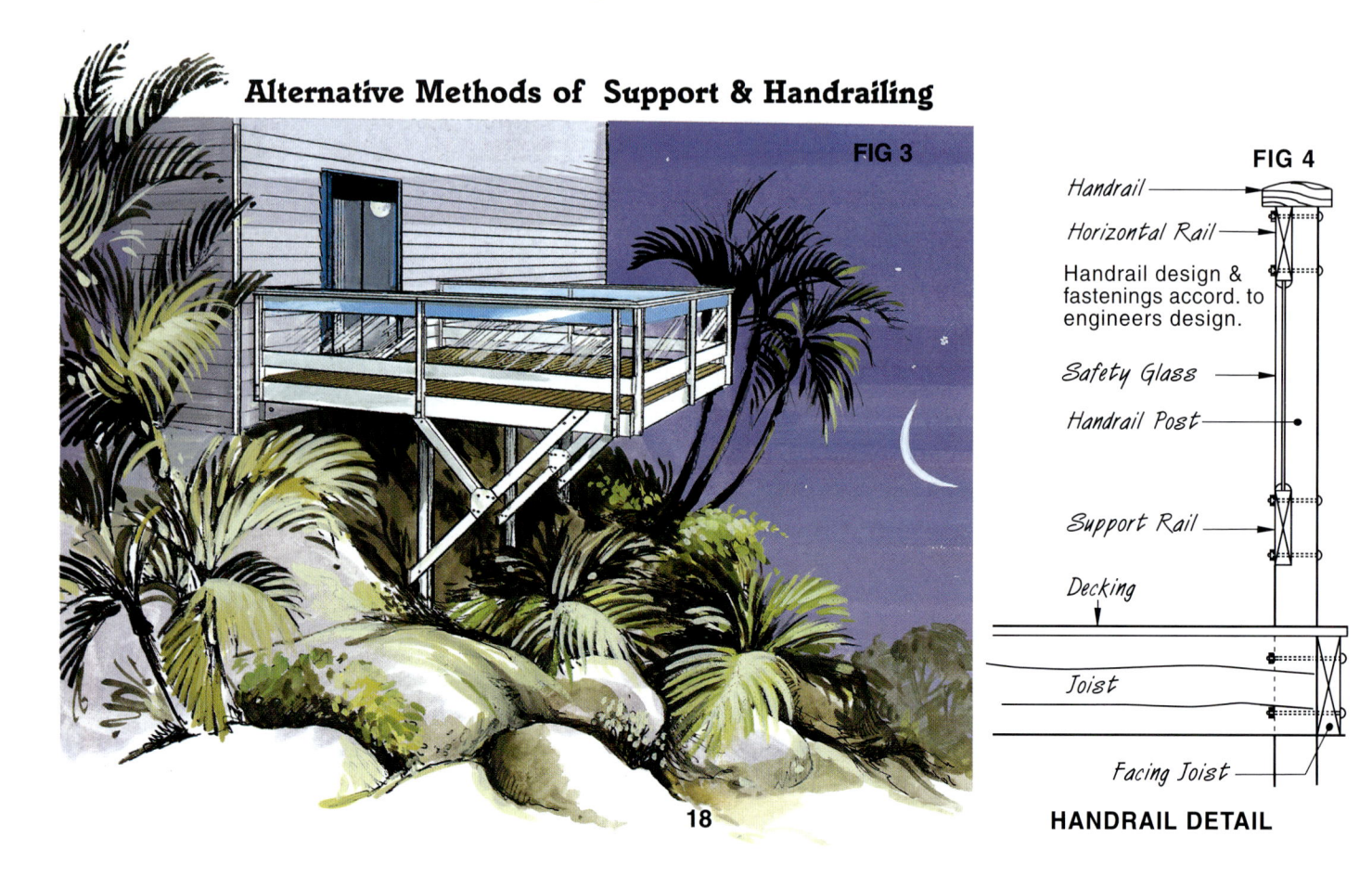

FIG 1

FIG 2

Handrail
Support Rail
Diagonal Cladding
Handrail Post
Support Rail
Decking
Joist
Facing Joist

HANDRAIL DETAIL

Alternative Methods of Support & Handrailing

FIG 3

FIG 4

Handrail
Horizontal Rail
Handrail design & fastenings accord. to engineers design.
Safety Glass
Handrail Post
Support Rail
Decking
Joist
Facing Joist

HANDRAIL DETAIL

Deck Handrailing Design

The hand rail design will provide the strongest architectural influence in the overall appearance, so take care with this element it can really make or break the design.

Ensure that the chosen style is in keeping or compliments the existing house. This is important when applying period designs.

FIG 1

Other Factors to Consider

While appearance is a major factor to consider, safety, privacy, views and some protection from wind may also be important considerations. The fully enclosed handrail as in fig 2 will satisfy the need for protection from wind and privacy when seated. Where views are an important factor vertical balustrades or even clear acrylic sheet or safety glass can be utilised.

FIG 2

Unusual Settings

This fully developed tree has provided a unique setting for an outdoors entertainment deck and at the same time utilised a steep otherwise unmanageable site.

You may wish to create your own unique setting by importing a mature tree to the site or some large boulders to bring a variation to the surrounding ground line.

Deck Construction

3

Deck Posts or Columns

Posts supporting bearers can be positioned flush with end of bearers or be set back* to reduce the bearer span and also for appearance if necessary. Posts can also extend through the deck to become pergola supports above.

Deck posts can be constructed using either H4*, or H5 treated timber or durability Class 1 hardwoods for embedment in-ground or H3 treated timber and hardwood durability Class 2 for above ground. The sapwood of hardwoods should be treated to the required 'H' level.

Alternatively gal. hollow steel posts, concrete filled fibre cement columns, brick or concrete block piers can be used.

* a). Set back should not be greater than the allowable cantilever of joists.
  b). H4 can be used in some States but is only suitable for moderate Hazard applications. If in doubt, use H5.

Concrete Footings to Posts

Footings should be taken to depths required in plans or specifications or see Tables and down to firm subsoils. The top surface of footings should slope away from stirrups or posts to prevent water ponding. Posts can be bolted into either high wind post supports or stirrups or be embedded directly into concrete.

Post & Footing Sectional Sizes

Select the correct post and footing sectional sizes or diameters from 'Tables Chapter'.

> **Hint:**
> Tamp the concrete well around posts or steel post supports to remove any honey combing where moisture could lodge.

High Wind Post Supports

These supports are ideal for both square and round posts. They should be fabricated according to the 'Australian Standards' (Code). Pryda anchors comply.

They are also less likely to corrode as there are no voids in which water can lodge as in stirrups with the hollow tube base.

How to Install

The post supports can be embedded in concrete prior to or after attaching the posts.

Step 1 Excavate the post holes.

Step 2 Pour the concrete and stretch string lines for aligning the post supports.

Step 3 Embed the post supports plumb and in alignment with the string lines. Keep the post ends 75mm clear of the footing or paved surface. Ensure the concrete surface slopes away from the steel legs.

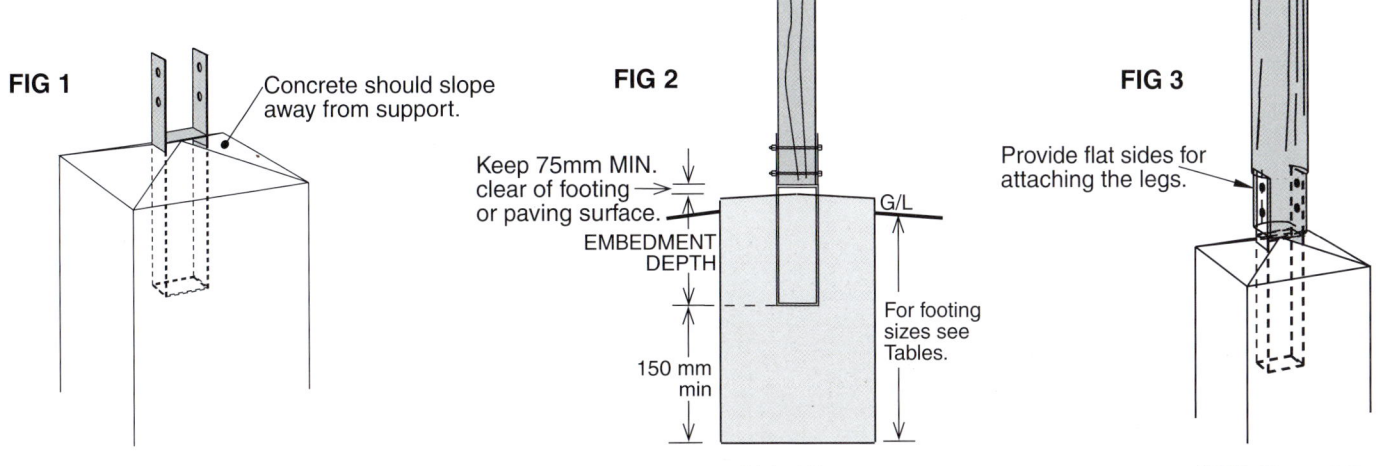

FIG 1 — Embedded Post Support — Concrete should slope away from support.

FIG 2 — Side View — Keep 75mm MIN. clear of footing or paving surface. EMBEDMENT DEPTH. 150 mm min. For footing sizes see Tables.

FIG 3 — With Round Post — Provide flat sides for attaching the legs.

Stirrup Post Supports

Stirrup fabrication should comply with the 'Australian Standards' (Code). The Pryda stirrup has a ribbed cross plate which enables the post to be supported without attracting moisture. On other brands which have a flat cross plate, raise the post to clear the plate to allow moisture to dry out. Some Councils require 12mm clearance.
Beware of the many lightweight stirrups available, as the welds can crack.

Note: High wind post anchors offer superior protection from corrosion as there are no voids in which moisture can lodge as is found on stirrups with the tube post.

How to Install
The anchors can be embedded in concrete prior to or after attaching the posts.

Step 1 Excavate the post holes.

Step 2 Pour the concrete and stretch string lines for aligning the stirrups.

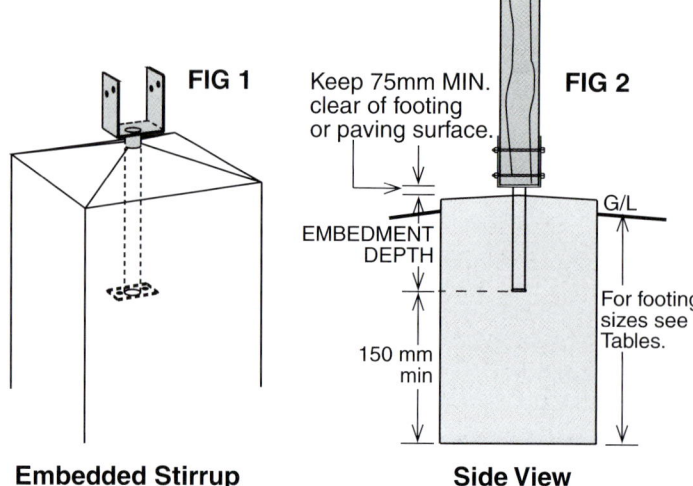

Step 3 Embed the stirrups plumb and in alignment with the string lines. Keep the post ends 75mm clear of the footing or paved surface. Ensure the concrete surface slopes away from the steel legs.

> **Hint:**
> To prevent moisture being trapped in the hollow tube stem, fill with polystyrene pressure pak foam.

Posts Embedded in Concrete

Round posts are most commonly used for this purpose although square sawn can be applied. Treated softwood H5 level treatment is preferable for embedded posts, H4 can be used on some States for moderate Hazard applications. If uncertain, use H5. Hardwood of Durability Class 1 can be used. In a continually moist situation use H6 treated softwood. The bottom ends of treated timber should not be trimmed as this could expose untreated heartwood.

The Footing
It is important to keep embedded timber as dry as possible this includes treated timber. Moisture should be capable of escaping after rain. This is difficult to achieve where posts are fully embedded. Always use no fines concrete. A common trade practice where the subsoil has sufficient bearing pressure, is to provide a 100mm depth of 20mm dia. gravel at the base of the post as in fig 4. However, where poor bearing pressure requires a concrete pad, the drainage gravel can be laid above the pad as in fig 3. Some Tradesmen insert a 20mm dia. plastic tube below the post through the pad into the ground to keep the bottom of the post dry (see fig 3).

How to Install
Excavate footing holes and lay the concrete or gravel pad. The posts are temporarily braced into plumb alignment with string lines and concreted into place. Use stiff concrete and ram well. Ensure the concrete surface is sloping away from the posts. Allow seven to fourteen days to harden before making insitu housings.

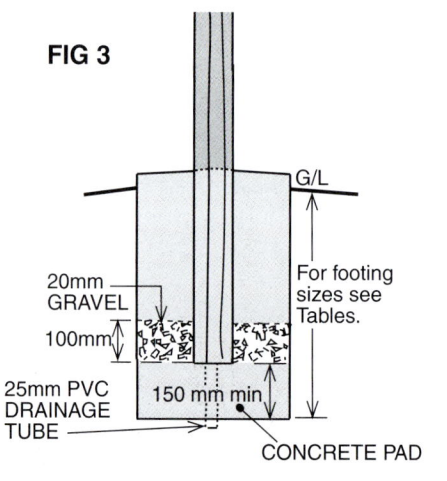

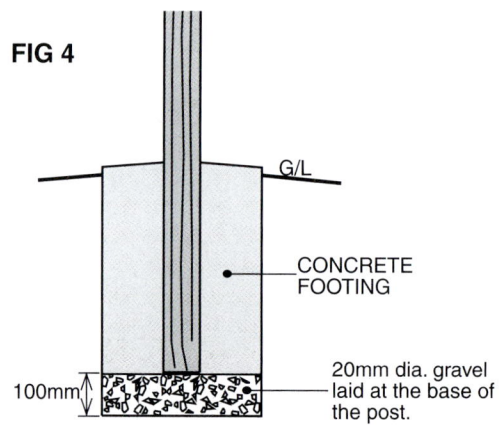

Alternative Columns

Brick or Concrete Block Piers for Tie Down

Brick piers and footings should comply with the current 'Australian Standards' (Code).

Where the brick or concrete block piers are to be used for tie down for high winds, 350 x 350mm brick piers or 200 x 200mm block columns are built to provide a hollow core for installing a tie down rod. The rod has a cog in the bottom and is embedded in the footing a min. of 150mm. The hollow core is grout filled (see figs 2 & 3).

Ant Capping

When installing bearers to piers or columns, it is essential that ant capping be laid in accordance with the 'Australian Standards' (Code).

Fibre Cement Columns

See fig 4 below for details.

Steel Columns

Steel columns and footings should comply with the current 'Australian Standards' (Code).
Square or round columns can be used. Ensure all fabrication and hole boring is complete before galvanising.

How to Install

Columns can be installed prior to or after constructing the deck or pergola. Posts are embedded in stiff concrete and temporarily braced into plumb alignment with string lines. Ensure when installing that all post tops are located at the right height prior to constructing the deck or pergola. Heights should be aligned to a string line.

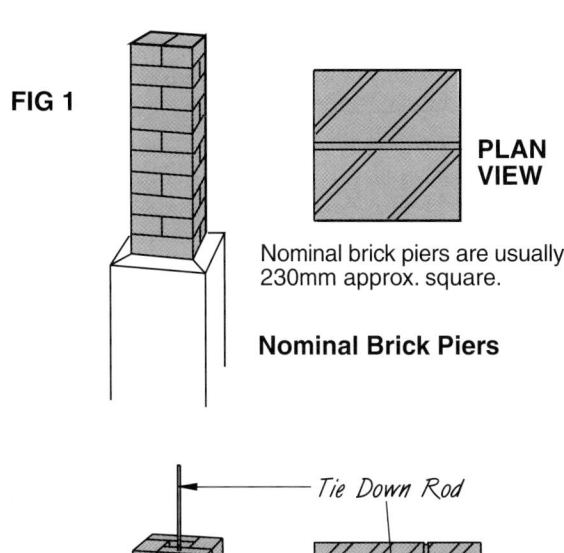

FIG 1

Nominal brick piers are usually 230mm approx. square.

Nominal Brick Piers

FIG 2

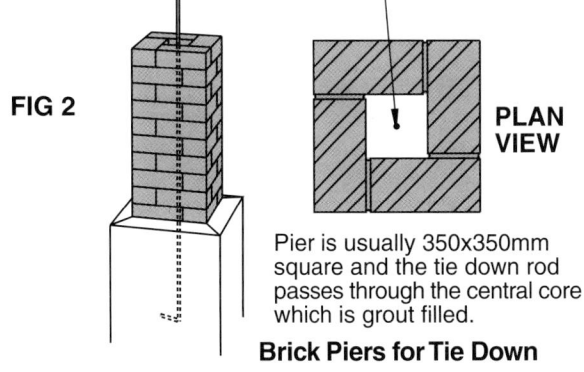

Pier is usually 350x350mm square and the tie down rod passes through the central core which is grout filled.

Brick Piers for Tie Down

FIG 3

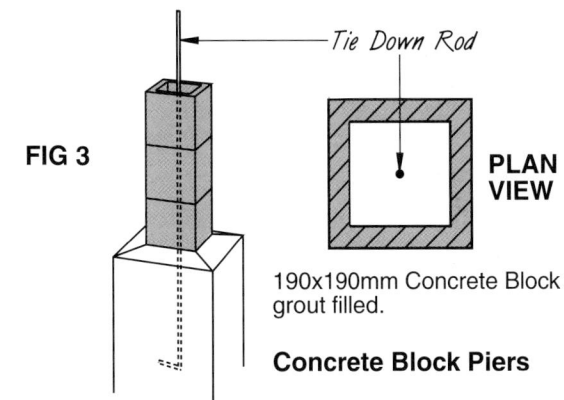

190x190mm Concrete Block grout filled.

Concrete Block Piers

FIG 4

Bearer bolted down to top of column.

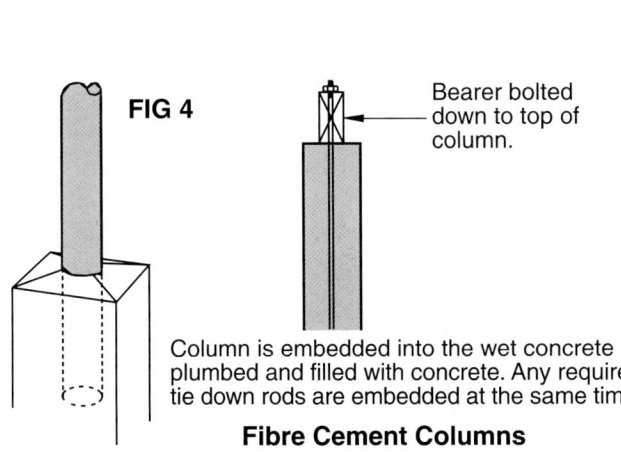

Column is embedded into the wet concrete plumbed and filled with concrete. Any required tie down rods are embedded at the same time.

Fibre Cement Columns

FIG 5

FIG 6

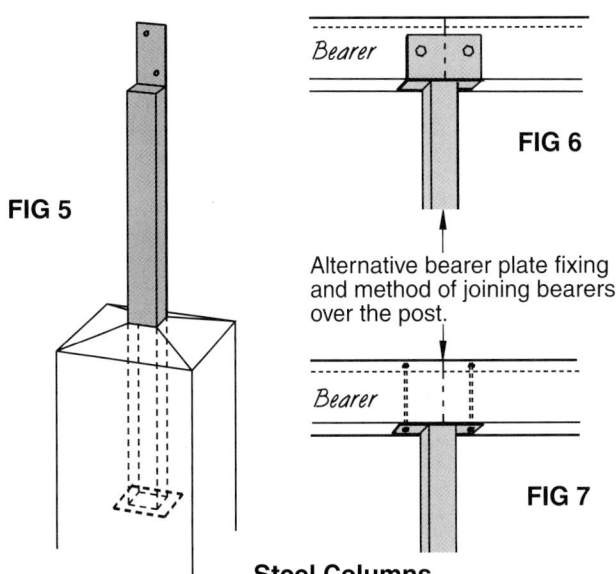

Alternative bearer plate fixing and method of joining bearers over the post.

FIG 7

Steel Columns

Post-to-Bearer Connections

See 'Table 8' for bearer sizes.

The bearer supports the joists through the outer edge and through mid span. Bearer ends can extend past the deck perimeter as a design feature or remain flush with the last joists.

For housing the bearer into the posts, see figs 1-4.

Where the table specifies two bearers e.g. 2/150x50mm, these should be located as a pair fastened on each side of the posts not laminated together. When installing bearers in pairs, ensure their top edges are both on the same level alignment see fig 5.

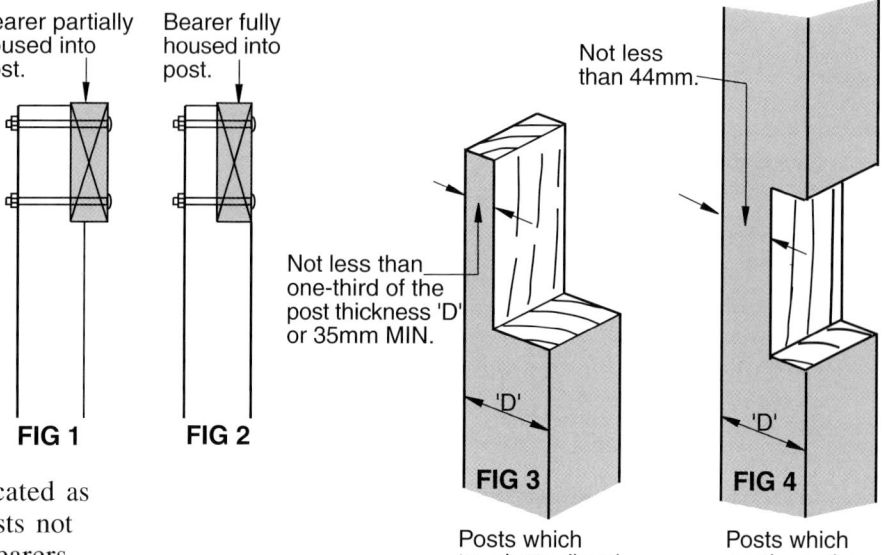

Bearers Less Than 70mm Thick

A single bearer less than 70mm thick supporting joists from underneath as in fig 7 should have a minimum sectional size of 200x50mm nominal and should not span more than 3000mm and should be bolted to the sides of posts as in figs 1-4 and *not* be mounted on top of posts.

Beside the above recommendation, bearers 35mm MIN. thick supporting joists from underneath should be mounted in pairs as in figs 5 & 6.

Alternatively, a single bearer 35 -50mm thick can be applied where the joists are mounted along the inside face of the bearer as in fig 8 using the appropriate stainless steel joist hangers or alternative appropriate support.

Fastening Bearers to Posts

Use galvanised or stainless steel cup head bolts. Clamp the bearer in place then drill the bolt holes 1mm MAX. larger in diameter than the bolts. Then fasten the bolts.

Note: All housings should be flood coated with a reputable wood preservative. Allow to dry then prime paint well.

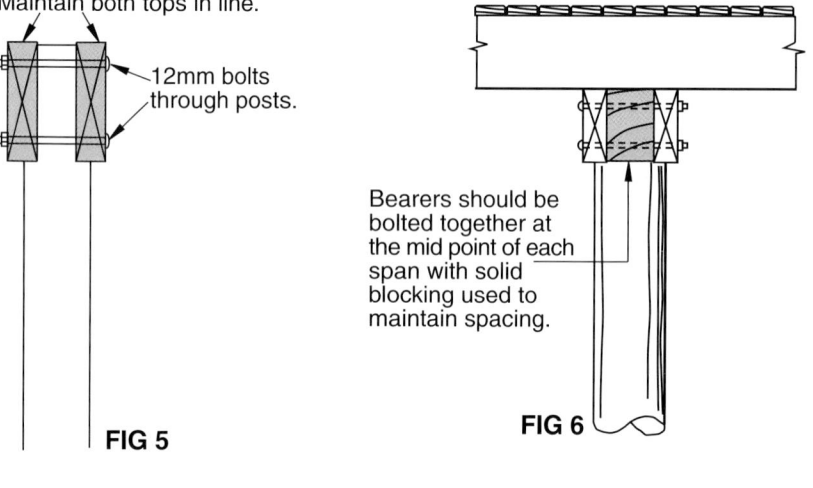

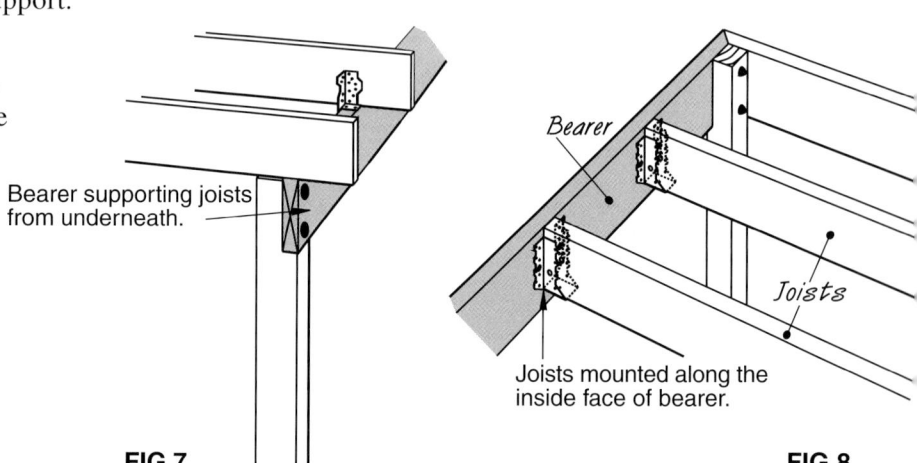

How to Make Housings in Round Posts

Making Housings in Post Tops

Step 1 Mark on the post tops the centre of the posts. Spring a chalk line through the post tops. If you don't have an assistant, drive a nail in one post at one end of each row of posts, then spring a chalk line through as in fig 1. Reverse the process to complete the line at the opposite end.

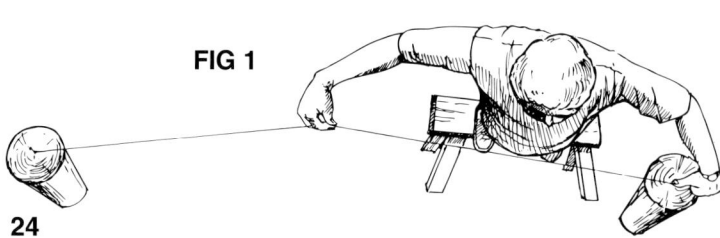

Step 2 Measure the exact thickness of the bearer and measure this distance back from the edge of the posts then mark a line through the post top parallel with the centre line as in figs 2 & 3 then plumb vertical lines down each side of the post using a level.

Step 3 Square a line around the post to indicate the bottom edge of the bearer. Use a piece of stiff cardboard or similar to wrap around the post to use as a squaring edge as in fig 2. Allow for the bearer top to be slightly above the post tops say 12-20mm.

Step 4 Saw the housing through.

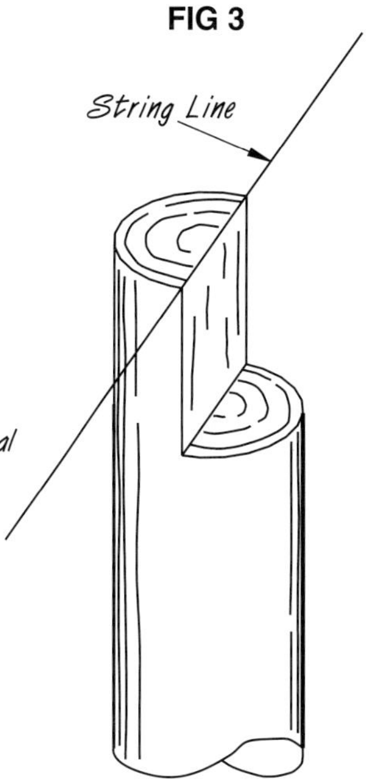

How to Make Mid Post Housings

Step 1 Mark a line on the two end posts to represent the top and bottom edges of the bearers. Where there are intermediate posts, spring a chalk line through.

Step 2 Using a piece of cardboard or similar to wrap around the posts as a square, mark the top and bottom edges of the housings (see fig 4).

Step 3 Mark vertical lines to represent the depth of the housings as in fig 5.

Step 4 Saw the housings to the required depths see fig 5 and chisel out the waste as in fig 6.

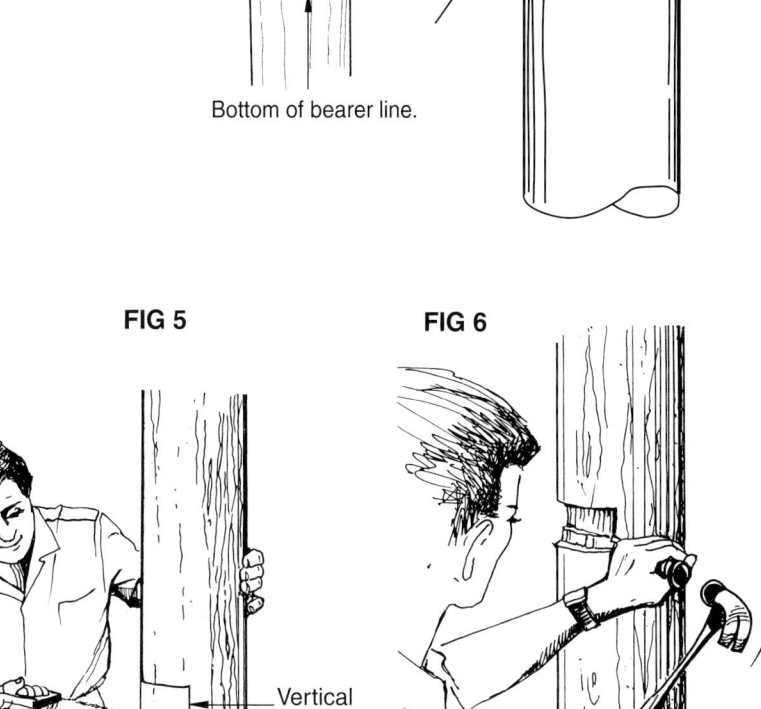

FIG 2 — Proposed Housing — Vertical Lines — Bottom of bearer line.

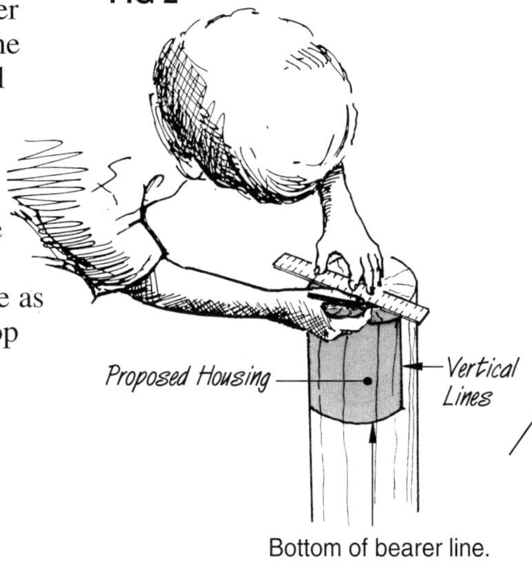

FIG 3 — String Line

FIG 4

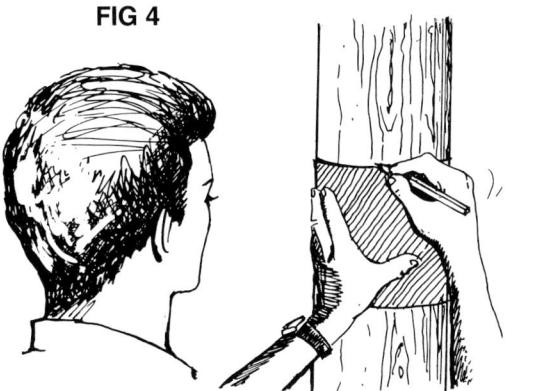

FIG 5 — Vertical Depth Lines

FIG 6

Fastening Bearers to Round Posts

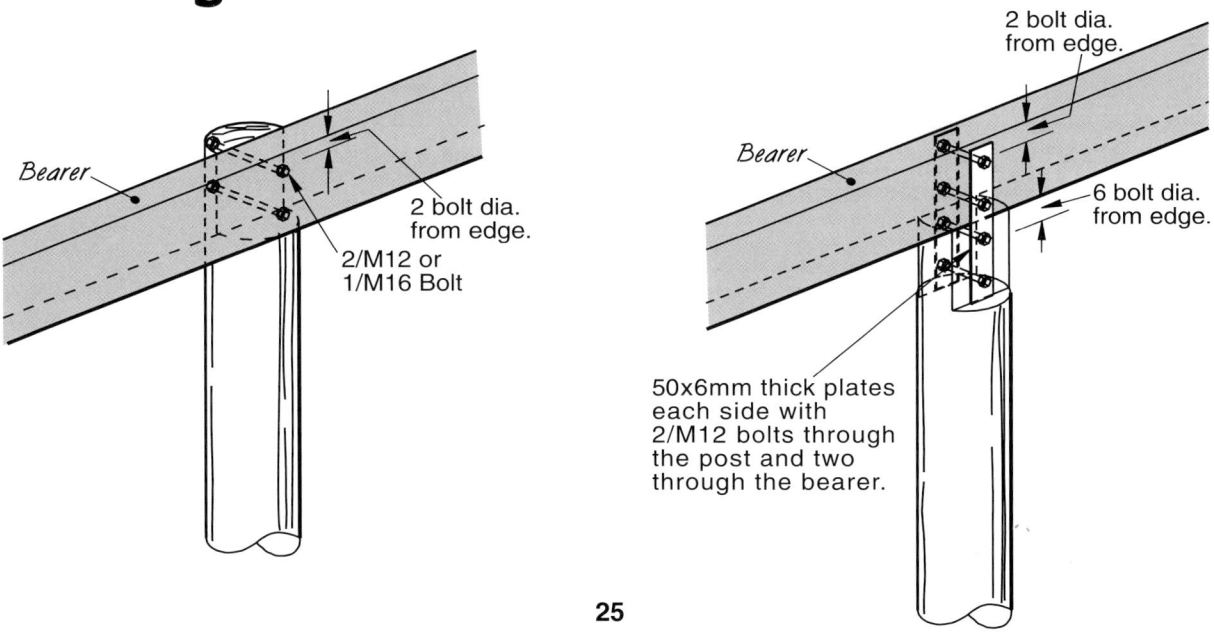

Bearer — 2 bolt dia. from edge. — 2/M12 or 1/M16 Bolt

Bearer — 2 bolt dia. from edge. — 6 bolt dia. from edge. — 50x6mm thick plates each side with 2/M12 bolts through the post and two through the bearer.

25

Attaching Joists to Bearers & Wall Ledgers

Joists can be skew nailed and preferably with hot dip galvanised or s.s. nails. Where splitting may occur, pilot holes should be drilled or use s.s. framing anchors.

Where joists are supported above the bearer or wall ledger as in figs 1 & 2, apply s.s. multigrips or skew nailing. Where they are face mounted as in figs 3 & 4. apply s.s. joist hangers or use the fig 5 method.

Which Joist Hanger?
Joist hangers are available in various widths and lengths and should be matched to fit the selected joists (see Tables).

How to Install Joists
Step 1 Joist positions should be marked on the top side of the bearer and wall ledger.

Step 2 Lay the two joists at each end of the deck as in fig 10 Page 49 then install any required wind bracing and continue to secure the remaining joists.

Keep all bows uppermost and when using Multigrips all the joists could be just tacked in position at first with a 50mm nail. When using joist hangers these are all positioned and fastened on one side only. The joists are installed and then the multigrips attached or all remaining nails are driven in the hangers.

Note: Multigrips should receive 10/30x2.8mm connector nails as in fig 2 and joist hangers nail quantity according to their size see Tables.

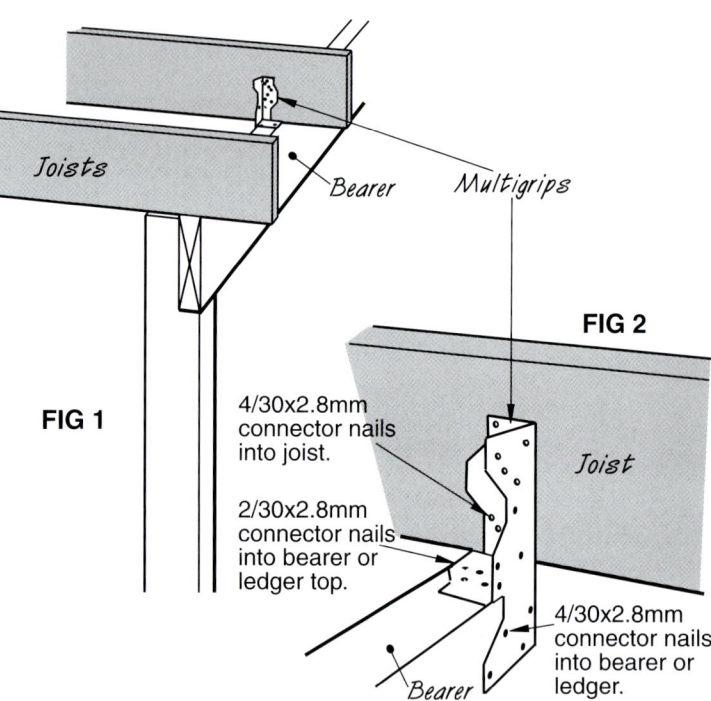

Joists Supported Above Bearers or Wall Ledgers

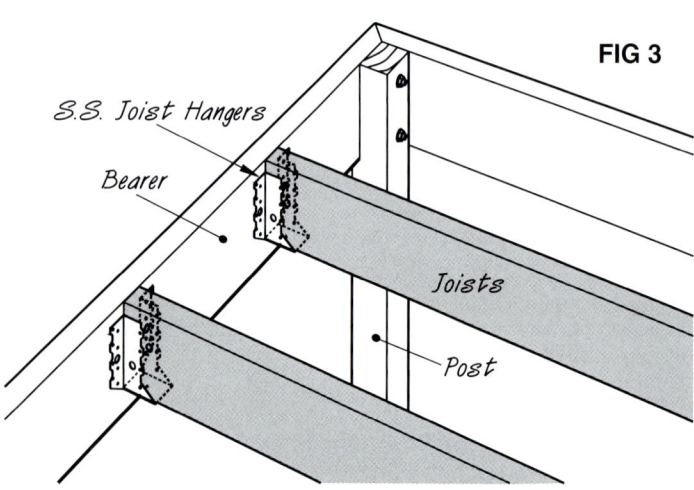

Joists Mounted on Inside Face of Bearers or Ledgers

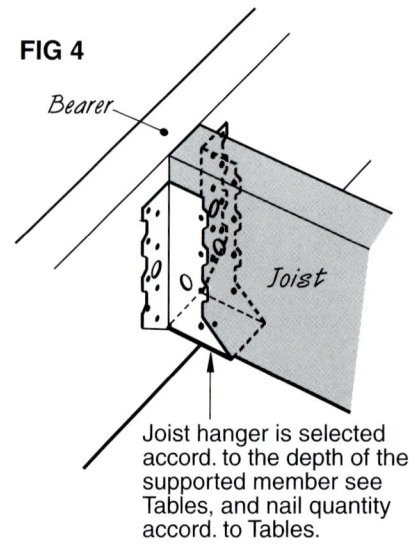

Joist hanger is selected accord. to the depth of the supported member see Tables, and nail quantity accord. to Tables.

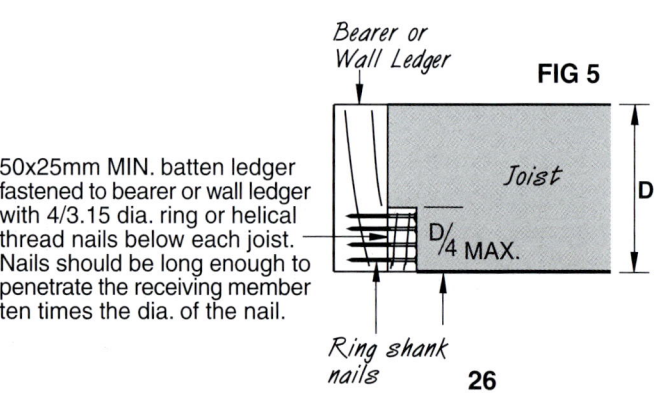

50x25mm MIN. batten ledger fastened to bearer or wall ledger with 4/3.15 dia. ring or helical thread nails below each joist. Nails should be long enough to penetrate the receiving member ten times the dia. of the nail.

Note: All framing anchors and fastenings should be corrosion proof.

Attaching Decks to Walls

Attaching Decks to Weatherboard Walls

The joists are supported either on top of a 100x50mm min. wall ledger as in fig 1 or against the face of the ledger as in fig 2. In the latter situation, the ledger is usually of the same depth as the joists.

The ledger is through bolted to the wall. Bolts should pass through the house bearer or similar solid timber. The wall or members to or through which the deck is to be fastened must be capable of adequately supporting the proposed deck without reducing the structural integrity for which they were originally intended. Apply 12mm gal. round head bolts with nuts and washers below every alternate deck joist.

The deck surface can terminate 12mm below the house floor, however if in future it is decided to lay compressed sheet material and paving tiles, it is better to terminate the deck a min. of 50mm and a max. of 150mm below the house floor (see figs 1 & 2).

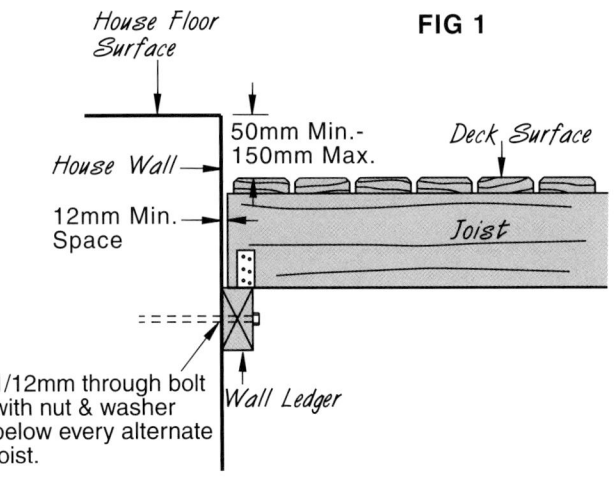

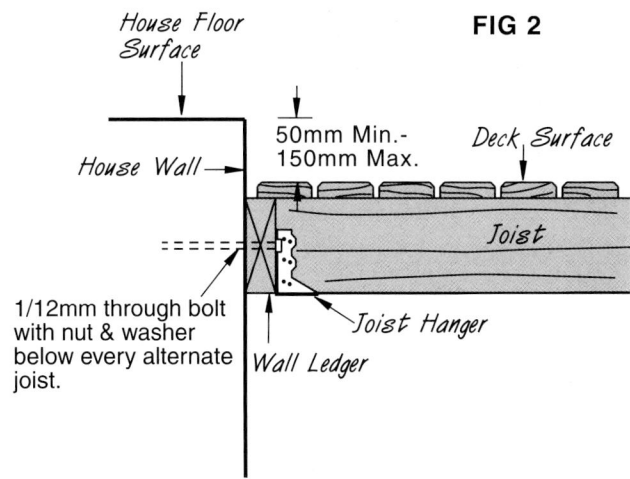

Note: Decks attached to houses must be protected against termites in accordance with AS3660, particularly decks close to the ground where inspection underneath may *not* be possible.

Attaching Decks to Brick Veneer or Double Brick Walls

Generally a Structural Engineers advice should be obtained for attaching decks directly to these walls.
Check also the Local Council specific requirements.

Alternative to attaching decks directly onto brick walls - piers, posts or columns can be constructed to support bearers parallel to the wall line as in fig 4 or at right angles to the wall as in fig 5.

Brick or block piers should have ant capping and steel or wood posts should be kept clear of the wall at least 50mm to enable visual maintenance for termite activity (see fig 7).
Brick piers required for high wind tie down should be 350 x 350mm to enable insertion of the tie down rod and grout.

Constructing Brick Piers

Step 1 Excavate footings to required depths.

Step 2 Construct piers plumb both ways and ensure their tops all arrive on the same level plane. Threaded starter tie down rods when required are embedded in the footing and extend up the pier via a connector nut. Keep the brick pier 5mm clear of the house wall and fill this gap later with long life brick silicone sealant, see Page 23 for further construction information.

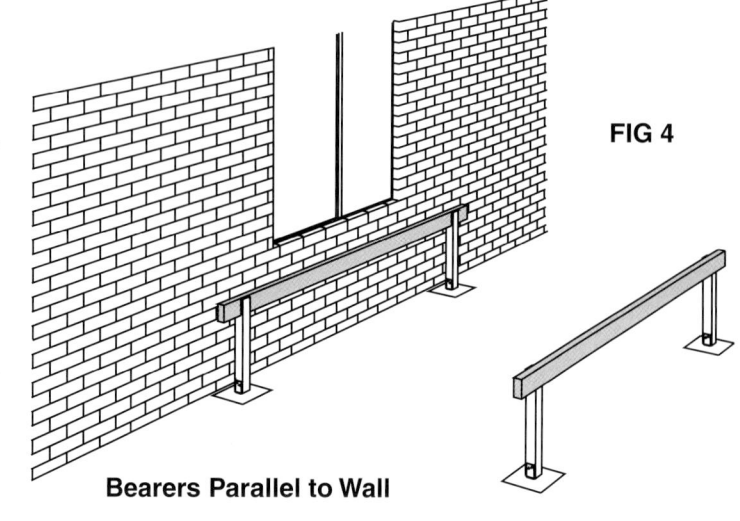

FIG 4
Bearers Parallel to Wall

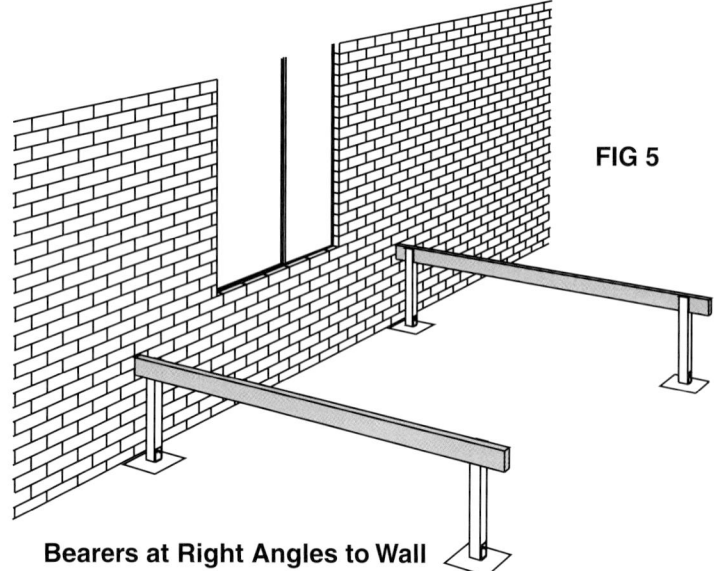

FIG 5
Bearers at Right Angles to Wall

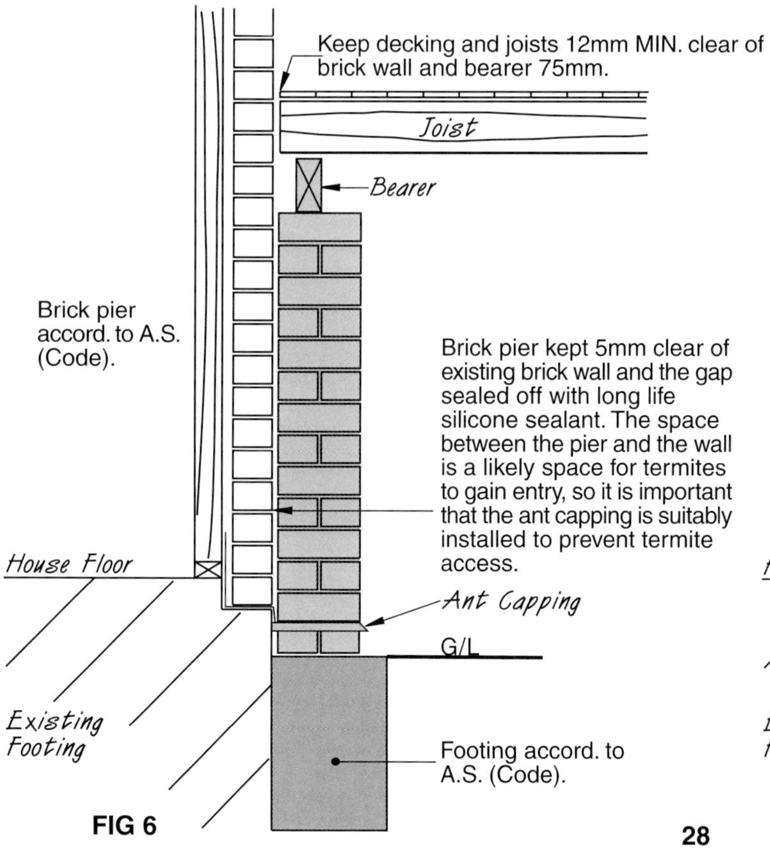

FIG 6 — Keep decking and joists 12mm MIN. clear of brick wall and bearer 75mm. Brick pier accord. to A.S. (Code). Brick pier kept 5mm clear of existing brick wall and the gap sealed off with long life silicone sealant. The space between the pier and the wall is a likely space for termites to gain entry, so it is important that the ant capping is suitably installed to prevent termite access. Ant Capping. House Floor. Existing Footing. Footing accord. to A.S. (Code). G/L.

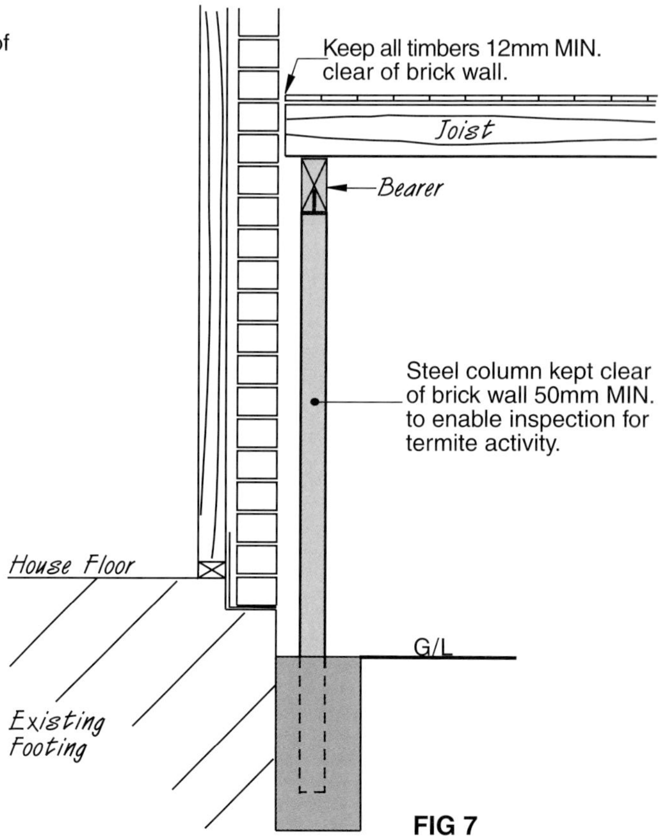

FIG 7 — Keep all timbers 12mm MIN. clear of brick wall. Steel column kept clear of brick wall 50mm MIN. to enable inspection for termite activity. House Floor. Existing Footing. G/L.

Bracing Decks

Bracing Decks Attached to the House

a). The following decks will not normally require bracing:
Decks which are securely bolted to the house and are not greater in height than 1200mm and where the posts are embedded in concrete a min. of 450mm or not greater than 1800mm high with posts embedded 600mm min.

b). Decks which are securely bolted to the house but are greater in height than twelve times the post width or diameter and with posts embedded in concrete less than 600mm should be braced.

c). Decks which have posts secured to stirrups or high wind post supports should be braced.

Amount of Bracing for 'b' & 'c'

For decks which are not greater than 2000mm wide measuring at right angles from the house wall and not greater in height than 1800mm, provide a pair of 90x45mm F7 min. opposing braces parallel to the house wall as in figs 1 or 2 for every 6 sq. metre of deck area.

Alternatively, apply 90 x 45mm F7 min. bracing in opposing pairs to the underside of joists as in figs 3 & 4.

All decks between 1800-3600mm high and greater in width that 2000mm measuring from the house wall with posts either attached to stirrups or embedded in concrete up to 450mm deep in the ground should have a pair of opposing braces in both directions that is at right angles to the house wall as well as parallel to the house wall for every 12 sq. metre of deck area.

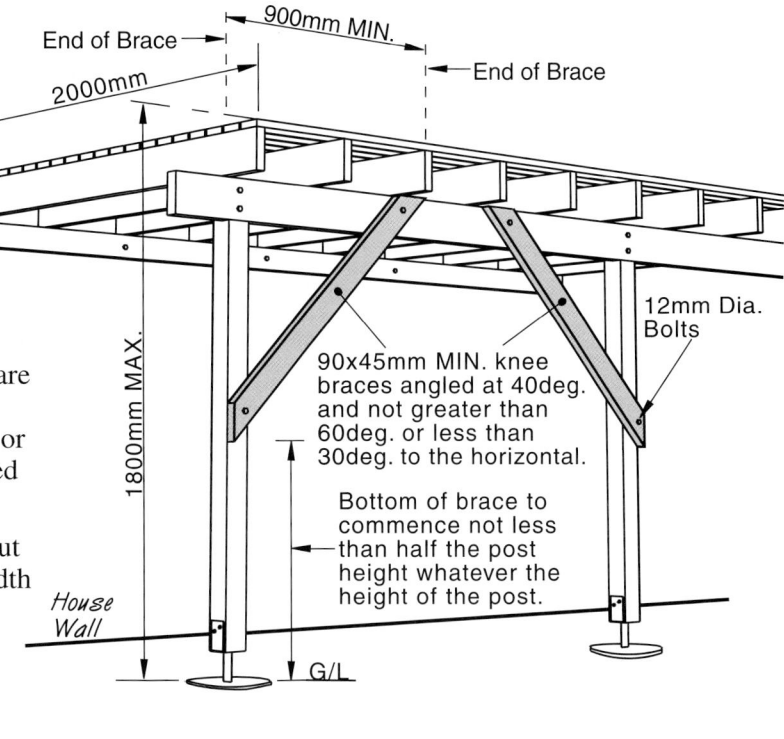

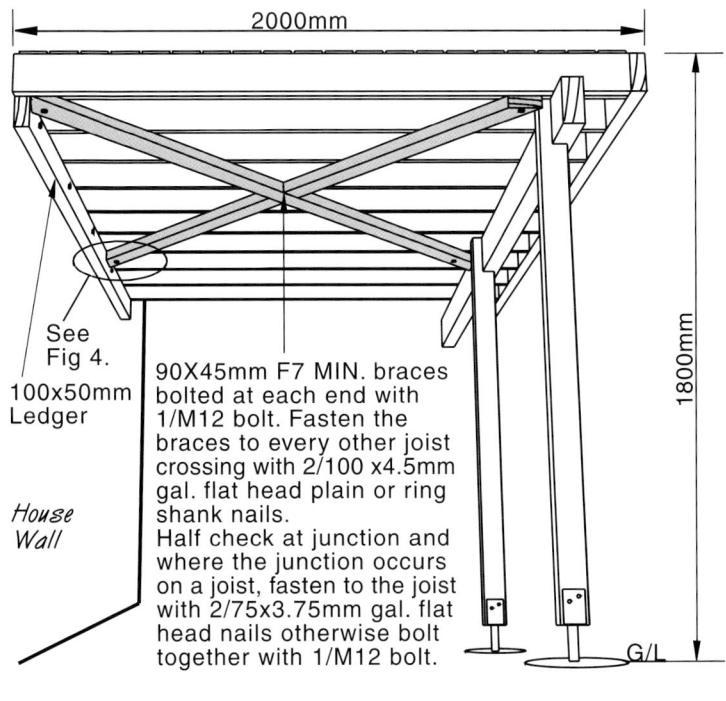

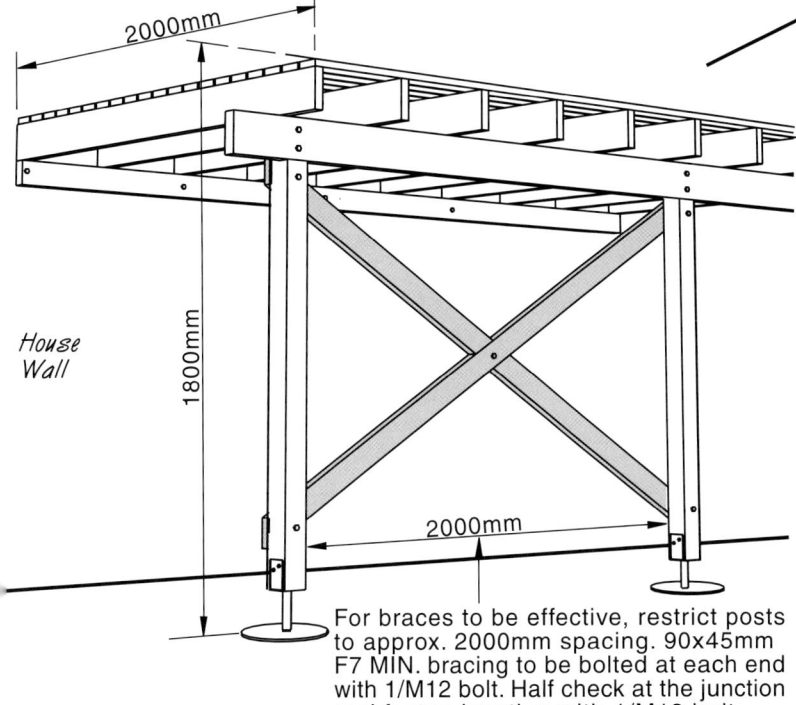

For braces to be effective, restrict posts to approx. 2000mm spacing. 90x45mm F7 MIN. bracing to be bolted at each end with 1/M12 bolt. Half check at the junction and fasten junction with 1/M12 bolt.

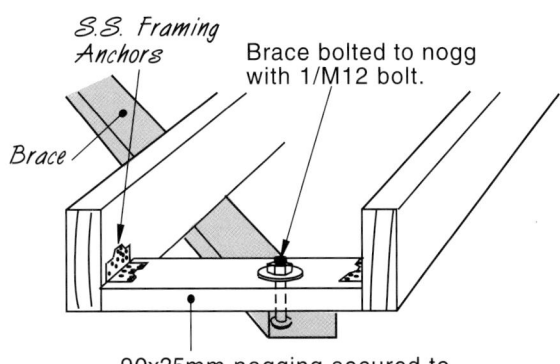

90x35mm nogging secured to joists with framing anchors each side or mini grip brackets with 6/30x 2.8mm dia. connector nails in each leg of each bracket.

Bracing Freestanding Decks

(free standing decks are those not attached to the house or any other structure)

a). Freestanding decks which are not over twelve times the post width or dia. high and where the posts are embedded up to 600mm deep in concrete do not require bracing.

b). Decks which are over twelve times the post width or dia. high but not greater that 3600mm and which have posts bolted in stirrups or embedded to a max. of 600mm should have a pair of 90x45mm F7 min. opposing braces in both directions for every 12 sq. metres of deck area as in figs 5 & 6.

Where it is desired to eliminate bracing, posts will need to be designed as cantilever posts and will require embedment in concrete to greater depths.

To obtain footing sizes and post embedment depths for cantilever posts for decks or pergolas up to 2100mm above ground see Tables.

To obtain footing sizes and post embedment depths for cantilever posts for decks or pergolas higher than 2100mm above ground consult a Structural Engineer.

Note: Posts are terminated at deck level for illustration purposes only.

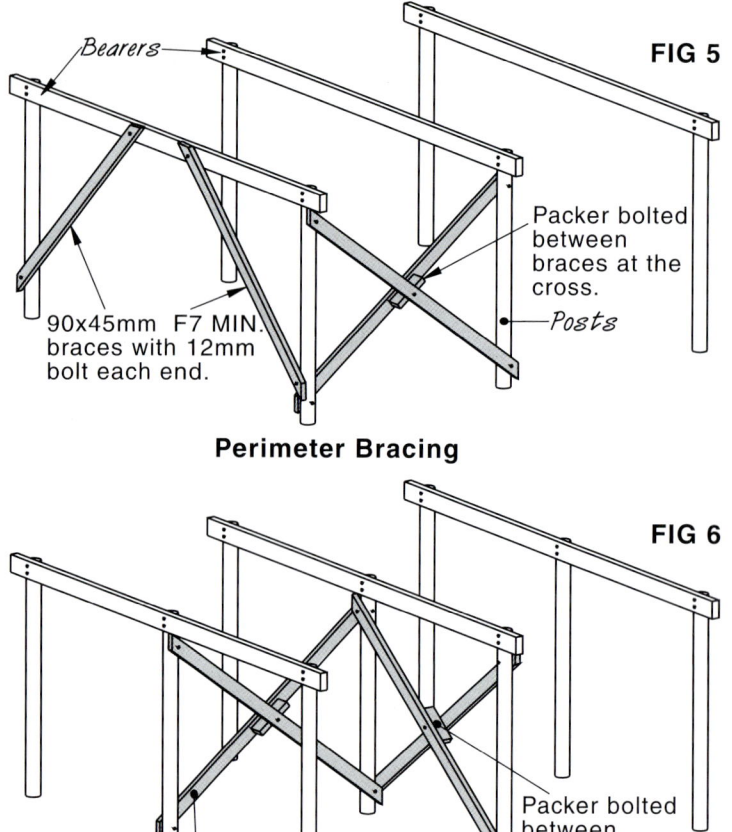

Perimeter Bracing (FIG 5)

Internal Bracing (FIG 6)

How to Install Bracing

Step 1 Attach the end joist at each end of the deck.

Step 2 Temporarily brace the structure into plumb and square alignment.

Step 3 Clamp or hold the bracing material in the proposed position. Mark the ends and trim to shape.

Step 4 Clamp back into position, drill the bolt holes and secure the bolts. The temporary braces can then be removed.

Where Posts & Bearers Aren't Aligned Flush
Attach a packer under one end as in fig 7.
The packer should be the full width of the brace.

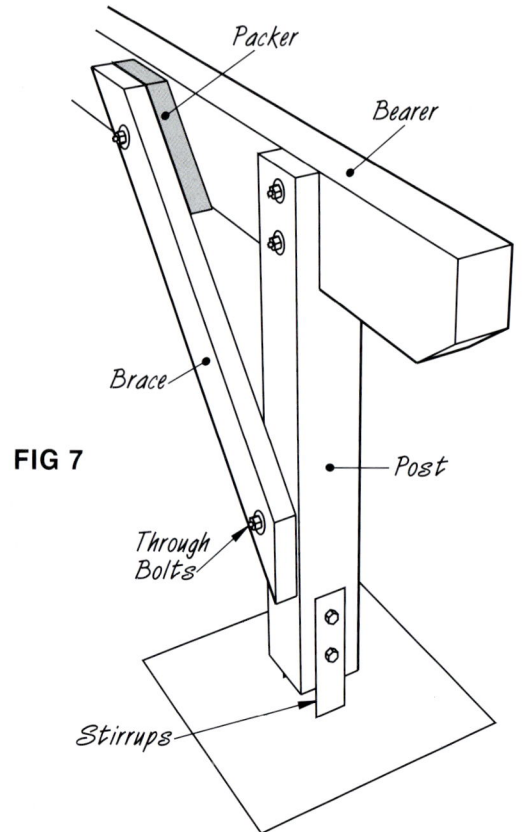

Bolt Positions in Braces

Braces should be bolted each end to posts or bearers or joists with 1/M12 round head gal. bolt with a 50mm washer. For distances of bolts from edges and ends of braces, see fig 8.

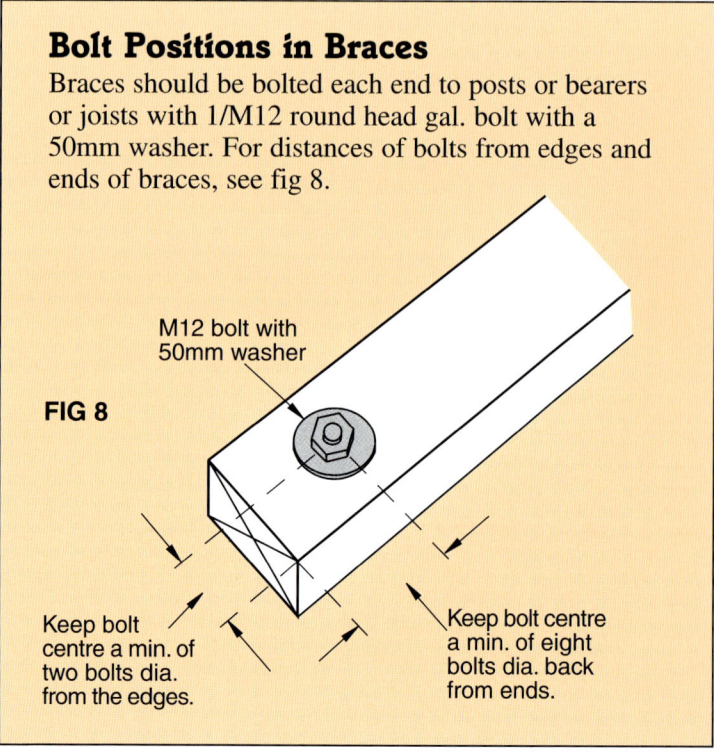

Ways to Conceal Bracing

Bracing need not be conspicious. Various methods can be applied to conceal them. Besides covering with lattice, battens or shrubbery, additional members of the same dimension can be installed to form a pattern as in figs 1 & 2. This pattern could be repeated in the handrailing to create a pleasing overall architectural design.

Where the deck contains additional posts internally, apply the braces to these rather than around the perimeter.

Bracing required anywhere on the perimeter of the deck could be attached to the rear sides of the posts to reduce the visual appearance of the full length of the braces.

The following suggestions could be visualised with the deck cantilevered beyond the posts as this is a common situation.

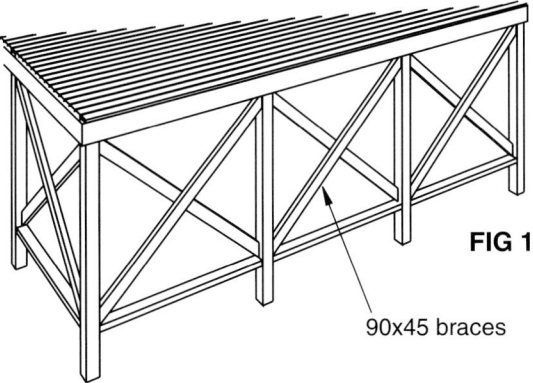

FIG 1

90x45 braces

Solid timber bracing applied as a repeating pattern.

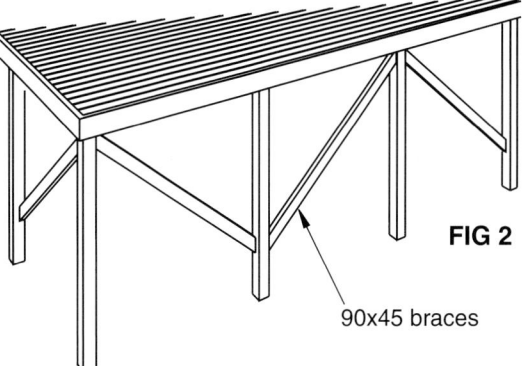

FIG 2

90x45 braces

Similar effect to fig 1 although over simplified. Will only compliment a particular application.

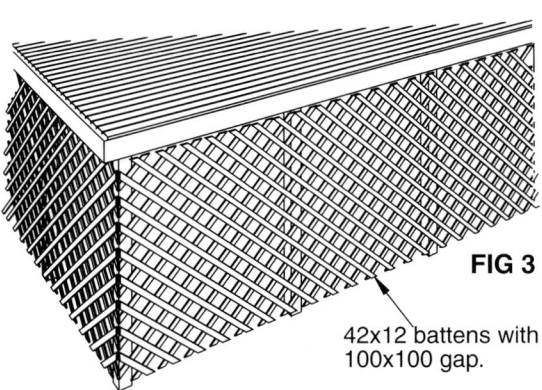

FIG 3

42x12 battens with 100x100 gap.

Lattice has been a traditional material for this application. Explore the variety of styles and varying member and opening sizes available.

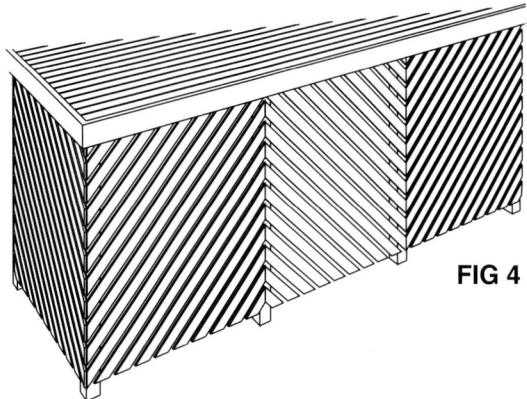

FIG 4

70-90mm herringbone battens with 12-20mm gaps between.

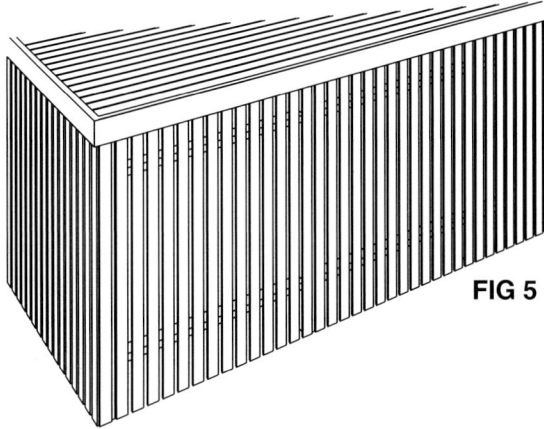

FIG 5

70-90mm wide vertical battens with 12-20mm gaps between.

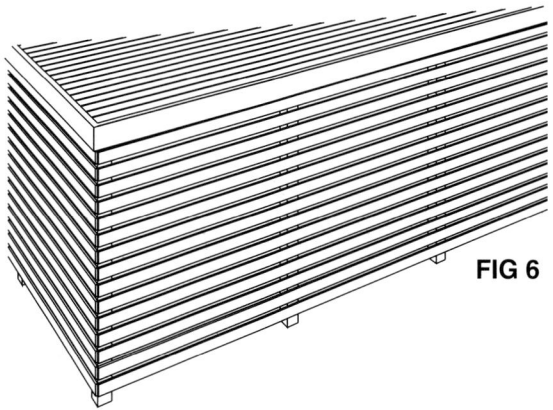

FIG 6

70-90mm wide horizontal battens with 12-20mm gaps between.

Decking (Flooring)

(to obtain decking thicknesses for specific joist spacings and for fastenings seeTables)

Timber to Use

Use either treated seasoned softwood H3 or seasoned hardwood durability Class 2 or better. Treated softwood and hardwood decking is available dressed all round with pencil corners as in fig 1 and in other styles and in various thicknesses and widths.

Decking Laid at an Angle to Joists

Joist spacings for decking laid at an angle to the joists should be measured along the same angle as the deckings as in figs 3 and 6.

FIG 1

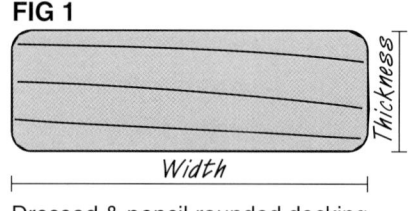

Dressed & pencil rounded decking

Deck Patterns

FIG 2

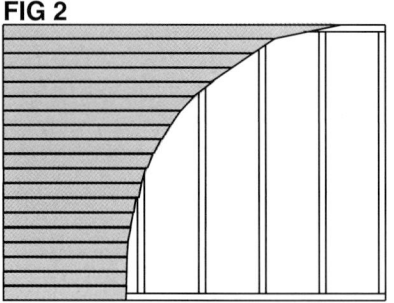

Decking at right angles to joists.

FIG 3

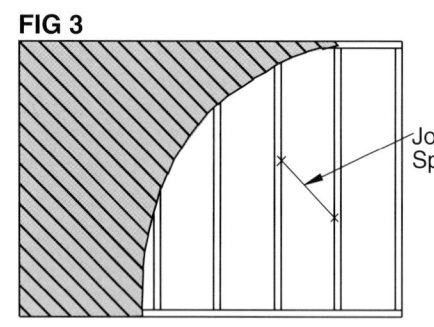

Decking at 45 deg. angle to joists will require decking ends around the perimeter to be cut on an angle.

FIG 4

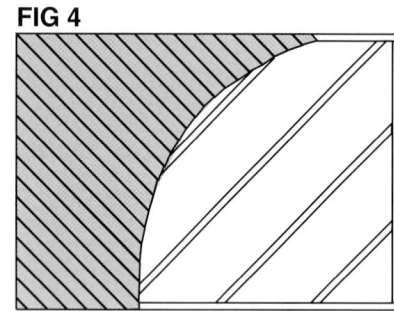

Joists angled at 90 deg. to decking will require all joist ends to be bevel cut.

FIG 5

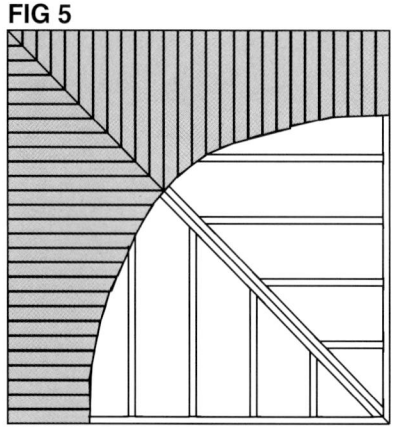

Mitred decking and joists.

FIG 6

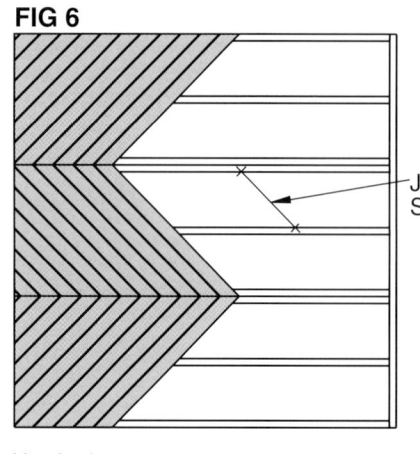

Herringbone pattern.

FIG 7

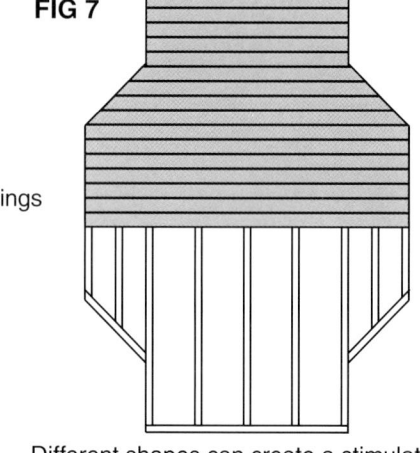

Different shapes can create a stimulating and interesting area.

FIG 8

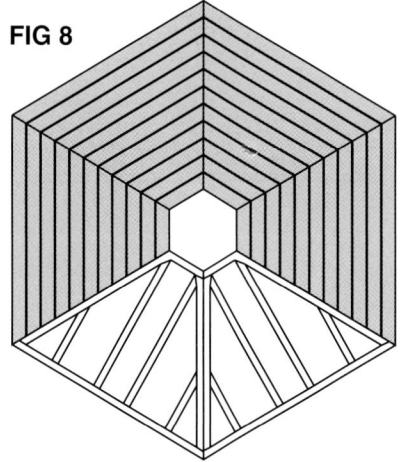

Hexagonal deck with joists meeting at a trimmed opening suitable to plant a shade tree.

FIG 9

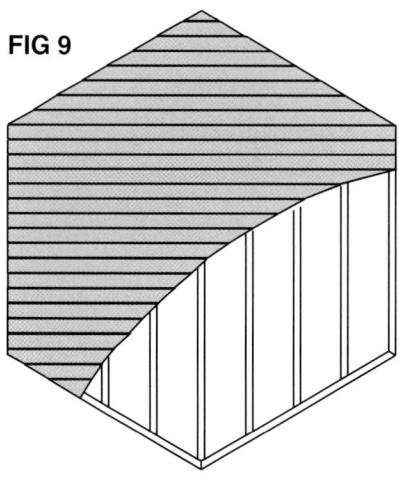

Hexagonal with joists and decking at right angles.

How to Lay Decking
(see Tables for correct nail or fastening selection)

Step 1 Check that the top surfaces of joists are all on the same level plane without bowed joists projecting above those adjacent. Use a long straightedge to check, then remove any high spots with a power plane.

Step 2 Lay the decking out loosely and partially nail the first board through the outer edge as in fig 1. Allow the board to overlap the front edge by 10-15mm as in fig 2 and extend each end a little past the proposed trimmed overhang points for trimming off later (see fig 3). Secure the board in straight alignment.

Stretch a string line through for straightening the first board.

Nailing Boards
Drive nails at a slight angle for a better hold (see fig 4) and drill pilot holes 80% of the nail diameter at ends and wherever splitting could occur. Offset (stagger) the pairs of nails on each board to prevent splitting the joists (see fig 5).

End Joins
Secure end to end joins centrally over joists (see fig 6) and avoid having joins occur consecutively as in fig 7 but rather alternate or stagger them as in fig 8.

Spacing Between Boards
Allow a 3-4mm space between seasoned boards.
To maintain equal spacing between boards, use a nail or a 3-4mm strip of ply or masonite.

A good method to avoid the spacer repeatedly falling through the boards is to drive a 100mm flat head nail through a piece of ply or masonite leaving the head protruding to use as a handle (see fig 9). Make three of these, one for each end of boards and one for the intermediate joist crossings.

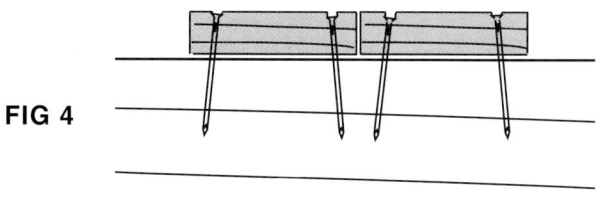
FIG 4
Angle nails slightly for a stronger hold.

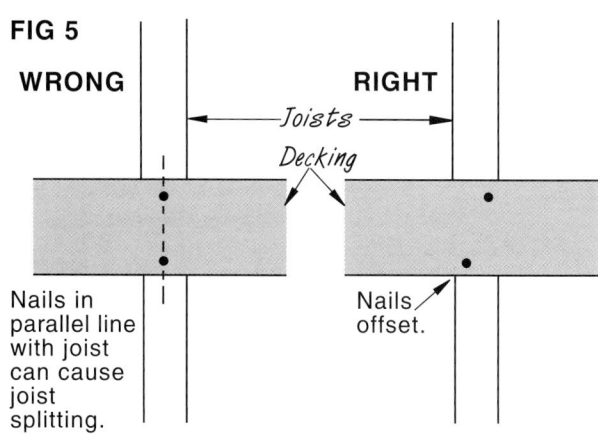
FIG 5 WRONG — RIGHT
Joists — Decking
Nails in parallel line with joist can cause joist splitting.
Nails offset.

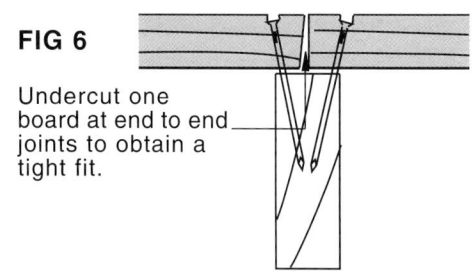
FIG 6
Undercut one board at end to end joints to obtain a tight fit.

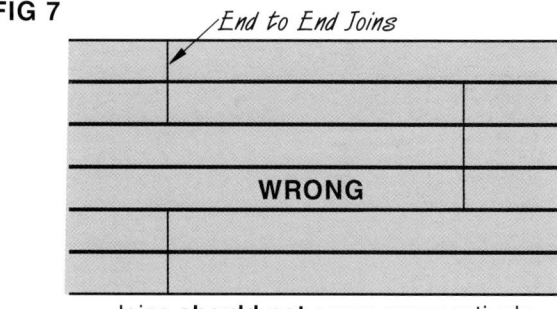
FIG 7
End to End Joins
WRONG
Joins **should not** occur consecutively.

FIG 8
RIGHT
Joints Staggered Apart

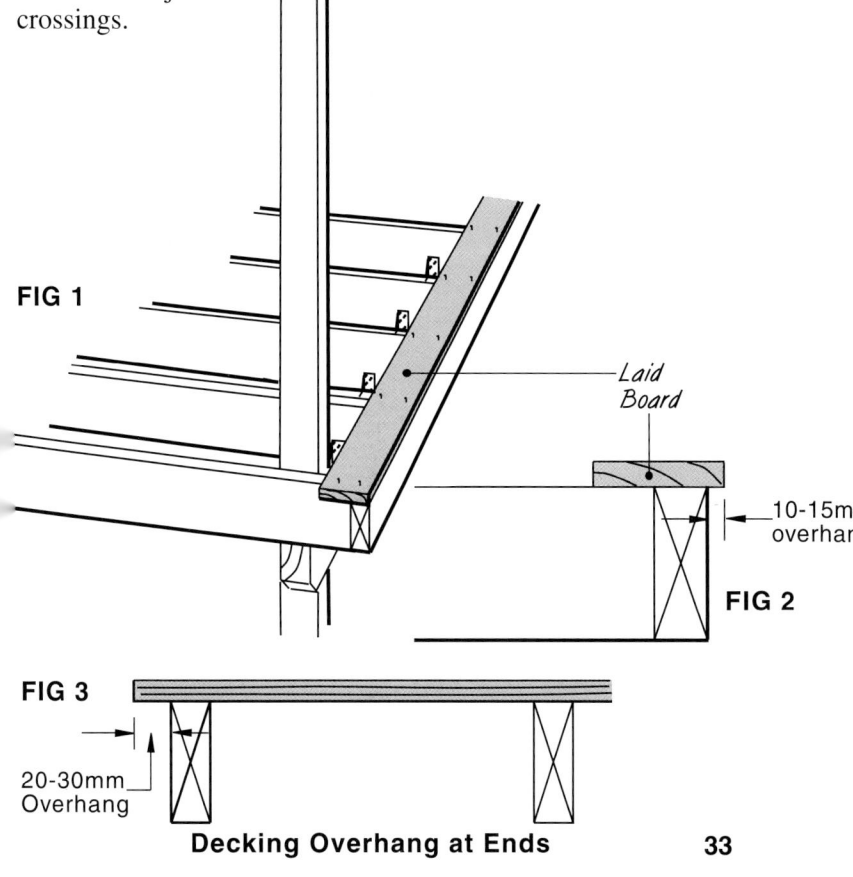
FIG 1
Laid Board
10-15mm overhang
FIG 2
FIG 3
20-30mm Overhang
Decking Overhang at Ends

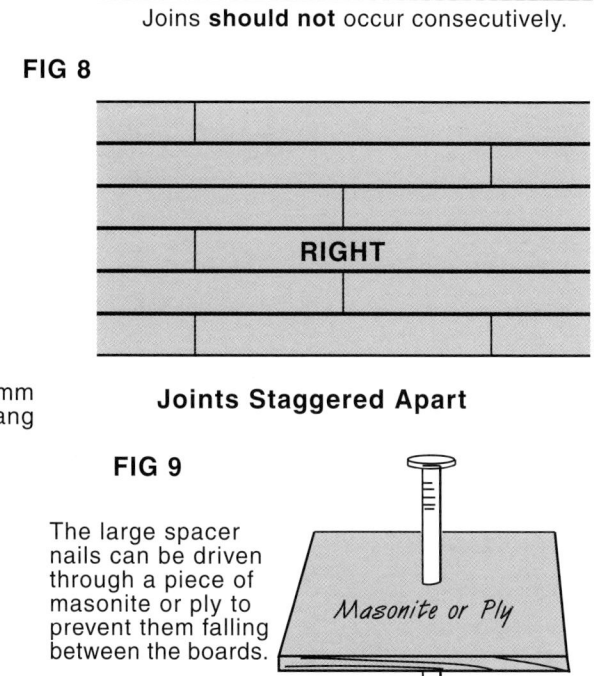
FIG 9
The large spacer nails can be driven through a piece of masonite or ply to prevent them falling between the boards.
Masonite or Ply

Straightening Each Board

After nailing each end, tack the remaining nails in the decking only at each joist crossing, this enables both hands to be free for leavering the board into straight alignment with one hand and for driving the nail with the other.

Apply the spacer centrally along the board or at the mid point of any bows. Where the bow is curving in against the last laid board, drive a chisel between them and lever the bow out see fig 9, then placing the spacer, drive the nail.

If the board is curving away from the last board laid, force it in as much as possible by hand then drive the chisel into the joist directly behind the board and lever it into alignment as in fig 10.

Continue to straighten the board working from mid spans or from the worst point of bows. After partially nailing the board at two or three mid. points, using the spacer, have an assistant sight the board from one end for straight.
Continue this process until the board is nailed at each joist crossing then after straightening, drive all the nails home.

Check for Creep

After aligning about a third of the boards, check the spacing remaining between the boards and the house wall. Check at each end and centrally see fig 11.
If one end is creeping closer than the other, open the spacing of the next few boards slightly to correct. Carry out this check periodically.

The Last Board

To avoid ending up with a very narrow last board, carry out a check on the loose boards at about a metre from the end by spacing them along the joist. The spacing may require slightly opening or closing. Check the ends and centre as well.

Trimming Decking Ends

Step 1 Mark the final trim overhang points of decking ends see fig 3 Page 33.

Step 2 Spring a chalk line through as in fig 12.

Step 3 Trim the ends with a circular saw see fig 13.

Step 4 Arris the sawn corner with a plane.

FIG 9 After nailing each end, drive the chisel between the boards to lever the bows straight.

Straightening a Bowed in Board

FIG 10 Drive the chisel into the joist to lever the board straight then drive the nail.

Straightening a Bowed out Board

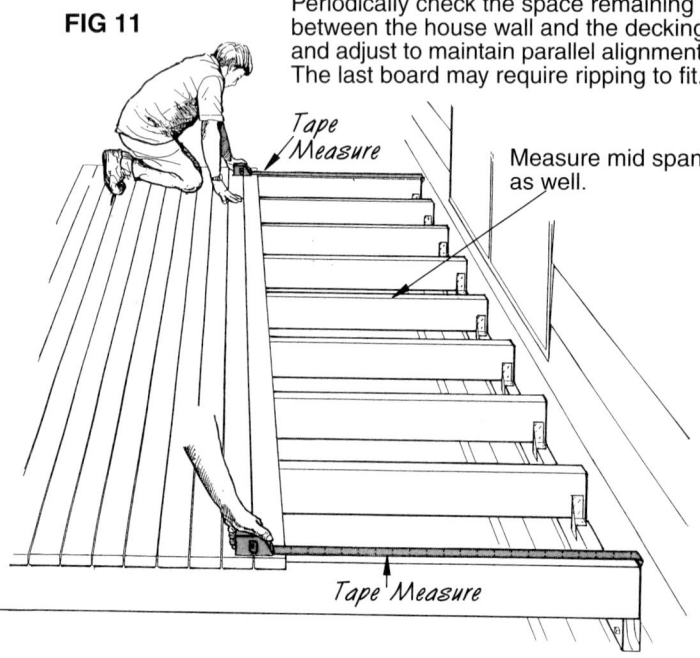

FIG 11 Periodically check the space remaining between the house wall and the decking and adjust to maintain parallel alignment. The last board may require ripping to fit.

Measure mid span as well.

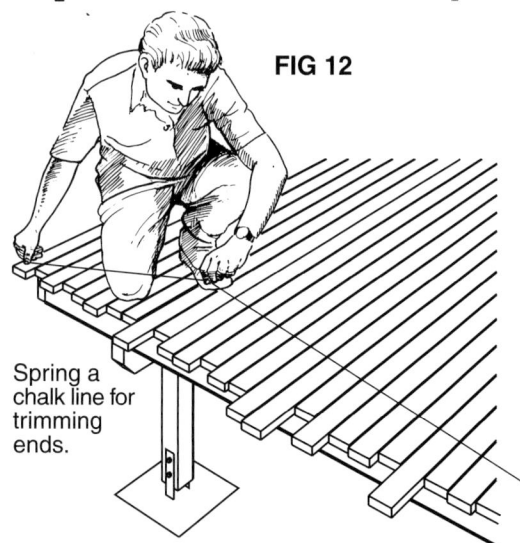

FIG 12 Spring a chalk line for trimming ends.

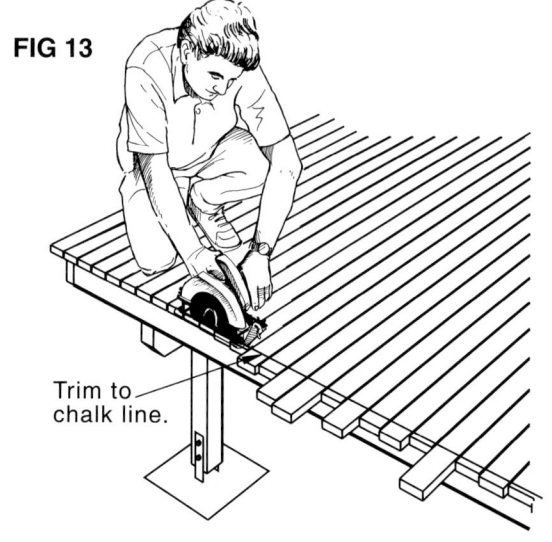

FIG 13 Trim to chalk line.

Waterproof & Tiled Decks

(utilising 'HardiPanel™ Compressed Decking System'. See 'James Hardie Decking Construction Product & Fixing Manual' for further information and other methods of construction).

Note: Timber sizes, footings, fastenings as well as handrails and their fastenings for this system must be provided by an Engineer as the tables in this manual are *not* suitable.

The following method of deck construction is suitable for decks located above habitable areas and utilises 'HardiPanel™ Compressed' as the base support. With this mortar bed method tiling can be laid across the area irrespective of the HardiPanel™ Compressed joint locations. (However when tiling without the mortar bed the tiles must **not** cross the sheet joins).

The following details should be observed:

a). The deck must have a fall of at least 1 in 100 to prevent ponding.

b). The finished deck or tiled surface should be a 50mm MIN. below the house floor surface, but preferably 150mm. Without such a set-down the deck system will inevitably leak and allow water to enter the ceiling of the area underneath.

c). HardiPanel™ Compressed should extend beyond the supporting frame 50mm MIN. and 100mm MAX. and a drip mould should be attached (see fig 1).

d). If deck is over 4.5m in any direction provide a movement joint.

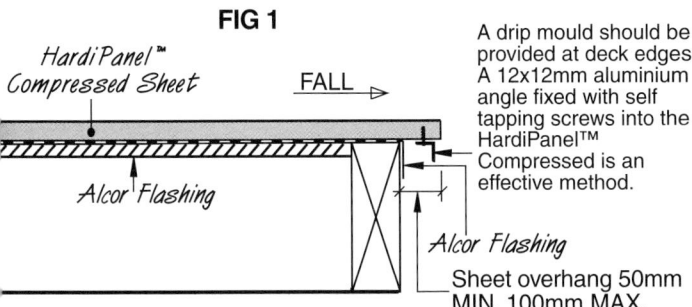

FIG 1

e). Tiles do **not** make decks waterproof. Waterproof membranes must be applied for this purpose.

f). Waterproofing with this method relies on the membrane applied directly over HardiPanel™ Compressed in Step 3 (see Page 36). Liquid membranes can be used or alternatively sheet membranes such as PVC.

g). To protect the waterproofing a wearing surface must be incorporated. This can be achieved by using Steps 4 & 5. Some integral liquid membranes can be coated with a suitable wearing surface.

Timber Framing for this Method

All framing should be treated. All joists and trimmers should be 45mm MIN. thick. The joint or gap between HardiPanel™ Compressed should be 5mm MIN. wide. For 900 wide x 15mm thick HardiPanel™ Compressed.

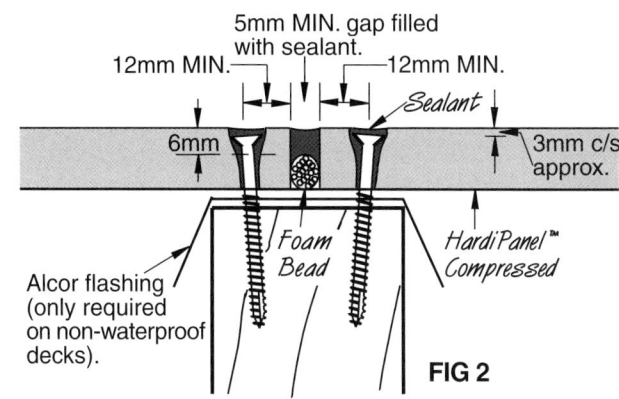

FIG 2

Joists are spaced at 453mm ¢ and 402mm ¢ for 1200mm wide sheets. For 1200x18mm thick sheets, space joists at 603mm ¢ and 453mm ¢ for 900x18mm. Sheet edges must be supported. Edges around the perimeter must **not** extend more than 100mm past the frame.

Laying the 'HardiPanel™ Compressed Decking System'

Sheets lying parallel with joists should be screw fixed with 10x50mm long galvanised steel countersunk screws at 450mm centres around the edges and through the centres of each sheet (see fig 2). Sheets lying across the joists should be fixed with three screws per joist for 900mm wide sheets and four screws per joist for 1200mm wide sheets, equally spaced.

Screws must **not** be closer than 12mm to a sheet edge or 50mm at corners. Before drilling screw holes, place a piece of adhesive tape in position and drill through the tape. This will help to prevent sealant soiling the deck surface during the next step.

Screw holes should be pre-drilled with a masonry bit and countersunk 3mm deep, allowing 1mm clearance over diameter of screw. Throughly clean screw holes then fill with sealant. Sealant must also be applied to the screw threads and to the top of the screws on completion to ensure a completely waterproof fastening. Remove adhesive tape.

Jointing

All sheets should be laid, positioned and screw fixed before the sealing of joints is begun. Joints should be clean, dry and free from dust to ensure satisfactory adhesion of sealant. Masking tape should be laid along both sides of the joint to assist with a neat clean finish. Remove tape immediately on completion.

Joints are sealed as follows:

a). Press continuous lengths of 9mm dia. polyethylene foam bead into the gaps between adjoining sheets, pressing down firmly on top of the joists or trimmers so as to finish approx. 6mm below the upper surface of the sheets.

b). Apply polyurethane sealant into the space immediately above the foam bead. Follow the recommendations outlined on the sealant cartridge for correct application.

c). The level of the sealant should be finished off slightly below the level of the sheet surface to avoid abrasion and scuffing. As the sealant quickly forms a tack free surface, it is essential that the joints be smoothed within 10 minutes of application.

d). Remove masking tape to leave a neat clean joint.

e). Avoid excessive foot traffic on the deck for at least twenty-four hours to allow sealant to set.

Steps of Construction

(for additional information on framing & other methods of laying the HardiPanel™ Compressed Decking System refer to the James Hardie External Deck Construction booklet).

Step 1 Construct floor framing.

Step 2 Lay the HardiPanel™ Compressed sheeting.

Step 3 Employ a Contractor to lay a waterproof flexible synthetic sheet material such as 1.2mm thick PVC sheeting applied across the HardiPanel™ Compressed surface. Request a waterproof guarantee from the Contractor covering materials and workmanship.

Step 4 Lay slip sheet as required by the waterproofing manufacturer.

This protects the membrane surface from damage and isolates substructure movement from any movement in the tiled surface system. This allows unbroken tile surfaces up to 4500x4500mm.

Step 5 Lay a 30mm thick mortar (compo) bed with 75x75x2.0mm or similar gal. mesh (not chicken wire) across the slip sheet in areas not greater than 4500x4500mm. For larger areas provide a movement joint. This doesn't have to be at the HardiPanel™ Compressed joints. Allow the mortar to cure for ten days min. before applying tiles.

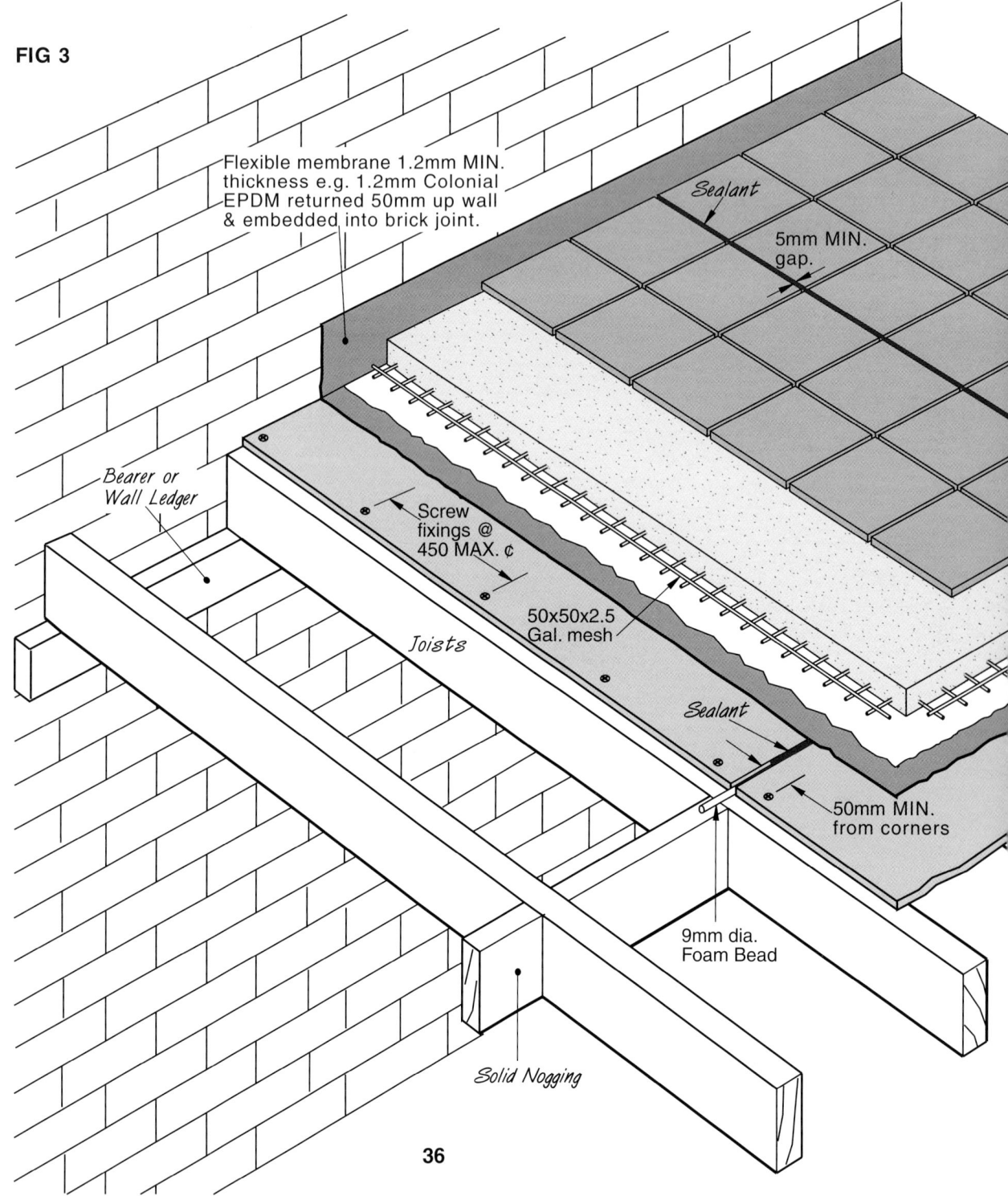

FIG 3

Prefinished metal overflashing

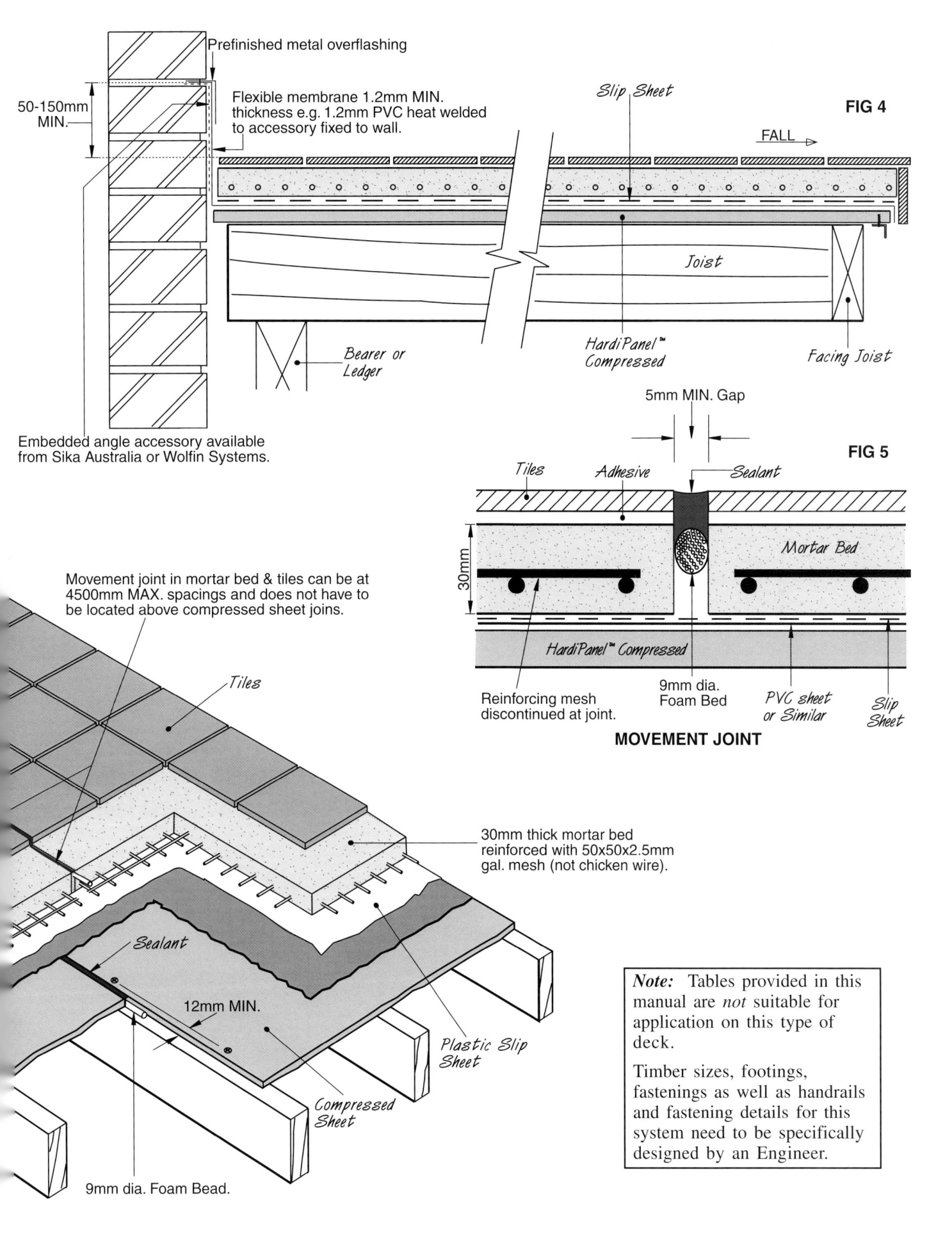

50-150mm MIN.

Flexible membrane 1.2mm MIN. thickness e.g. 1.2mm PVC heat welded to accessory fixed to wall.

Slip Sheet

FIG 4

FALL →

Joist

Bearer or Ledger

HardiPanel™ Compressed

Facing Joist

Embedded angle accessory available from Sika Australia or Wolfin Systems.

5mm MIN. Gap

FIG 5

Tiles — *Adhesive* — *Sealant*

30mm

Mortar Bed

HardiPanel™ Compressed

Reinforcing mesh discontinued at joint.

9mm dia. Foam Bed

PVC sheet or Similar

Slip Sheet

MOVEMENT JOINT

Movement joint in mortar bed & tiles can be at 4500mm MAX. spacings and does not have to be located above compressed sheet joins.

Tiles

30mm thick mortar bed reinforced with 50x50x2.5mm gal. mesh (not chicken wire).

Sealant

12mm MIN.

Plastic Slip Sheet

Compressed Sheet

9mm dia. Foam Bead.

Note: Tables provided in this manual are *not* suitable for application on this type of deck.

Timber sizes, footings, fastenings as well as handrails and fastening details for this system need to be specifically designed by an Engineer.

Joint Sealants
Selleys or Dow Corning Brick & Concrete Crack Sealant.

37

Building Outdoor Steps

(see Tables for stringers & tread sizes)

Timbers to Select
Hardwoods durability Class 2 or better or treated softwood H3. Treated softwoods will perform better if seasoned.

Getting the Proportions Right
For steps to be comfortable to climb, the proportion between tread and risers needs to be right. If you are not sure, use the following proportion calculation to check: *The going plus twice the riser should equal between 550-675mm alternatively, the sum of 1 riser plus 1 tread should equal between 430mm and 460mm.*

Risers should not be greater than 190mm high and treads should not be less than 250mm wide.

Important: Riser and tread dimensions should be the same for the last ones at the top and bottom to avoid injuries.

How to Establish the Proportion
(See example Fig 1). Obtain the total rise and divide it until you arrive at a riser height of between 150-175mm as this is a good average height. Then obtain the 'total going' and divide it until you arrive at a tread width of between 250-275mm as this is also a good average width. Apply the proportion calculation as a check.

Stringers
Step treads are supported by the stringers either directly with step shaped stringers as in fig 3 and trenches as in figs 5 & 6 or indirectly by attached battens as in fig 4 or triangular shaped wedges or tread supports as in fig 7.

Treads
Treads can be laid in one single piece as in fig 4 or as a pair with a space between as in fig 3. Single solid timber treads are more subject to distortion through exposure than the narrower pairs.

Note: Use only low shrinkage or seasoned Durability Class 1 or H3 or 4 treated timber for stringers.

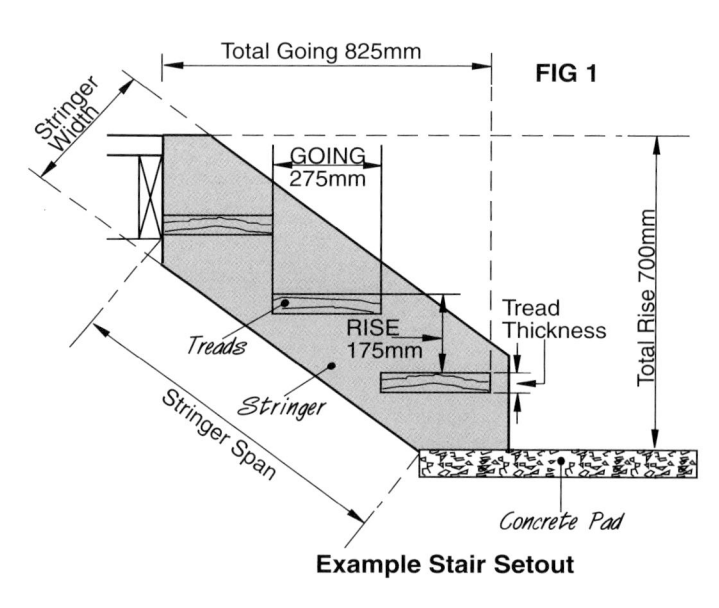

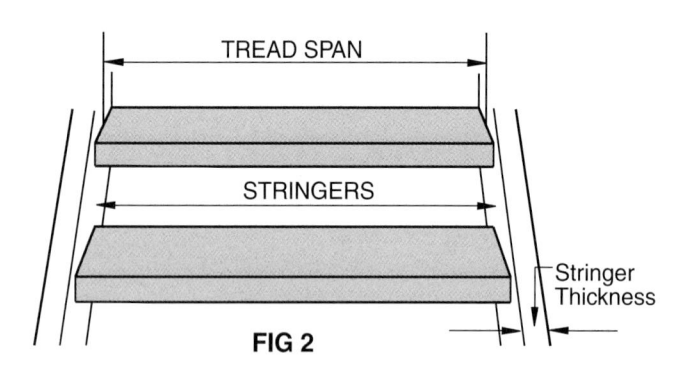

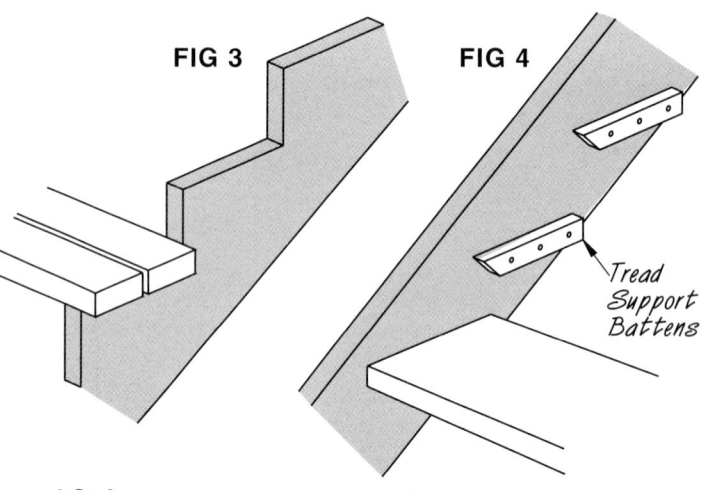

FIG 1 — Example Stair Setout

FIG 2

FIG 3 — Step Shaped Stringers

FIG 4 — Attached Stringer Battens

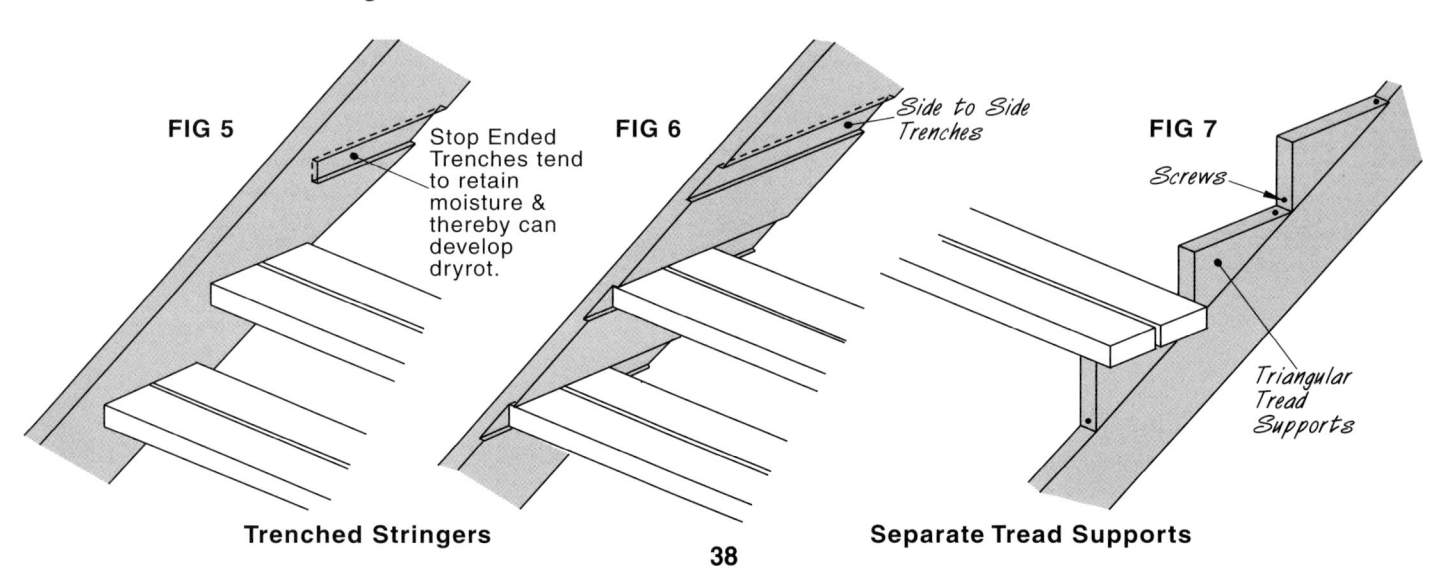

FIG 5 / FIG 6 — Trenched Stringers (Stop Ended Trenches tend to retain moisture & thereby can develop dryrot. Side to Side Trenches)

FIG 7 — Separate Tread Supports (Screws, Triangular Tread Supports)

Anchoring Stairs to Decks

Stairs are usually adjoined to the deck by the stringers and secured by fastenings through the stringers into the deck joists as in fig 8 or by galvanised angle brackets as in fig 9 or they may be housed directly into the deck. However these housings are prone to rot. Steel stringers are fastened to the deck with bolts through flat plates welded to the stringer ends as in fig 10.

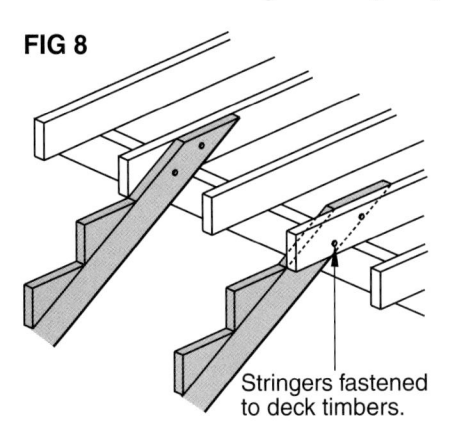

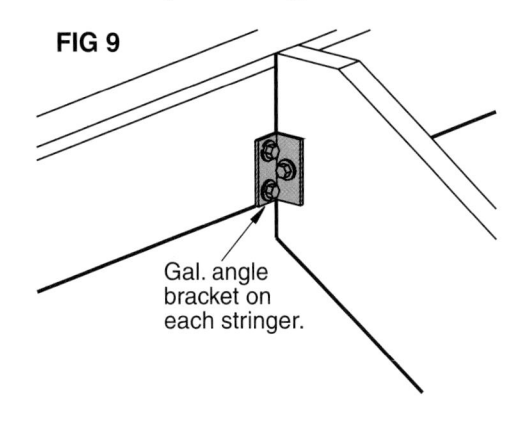

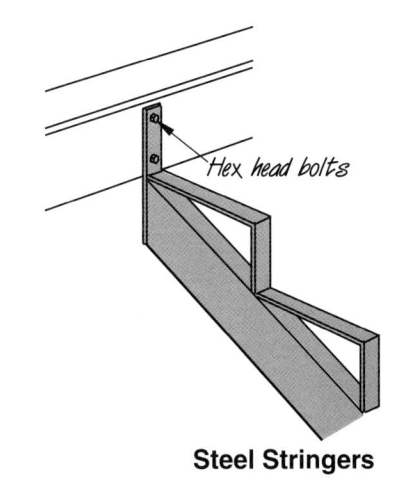

FIG 8

Stringers fastened to deck timbers.

FIG 9

Gal. angle bracket on each stringer.

Hex head bolts

Steel Stringers

Anchoring Stringers at the Bottom Ends

Timber stairs can be anchored at the bottom ends by fabricated hot dipped galvanised brackets bolted to each stringer as in figs 11 & 12 with the bracket embedded in concrete. Drill bolt holes though brackets before galvanising. Keep underside of brackets clear of the concrete pad or path by 12-20mm.

Steel Stringers

Steel stringers have their lower ends embedded in concrete or sometimes bolted to a concrete pad. To prevent corrosion, take care that all honey combing is removed around embedded stringers and that the concrete surface slopes away from the stringers. Ensure moisture cannot enter the stringers throughout their length.

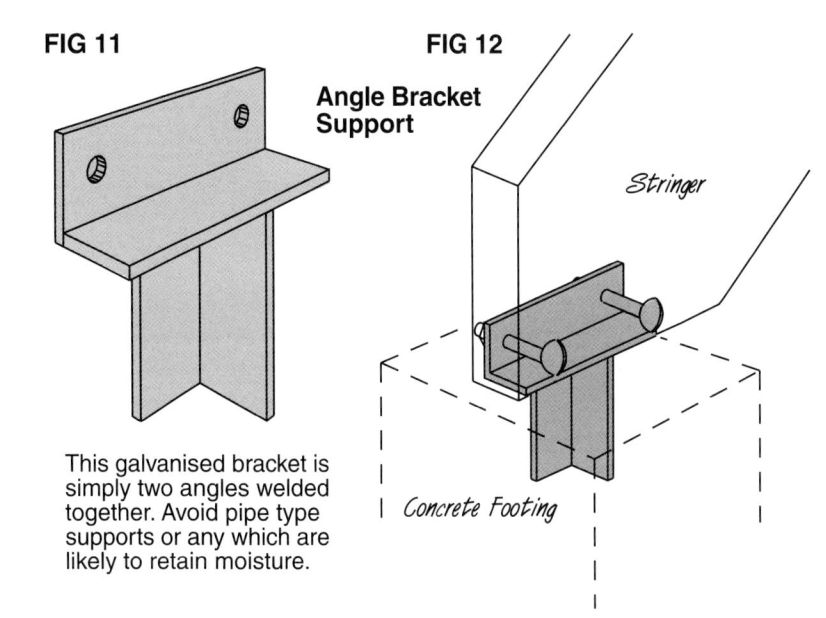

FIG 11

Angle Bracket Support

This galvanised bracket is simply two angles welded together. Avoid pipe type supports or any which are likely to retain moisture.

FIG 12

Stringer

Concrete Footing

Restraining Long Stringers

Stringers need to be restrained either by an adjacent wall or column or by 10mm gal. bolts under the treads at 1350mm centres max. The bolts are taken through both stringers and washers and nuts attached.

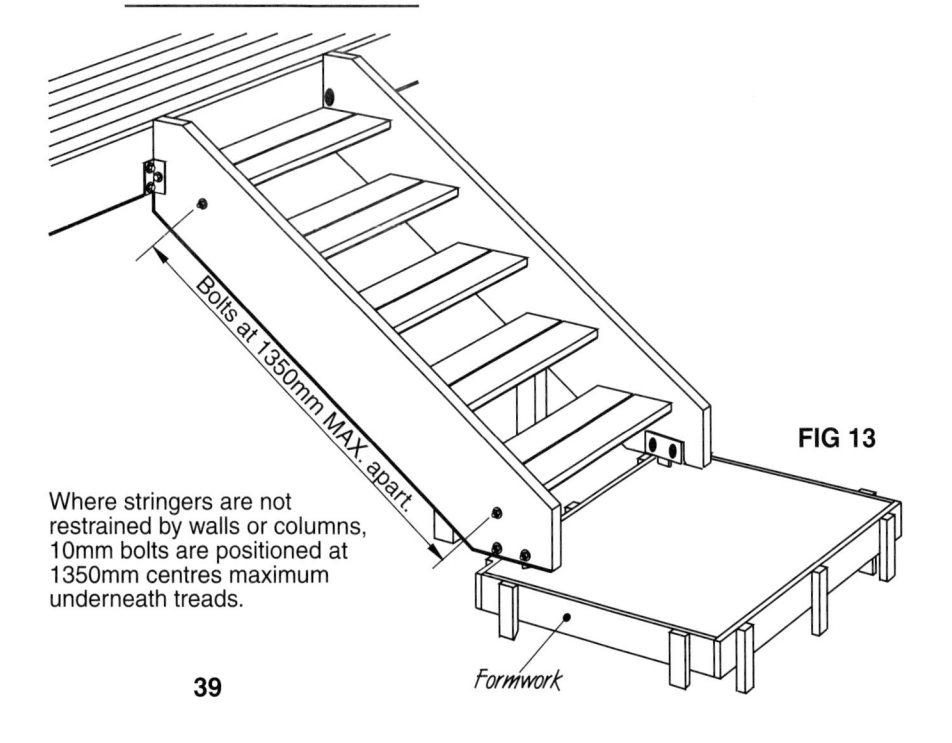

Where stringers are not restrained by walls or columns, 10mm bolts are positioned at 1350mm centres maximum underneath treads.

Bolts at 1350mm MAX. apart

FIG 13

Formwork

How to Construct Steps

Decide which tread supporting method to adopt (see figs 3 to 7).

Step 1 Working from a pair of sawstools, mark on both stringers the tread and riser outline as in fig 14. To obtain tread and riser measurements (see Page 38).

Step 2 Cut and fasten any tread support battens or triangular supports or cut any trenches required. Cut ends of stringers to shape. Prime paint all trenches, housings and raw ends and edges with oil based wood primer.

Step 3 Install treads fastening the top and bottom ones first.

Step 4 Bolt gal. anchoring brackets to the stringers. Raise steps into position and mark footing hole positions to receive the lower supporting brackets. Remove stairs and excavate footing holes.

Step 5 Bolt stairs in position and support their lower ends on temporary props or blocks (see fig 15).

Step 6 Construct formwork for the concrete pad at the lower end and pour concrete to footing holes and pad.

Allow concrete to harden 48 hours or more before removing the supports.

Handrailing

(for selecting handrail sizes see Tables)

What Timber to Use

Treated softwood H3 or hardwood durability Class 1 or 2. Seasoned timbers will perform better.

Heights Spacings & Spans (see figs 1 & 2)

Check with Local Council or Building Certifier regarding the most recent requirements for handrail heights above deck and step nosings and maximum spacings or openings between handrail members. Also check if the chosen design is permissible.

Where the chosen handrail design incorporates horizontal rails which create a laddered structure, safety glass or even acrylic sheet fitted on the inside of the handrail may be required by building regulations to prevent children climbing.

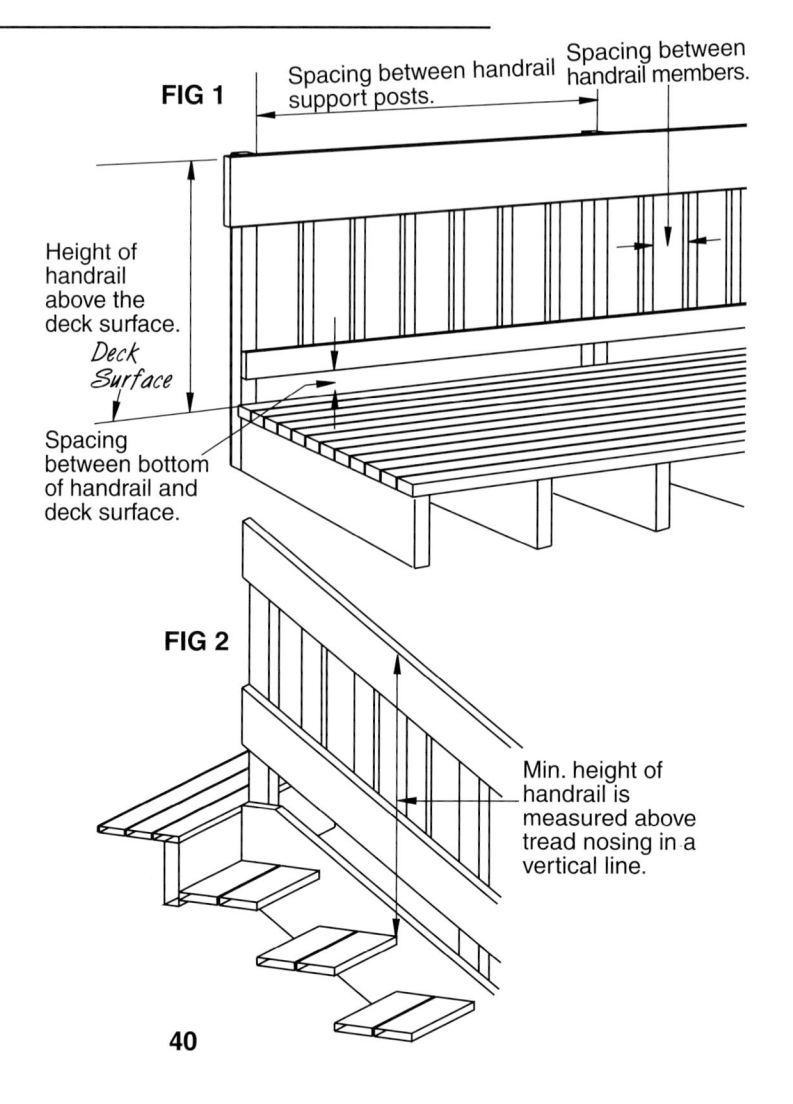

Handrailing

(for selecting handrail sizes see the Tables on Page 111)

Important Note: Handrail design and construction is critical and litigation for injury or even death could confront the builder even years after construction. Many common designs and methods of construction are suspect, in fact only a few could be considered safe. Weakening of the structure through wood rot and corrosion of fasteners is a common fault. You will need better coatings than hot dip gal. near the coast and in all situations handrail fastenings must *never* fail. Look for a system that has built-in permanent reliability.

Design Requirements

The handrail heights and spacing requirements in the BCA are illustrated in the box opposite. Check with the Local Council Building Depart. for any more recent changes to these requirements nationally or locally before adopting them.

What Timber to Use

H3 level treated softwood or hardwood Durability Class 1 or 2. Seasoned timber will perform better in exposed situations. Species suggested are: Jarrah, Ironbark, Spotted Gum, Kevila or Merbau.

Handrail Timber Sizes

For the size of handrail posts, rails and balusters, see Tables in Chapter 8.

Handrail Design & Fastening

Either of the following two methods are recommended.

A. Handrails can be cut and housed between the posts as in figs 2, 3 or 4;

B. Rails can be bolted to the face of posts as in figs 5 & 6. Use through bolts. The nuts can be c/s on the back side.

When employing 'Method A', it is important the joints are properly designed to resist outward pressure from people leaning against them. Fig 1 on Page 42 is a suggested joint (but it must be rot proof and figs 3 & 4 Page 42 are suggested fastening methods. Manufactured designs may provide purpose made brackets.

Note: A simple butt joint with skew nailing should *never* be applied to handrails.

Deck posts continue above deck to become handrail posts and sometimes also continue to become pergola posts. Vertical balusters can be attached at the lower ends to the facing joist as in fig 5 or to a rail as in fig 6.

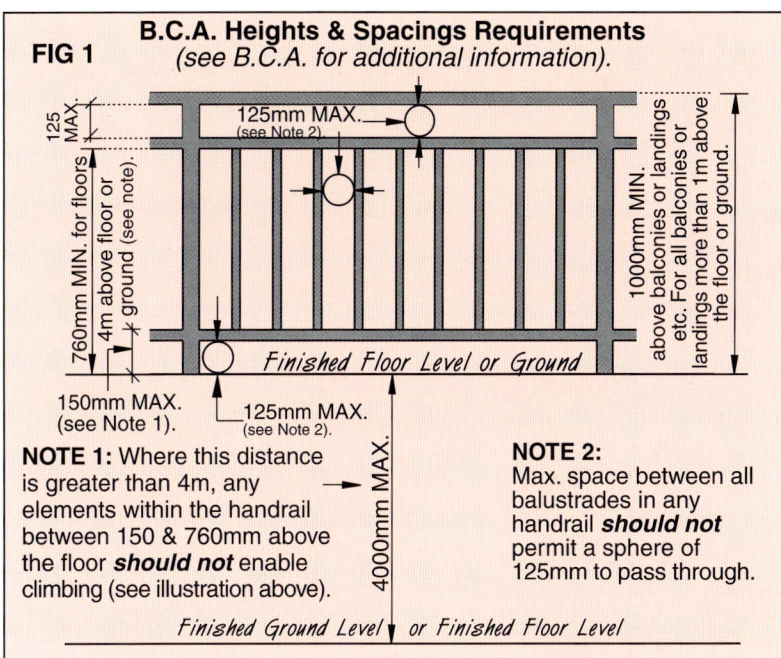

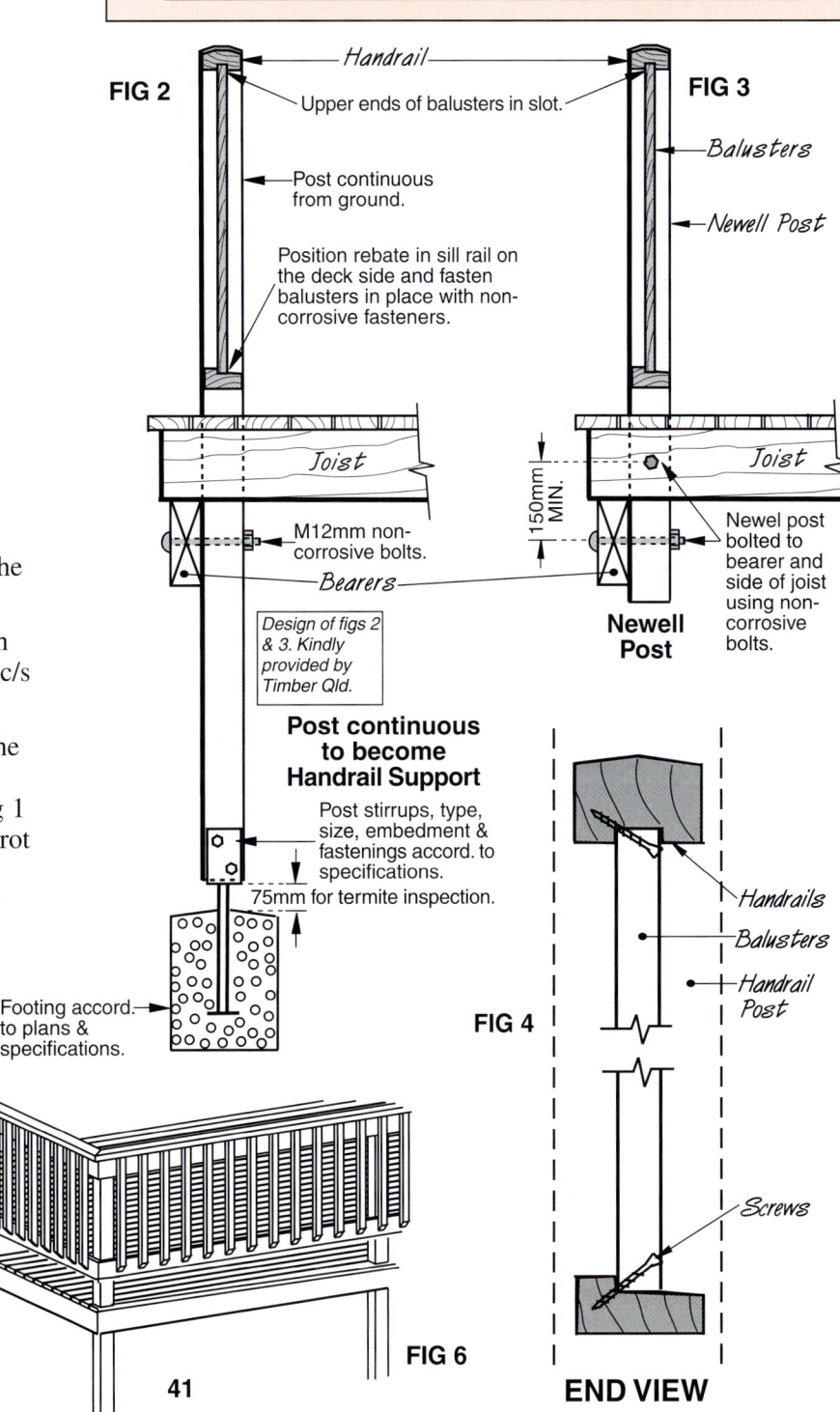

FIG 1 — B.C.A. Heights & Spacings Requirements *(see B.C.A. for additional information).*

125mm MAX. (see Note 2)
760mm MIN. for floors 4m above floor or ground (see note)
1000mm MIN. above balconies or landings etc. For all balconies or landings more than 1m above the floor or ground.
150mm MAX. (see Note 1).
125mm MAX. (see Note 2)
4000mm MAX.
Finished Floor Level or Ground
Finished Ground Level or Finished Floor Level

NOTE 1: Where this distance is greater than 4m, any elements within the handrail between 150 & 760mm above the floor *should not* enable climbing (see illustration above).

NOTE 2: Max. space between all balustrades in any handrail *should not* permit a sphere of 125mm to pass through.

FIG 2 — Handrail; Upper ends of balusters in slot; Post continuous from ground; Position rebate in sill rail on the deck side and fasten balusters in place with non-corrosive fasteners; M12mm non-corrosive bolts; Bearers; Design of figs 2 & 3. Kindly provided by Timber Qld.

Post continuous to become Handrail Support — Post stirrups, type, size, embedment & fastenings accord. to specifications. 75mm for termite inspection. Footing accord. to plans & specifications.

FIG 3 — Balusters; Newell Post; Joist; 150mm MIN.; Newel post bolted to bearer and side of joist using non-corrosive bolts. **Newell Post**

FIG 4 / END VIEW — Handrails; Balusters; Handrail Post; Screws

FIG 5

FIG 6

41

How to Construct 'Method A'

Step 1 Mark height positions of top and bottom rails.

Step 2 If rails are to be housed into posts, make the housings and cut the rails to length.

Step 3 Install rails and fasten securely.

Step 4 Cut and attach balusters.

Fastening Balusters

Refer to your plans or specifications for the correct fastener or select from Pages 86&87. In figs 4, Page 41, the upper ends of the balusters are fastened in a slot and the lower ends into a rebate. Don't use a slot in the lower rails as the ends of a baluster can't dry out as well after wet weather even if holes are drilled between them.

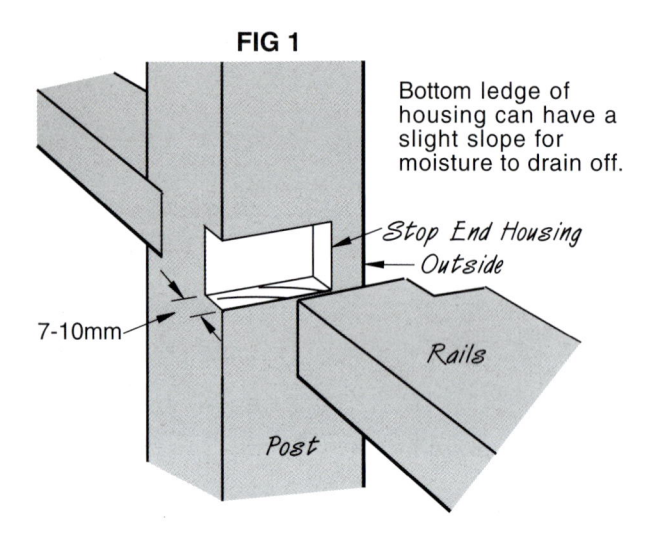

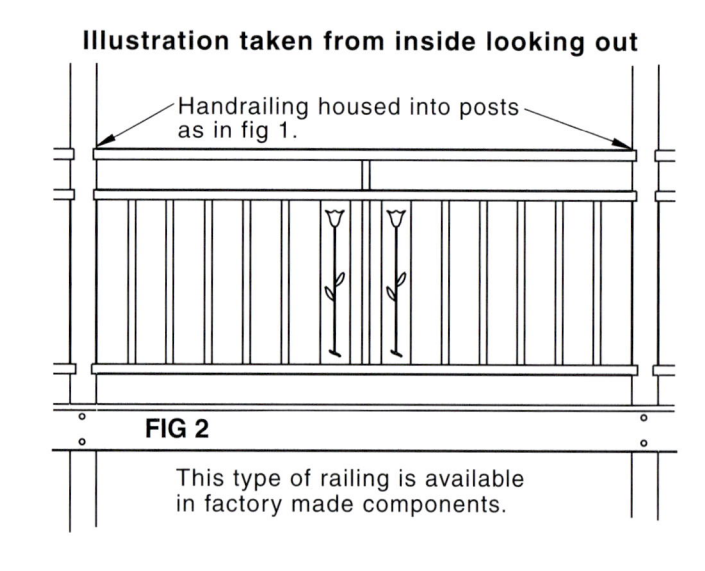

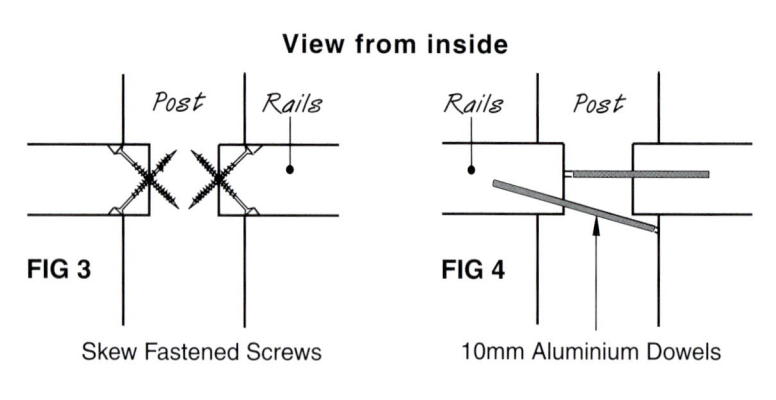

Illustration taken from inside looking out

FIG 2

This type of railing is available in factory made components.

FIG 1

Bottom ledge of housing can have a slight slope for moisture to drain off.

7-10mm

View from inside

FIG 3 — Skew Fastened Screws

FIG 4 — 10mm Aluminium Dowels

How to Construct 'Method B'

This is the simplest and most economical method as only one support rail for balusters is necessary. However, it does require the top rail to project outside the posts the same distance as the bottom rail, see fig 5, Page 41.

Step 1 Where the deck posts are trimmed to handrail height, spring a chalk line through at the required height and extend this height mark onto the house wall. Where a wall post is required as in fig 5, this can be cut and fastened to the wall. Use one 10mm dia. coach screw top and bottom into weatherboard walls and 10mm dyna bolts or similar into masonry walls. Trim all posts to height.

Step 2 Cut and attach the top rail (where lower or mid rails are required, attach these first). Corners can be either mitre joined or overlapped. Fasten the rails with through bolts.

Step 3 Baluster positions are then marked along the rails. Ensure they are plumb. Attach the balusters with screws as required.

> **Hints:**
> After cutting all handrail members and making housings, flood coat with a water repellent preservative and/or prime coat with the chosen paint or stain.

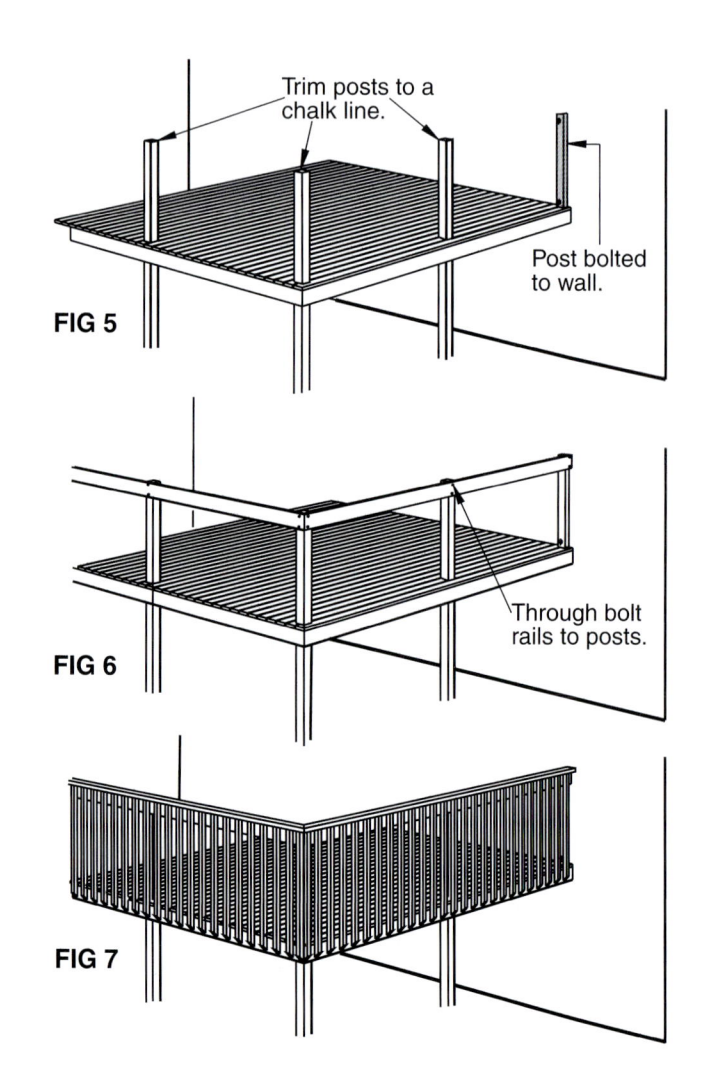

FIG 5 — Trim posts to a chalk line. Post bolted to wall.

FIG 6 — Through bolt rails to posts.

FIG 7

Handrail Designs & Construction Details

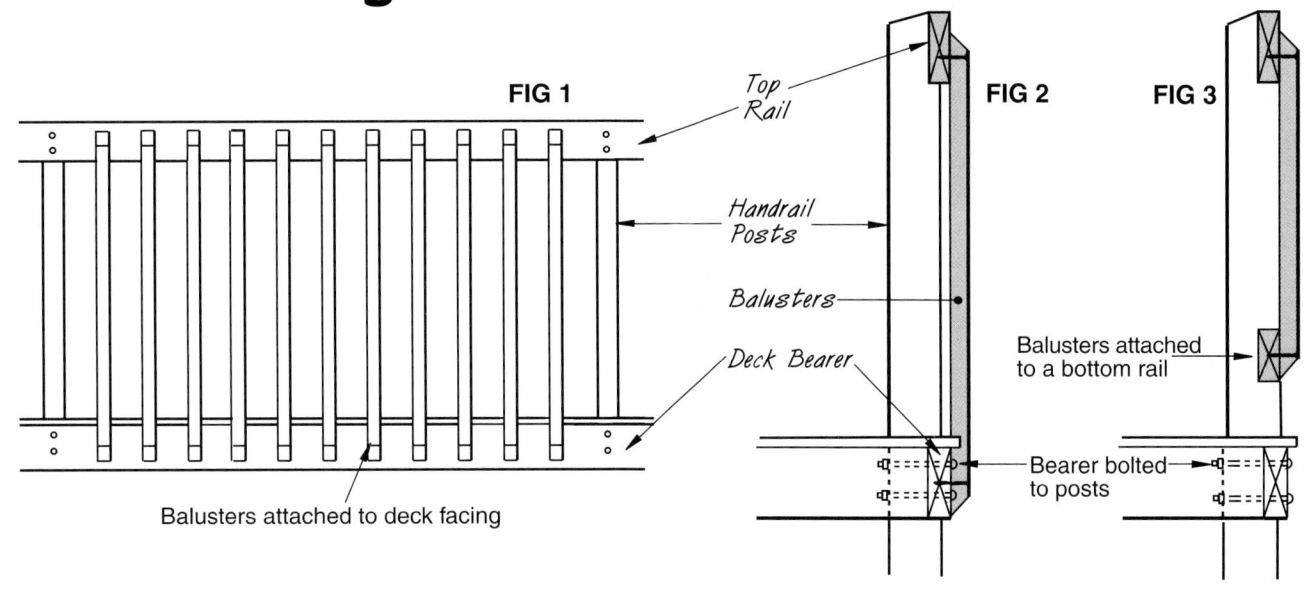

FIG 1 — Balusters attached to deck facing

FIG 2 — Top Rail, Handrail Posts, Balusters, Deck Bearer, Bearer bolted to posts

FIG 3 — Balusters attached to a bottom rail

Vertical Balusters

Vertical balusters attached at the bottom end to the deck facing as in fig 1 offer a simple low cost design with a high safety factor. Screw fasten the balusters and keep their top ends below the rail tops to enable hands to slide along the rail without injury.

A common variation is to install a bottom rail as in figs 3 & 4. Terminating the balusters above the deck as in fig 3 provides a horizontal space. The combined effect visually reduces the railing height.

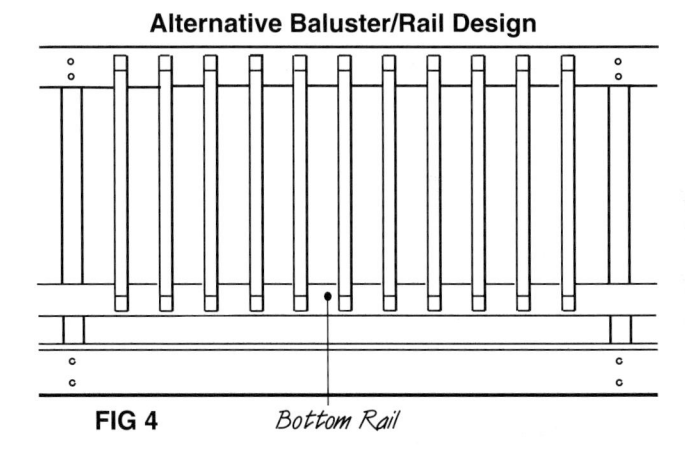

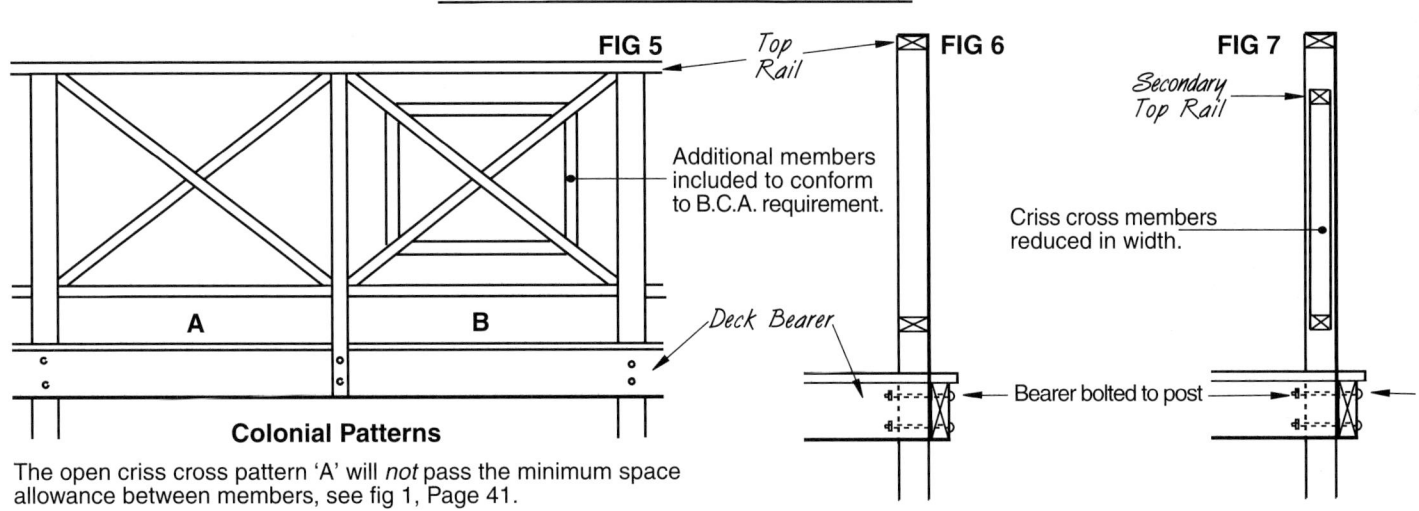

Alternative Baluster/Rail Design

FIG 4 — Bottom Rail

FIG 5 — Colonial Patterns (A, B)

The open criss cross pattern 'A' will *not* pass the minimum space allowance between members, see fig 1, Page 41.

FIG 6 — Top Rail, Additional members included to conform to B.C.A. requirement. Deck Bearer, Bearer bolted to post

FIG 7 — Secondary Top Rail, Criss cross members reduced in width.

Criss Cross Alternatives

Criss cross patterns are widely applied to traditional Australian architecture. The top rail is best fastened down into the post end grain with screws. The lower rail could be housed into posts and end grain or skew screw fastened. Where Authorities require the openings to be reduced for safety, additional members are cut in between the criss cross. The criss cross can be constructed with timber the full rail width or reduced to slender members of approx. 40x40mm to reduce the visual weight of the design as in figs 7 & 8.

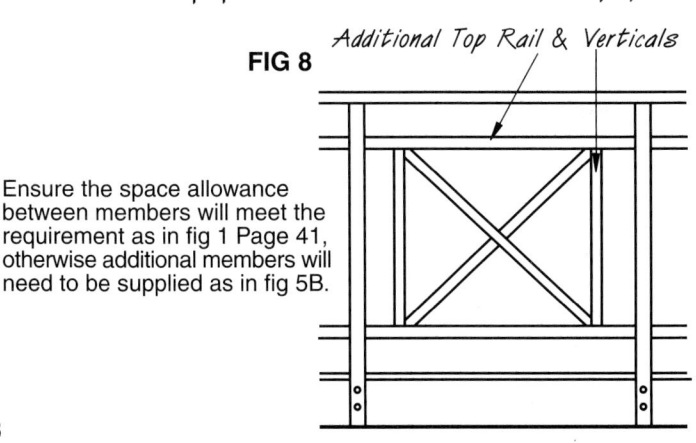

FIG 8 — Additional Top Rail & Verticals

Ensure the space allowance between members will meet the requirement as in fig 1 Page 41, otherwise additional members will need to be supplied as in fig 5B.

Timber Lattice Panelling

Timber lattice applied to handrails associates well with tropical and some 'old worlde' designs especially some Queenslanders.

For safety the battens should be 12mm min. thick on each side. The timber should be treated H3 and fastenings should be non corrosive.

Panels can be fitted into a grooved or (slotted) top rail and end posts and into a rebate at the lower end. Lattice provides a degree of privacy and but will still allow breeze and sunlight penetration. The smaller opening patterns usually hold a better achitectural appearance for handrailing.

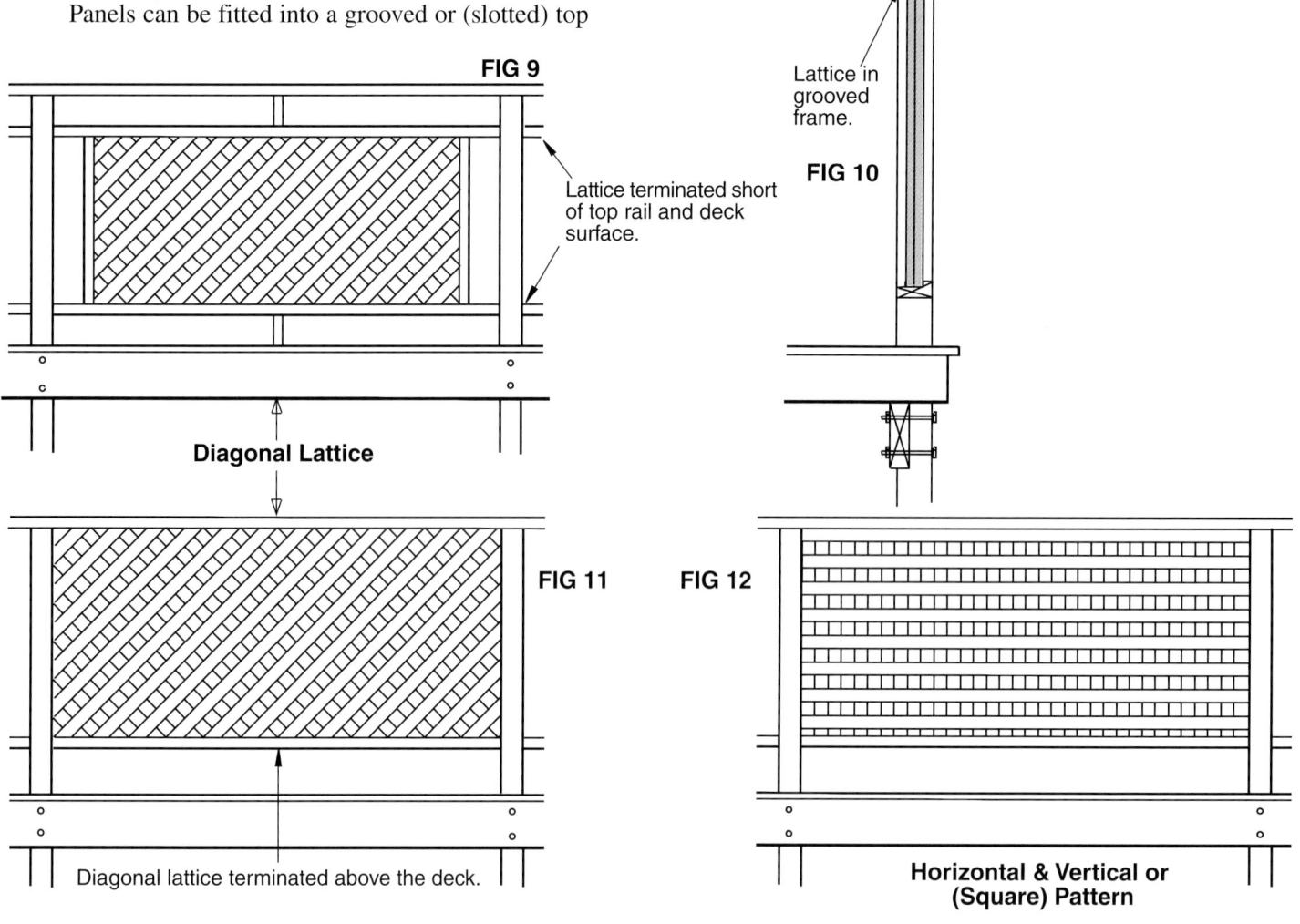

FIG 9 — Lattice terminated short of top rail and deck surface.

Diagonal Lattice

FIG 10 — Lattice in grooved frame.

FIG 11 — Diagonal lattice terminated above the deck.

FIG 12 — Horizontal & Vertical or (Square) Pattern

Glass Panels

Glass permits unempeded access to views and protection from wind. Glass should be safety glass and preferably laminated. The glass should be designed in accord. with the A.S. (Code).

Enquire at local glazier for installation details.

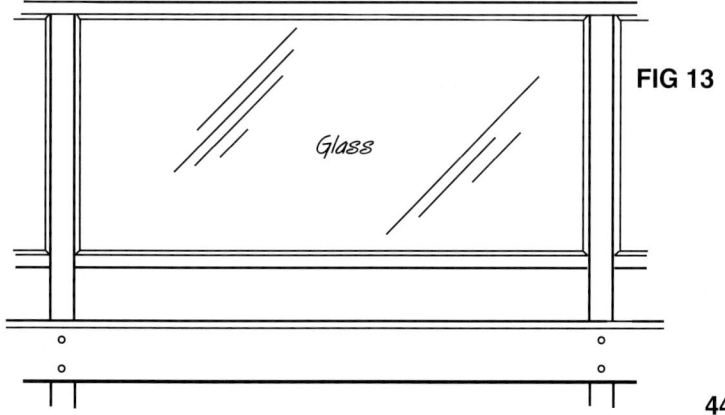

FIG 13

'Olde Worlde' Baluster Patterns

A multitude of designs are possible utilising round dowels, square balusters and battens and with routered patterns as in fig 19.

The top rails are screw fixed into the post end grains and the other rails housed with stop ended (half housings) into posts and dowelled or skew screw fastened. The pattern should be in keeping with the house style or period.

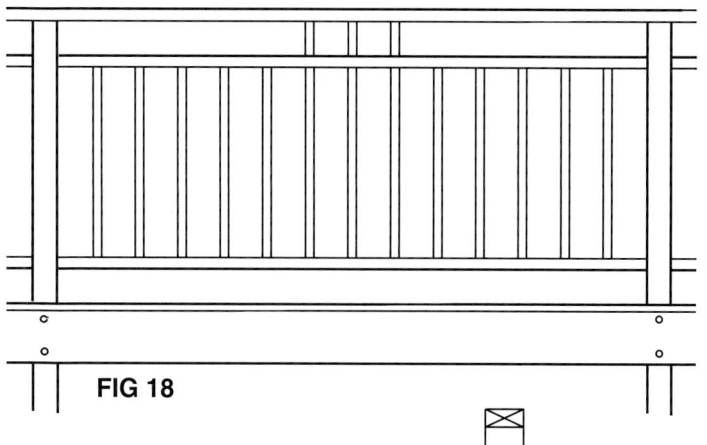

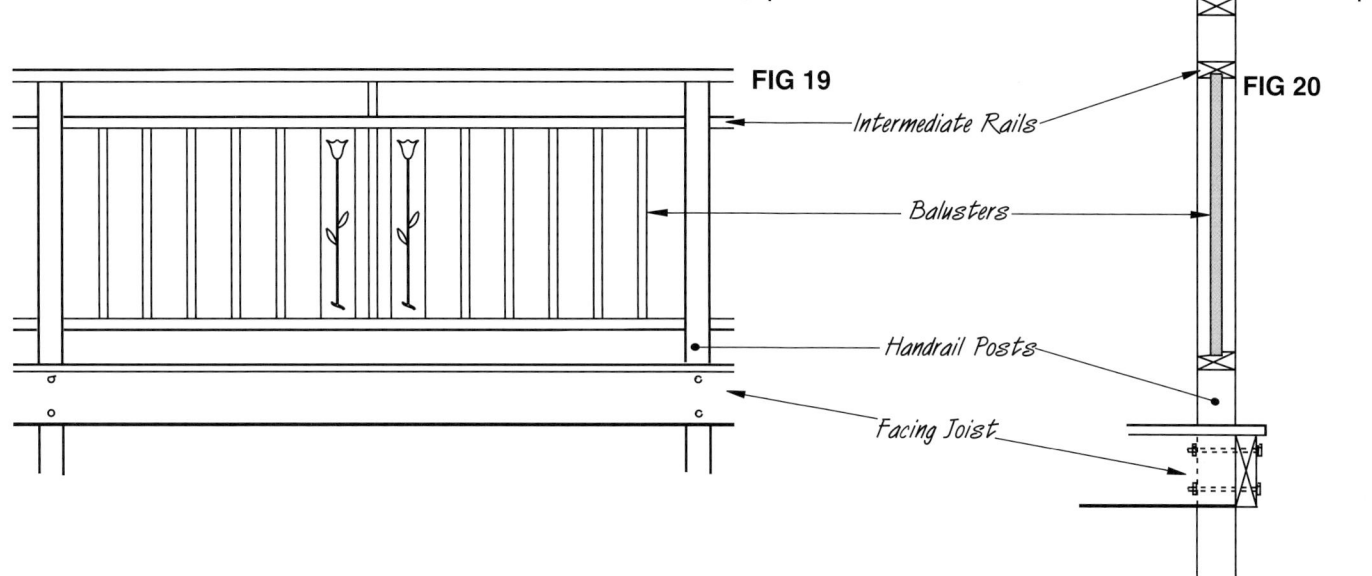

FIG 18

FIG 19

FIG 20
- Intermediate Rails
- Balusters
- Handrail Posts
- Facing Joist

Solid Timber Diagonal Planking

These handrails mainly suit modern or Post 1950's architecture. They provide privacy and good wind protection. Western Red Cedar is the most commonly applied material when wood stain finishes are required. Treated wood could be used if solid 100% acrylic paint finishes are applied and where the timber is a min. of 18mm thick and seasoned.

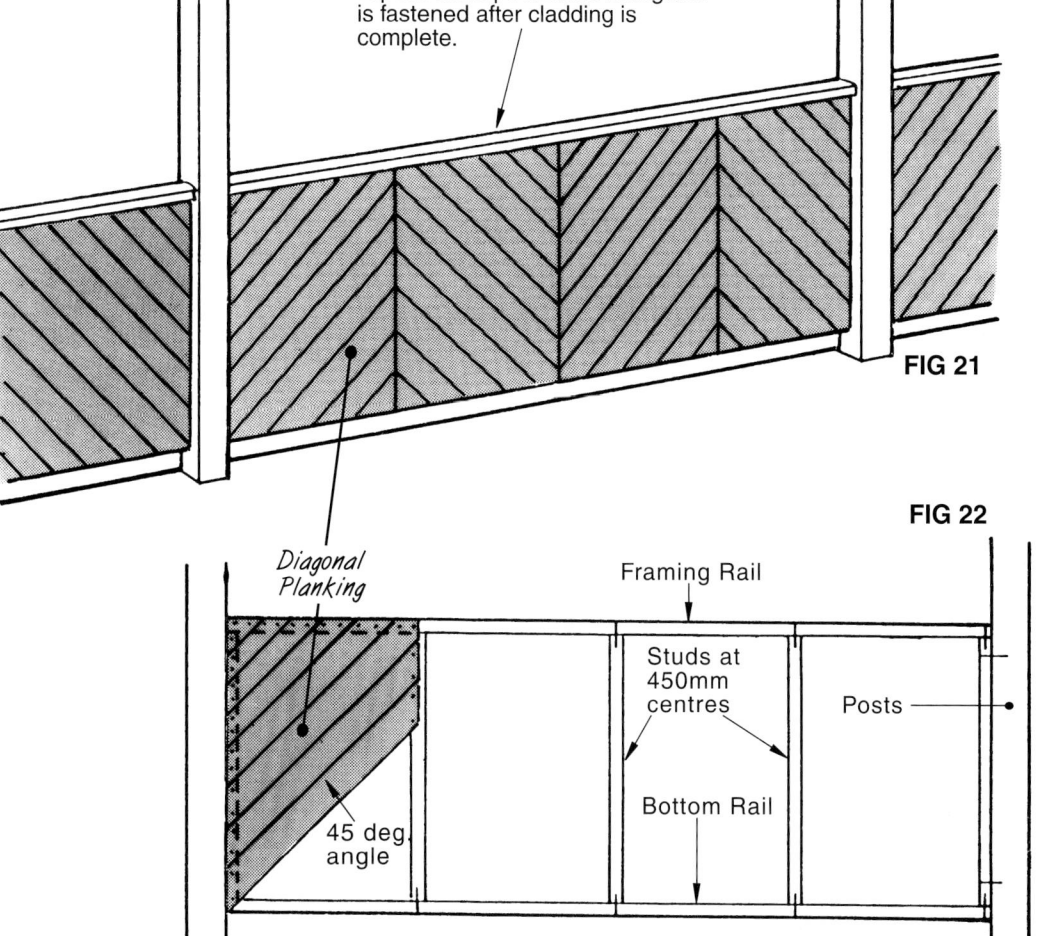

Top rail overlaps cladded railing and is fastened after cladding is complete.

FIG 21

FIG 22
- Diagonal Planking
- 45 deg. angle
- Framing Rail
- Studs at 450mm centres
- Bottom Rail
- Posts

4 How to Build Decks

Building Decks Attached to the House

One of the following two building methods are commonly applied:

Method A (commonly applied to low decks up to 1500mm high) — The posts or the stirrups are embedded in concrete or the permanent posts are bolted to stirrups and embedded in concrete at the commencement.

Method B (ideal for decks over 1500mm high and for pergolas) — The beams and joists are supported on temporary posts and the permanent posts are installed later, (see fig 6 Page 74).

This method enables the Builder to commence building without waiting for concrete to harden around stirrups and the temporary posts make it simpler to bring the supporting bearer into alignment.

Where to Begin (Method A)
Prepare a plan of the proposed deck (see Page 6) and make a 'Material List' from Page 9.

Step 1 *Installing the Ledger or Bearer*
For Weatherboard or BK Veneer Houses:
Mark on the house wall in pencil the proposed deck surface height (not less than 50mm and not more than 150mm below the house floor surface), then measure down from this point and mark the top side of the proposed wall ledger position, (see fig 1).

Spring a chalk line along the wall to represent the top of the wall ledger. Mark the proposed ends of the deck on the chalk line. Trim the wall ledger to length. Prime paint its ends and rear side and bolt into position with 12mm bolts below every alternate joist through the house bearer or framing with nuts and washers.

Where columns or piers are to support a bearer instead of a wall ledger along the wall line (as in BK Veneer), these are constructed to the bottom of bearer height see fig 2 and also Page 28 for further details. The bearer can then be trimmed to length and bolted to the columns as in fig 2.

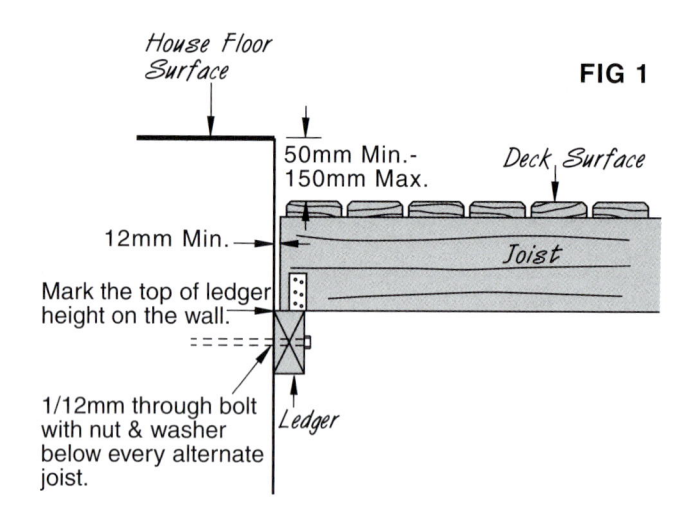

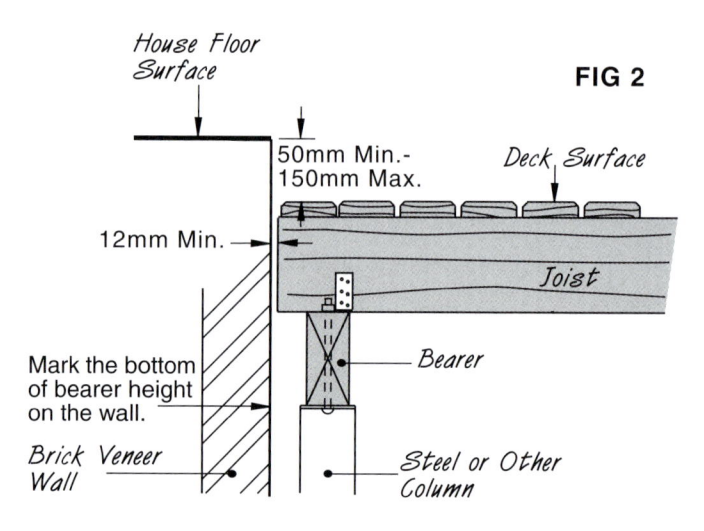

FIG 1

FIG 2

Step 2 *Squaring the Deck Area*
Attach temporary profile battens on the wall approximately 300mm above ground as in fig 4. Plumb lines down to the battens from each end of the wall ledger or bearer.

Drive two pegs to indicate the outer corners of the deck. Square these off the wall line but only roughly at this stage. Use either a large rafter square or the 3,4,5 method as in fig 3. Erect corner profile hurdles 600mm clear of the pegs and on the same level plane as the wall profile battens (see fig 4).

Cont.

Mark on the profiles the length and width of the outer sides of the deck or the points which correspond with the ends of the wall ledger or bearer. Attach string lines as in fig 4 then bring the area into square alignment by taking diagonal measurements. (Adjust two side lines together until both diagonal measurements correspond). Drive pegs to represent the centre of the post holes.

To bring the outer pegs into square alignment, measure a triangle using multiples of 3, 4, & 5. When the measurements intersect the outer lines are square.

FIG 3

To bring into square alignment adjust both outer nails together until both diagonal measurements correspond

FIG 4

Step 3 *Embedding the Stirrups or Posts*

Excavate the post holes to the specified depths and widths. Drive nails in the profiles to indicate the outer sides of the posts and reattach the string lines as in fig 8. Concrete the gal. stirrups with posts attached or stirrups only into the holes with rammed stiff concrete. Align them to the string lines or position them by measuring from a string line. Check them for plumb and square. For further information, (see Pages 21-23). Repeat this check as the concrete hardens. Stirrups with hollow pipe supports should be filled with expanding polystyrene foam (pressure pak) to prevent them holding moisture. Alternatively, for economy, use the high wind post supports, see fig 5.

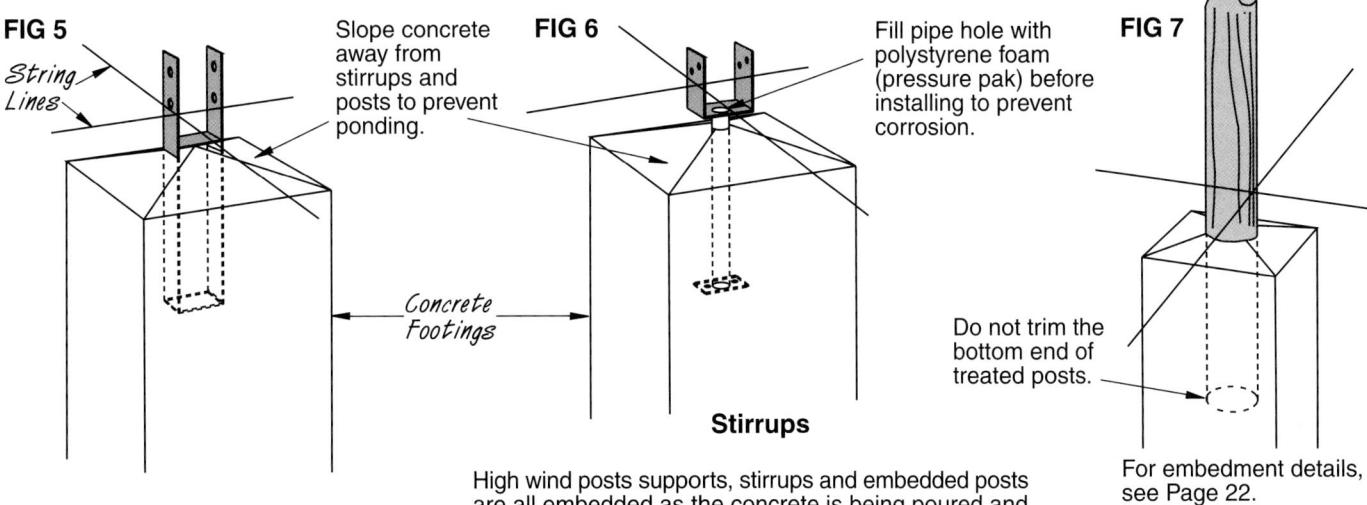

FIG 5 — Slope concrete away from stirrups and posts to prevent ponding.

FIG 6 — Fill pipe hole with polystyrene foam (pressure pak) before installing to prevent corrosion.

FIG 7 — Do not trim the bottom end of treated posts. For embedment details, see Page 22.

High Wind Post Supports

Stirrups

High wind posts supports, stirrups and embedded posts are all embedded as the concrete is being poured and aligned to string lines. Check them for correct height and plumb with a level on both sides.

Embedded Posts

It is easier to align and plumb the stirrups into wet concrete when the posts are attached, however, for those who prefer to install the stirrups first, follow on with Step 4.

Whichever method is used, you need to make bearer housing before erecting posts, see Pages 24 & 25.

Step 4 *Installing Posts into Stirrups*

Allow the concrete to harden for a min. of 48 hours before continuing. Square and shape the post bottoms to fit into the stirrups and clamp them into place. Plumb the posts and tighten the clamps. Drill the bolt holes.

Post top heights can be trimmed now or later. To do this now, firstly establish a level line taken from the wall ledger then measure up from this. You must include the bearer, joist or decking depths then add on the handrail height.

FIG 8

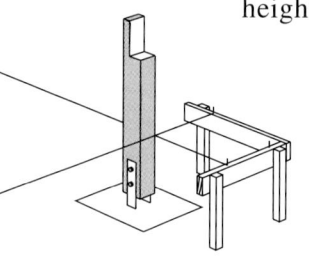

Remove and place the posts on a pair of saw stools to square and trim to length. Mark and cut the bearer housings (see Pages 24 & 25). Coat with preservative and prime paint housings, cut ends and bolt holes. Bolt posts into position and check for plumb both ways.

Step 5 *Installing the Bearer*

Trim bearer to length and bolt into the post housings with 2/12mm gal. cup head bolts with nuts and washers at each end (see fig 9).

Step 6 *Installing the Joists*

Mark each joist position on the top edges of the ledger and the bearer as in fig 9. Space them according to plans. If the last space is shorter than the rest it doesn't matter. Alternatively, equalise the last two spaces.

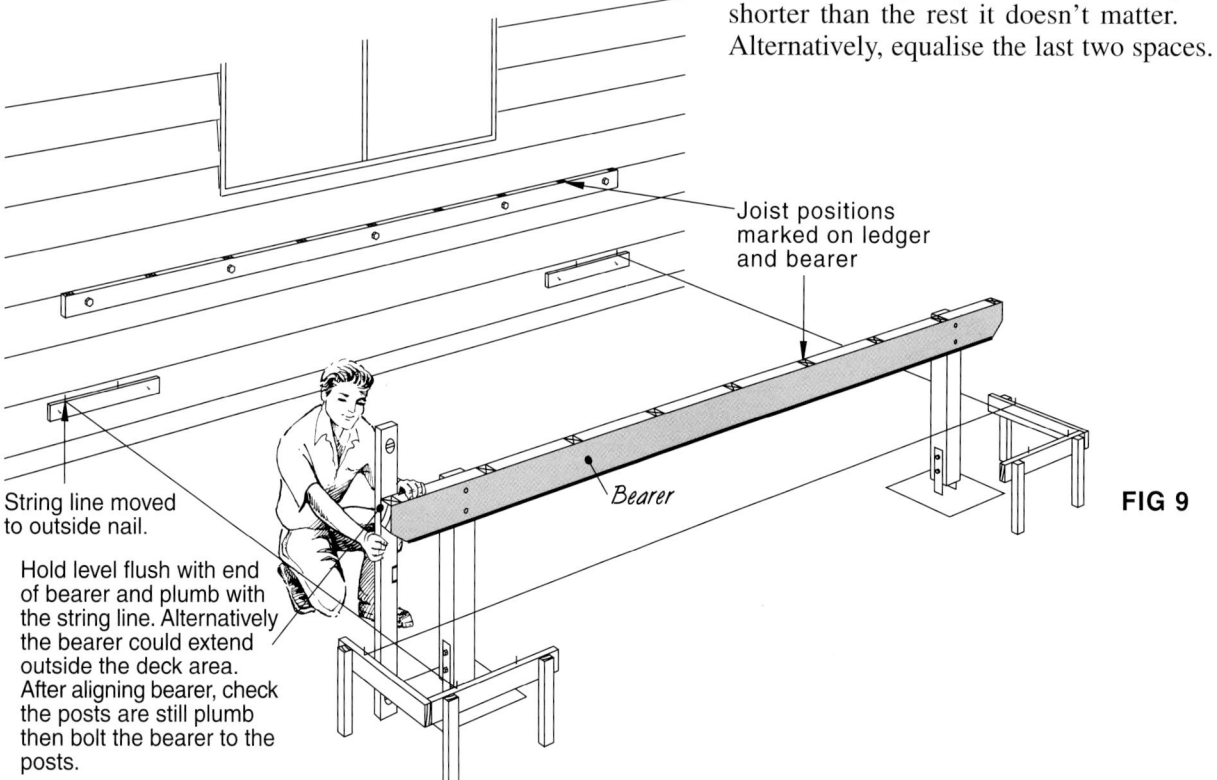

FIG 9

48

Square and trim the ledger end only of each joist and fix the two end joists to the ledger as in fig 10. Bring the posts and bearer into plumb alignment and secure the joists to the bearer.

Step 7 *Apply Any Bracing*

Bring the structure into square alignment and temporarily brace, then cut and bolt into position any required permanent wind bracing, (see figs 10 & 11). Continue to install the remaining joists keeping all bows uppermost. Leave trimming of joist ends until all joists are laid then spring a chalk line through, square each one and trim to length.

Attach a facing joist through the ends of the joists. This gives a better finished appearance.

Prime paint the top edge of each joist using the same colour as the finished decking to give a better appearance between the laid boards.

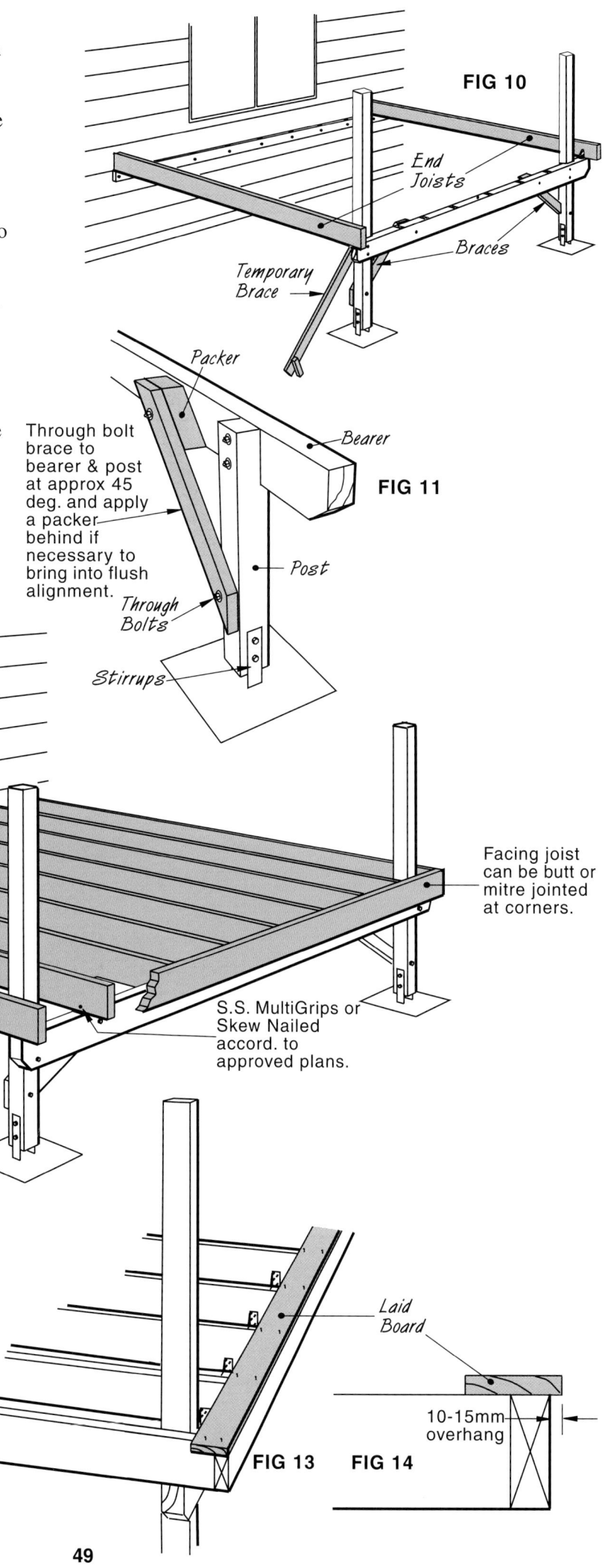

FIG 10

Through bolt brace to bearer & post at approx 45 deg. and apply a packer behind if necessary to bring into flush alignment.

FIG 11

Facing joist can be butt or mitre jointed at corners.

S.S. MultiGrips or Skew Nailed accord. to approved plans.

FIG 12

Applying the Deck Flooring

Use a straightedge to check the tops of joists for any bows or bumps projecting above surrounding joists.

Remove any high spots with a power planer. Install any required handrail newell posts as in fig 3 Page 41. Lay the decking out loosely. Attach the first board through the outer edge (see fig 13). Allow it to overhang the edge by 10-15mm as in fig 14. Ensure it is straight as the following boards will follow its alignment.

For complete instructions on laying decking, (see Pages 33 & 34).

FIG 13   FIG 14   10-15mm overhang

How to Build the Handrail

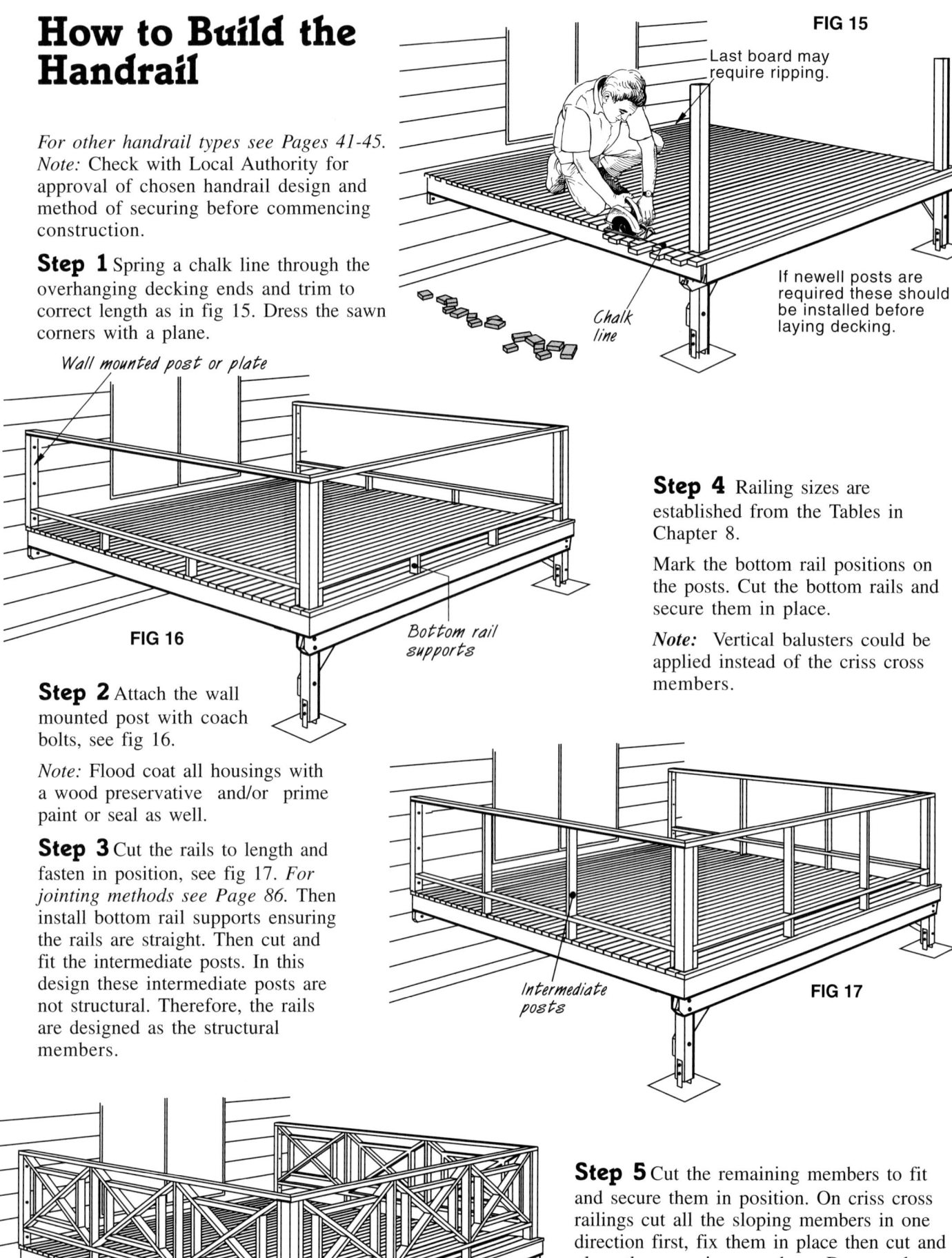

For other handrail types see Pages 41-45.
Note: Check with Local Authority for approval of chosen handrail design and method of securing before commencing construction.

Step 1 Spring a chalk line through the overhanging decking ends and trim to correct length as in fig 15. Dress the sawn corners with a plane.

FIG 15 — Last board may require ripping. Chalk line. If newell posts are required these should be installed before laying decking.

FIG 16 — Wall mounted post or plate. Bottom rail supports.

Step 2 Attach the wall mounted post with coach bolts, see fig 16.

Note: Flood coat all housings with a wood preservative and/or prime paint or seal as well.

Step 3 Cut the rails to length and fasten in position, see fig 17. *For jointing methods see Page 86.* Then install bottom rail supports ensuring the rails are straight. Then cut and fit the intermediate posts. In this design these intermediate posts are not structural. Therefore, the rails are designed as the structural members.

Step 4 Railing sizes are established from the Tables in Chapter 8.

Mark the bottom rail positions on the posts. Cut the bottom rails and secure them in place.

Note: Vertical balusters could be applied instead of the criss cross members.

FIG 17 — Intermediate posts.

Step 5 Cut the remaining members to fit and secure them in position. On criss cross railings cut all the sloping members in one direction first, fix them in place then cut and place the opposing members. Dress and sandpaper all sharp corners. The deck is then ready for painting.

Note: Check fig 1, Page 41 to ensure the spacings between members is acceptable to the BCA. Also if criss cross is applied, you will need to ensure it is unclimbable by applying acrylic or safety glass behind.

FIG 18

Building a Freestanding Deck

Freestanding decks are those unattached to any other structure. Posts are frequently embedded but stirrups can be used.

Posts embedded as cantilever posts as in Table 5 will enable the deck to be constructed without wind bracing.

The following instructions are for embedded posts (for applying stirrups or high wind post supports see Page 21).

The design illustrated utilises round posts, however square ones could be substituted see Tables.

Where to Begin

Step 1 *Setting Out the Site*

Prepare a plan of the deck and make a material list.

Drive pegs to indicate each corner. Carry out a rough squaring of the area by taking diagonal measurements between the pegs and adjust the pegs until both diagonal measurements correspond (see fig 1).

Sloping Sites

To square the area on a sloping site, the measurements must be carried out on a level plane to be accurate as in fig 2.

Drive a peg at the highest point then when driving the remaining pegs, maintain their tops level with the highest peg. Use either a string line level or an automatic level.

FIG 1

PROPOSED DECK AREA

Tape Measure

Both diagonal measurements should correspond.

Take diagonal measurements to bring the pegs into approximately square.

Highest Peg

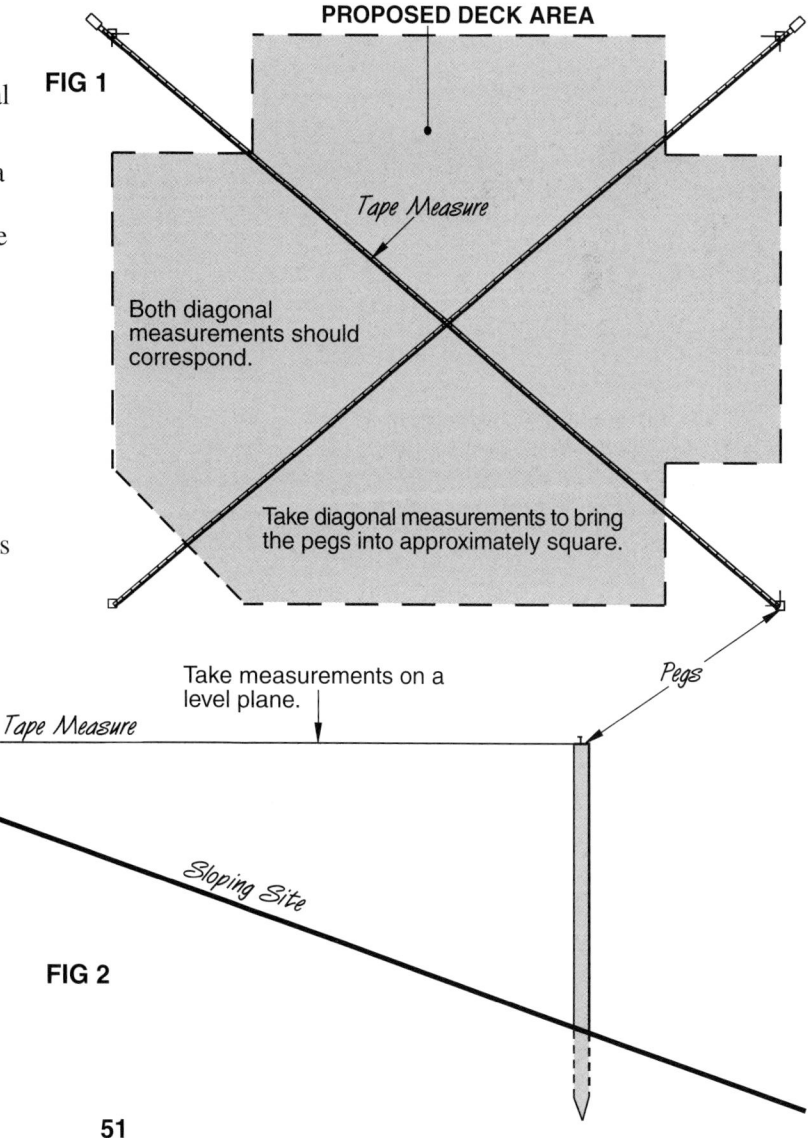

Tape Measure

Take measurements on a level plane.

Pegs

Sloping Site

FIG 2

Cont.

Step 2 *Locating Post Positions*

Construct profile hurdles about 600mm outside of each corner. Keep the tops of profiles all on the same level plane. Mark the outside alignment of the outer rows of posts on the profile tops and drive a nail at these points. (These may be set back from the deck perimeter).

Stretch a string line through all of these points, (see fig 3). Square the area carefully this time taking diagonal measurements between the string line intersections. Adjust one pair of nails together along one side until both measurements correspond.

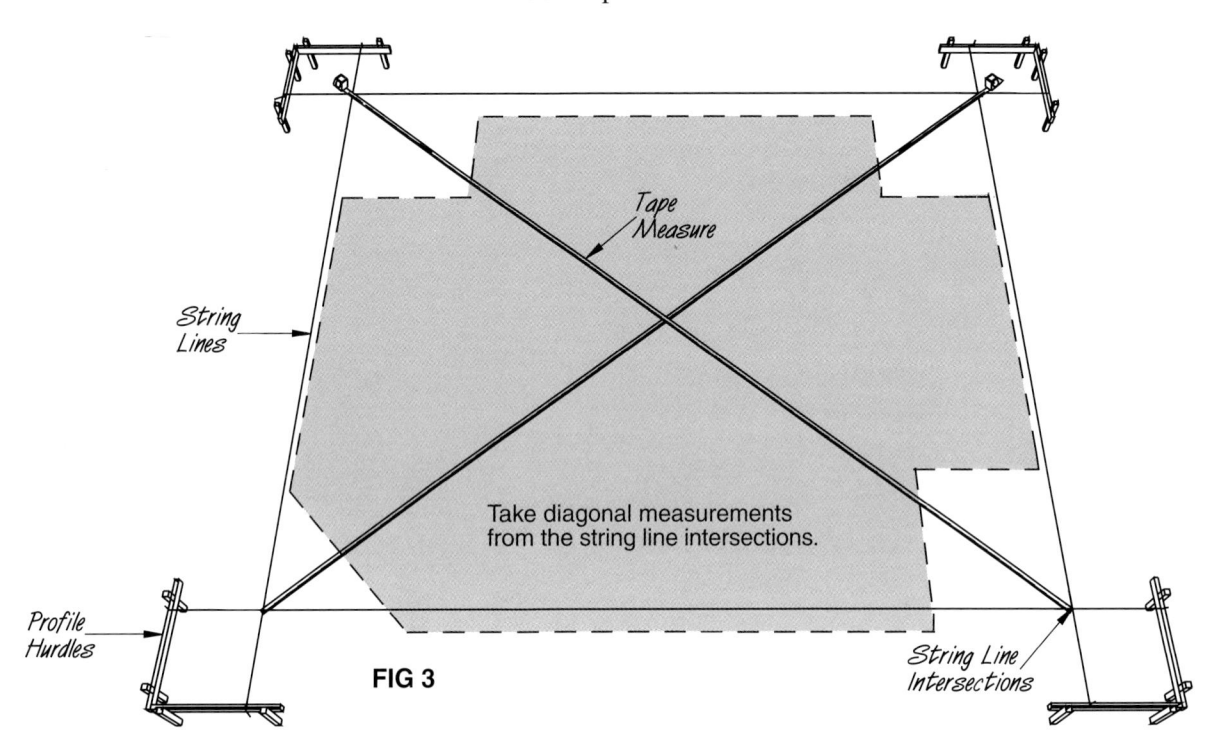

FIG 3

Take diagonal measurements from the string line intersections.

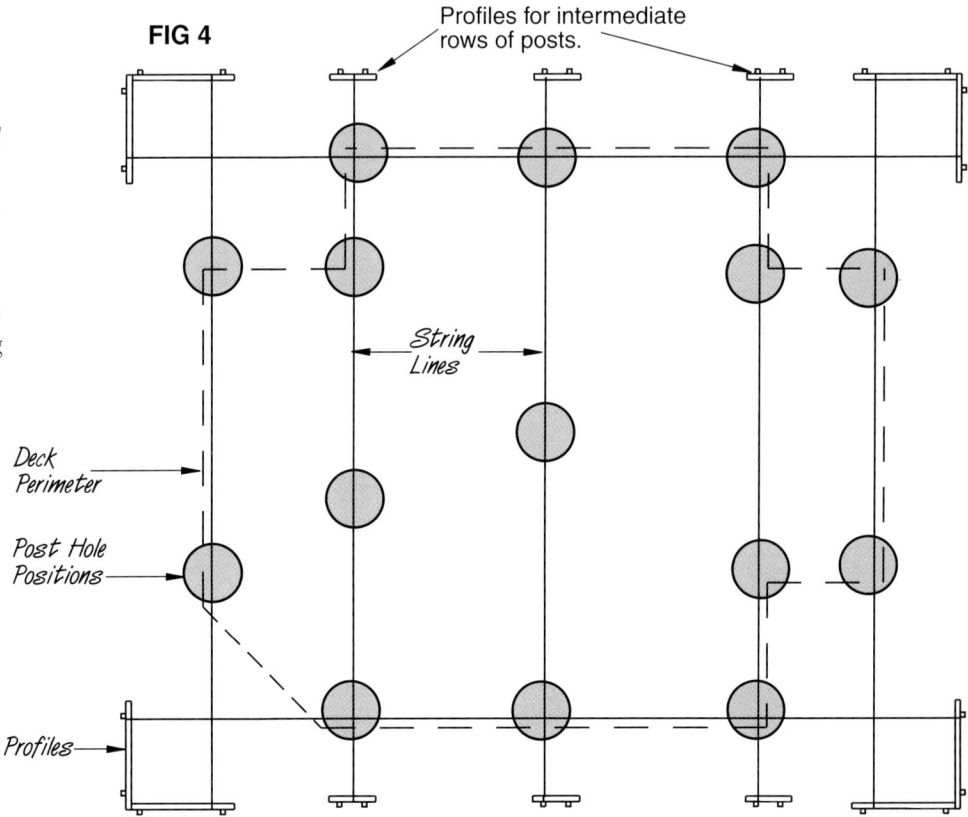

Locating the Post Holes

Construct profiles for any intermediate rows of posts as in fig 4.

Mark on all profiles the centres of the rows of posts. Drive nails at these points and stretch string lines through.

Using a tape measure along the string lines, mark and peg the centre of each post hole.

FIG 4

Profiles for intermediate rows of posts.

52

Cont.

Step 3 *Excavate the Post Holes*
For a number of holes, employ a mechanical hole borer. Ensure the correct dia. and depth is obtained. If the hole bottoms are soft take them down to firm bottoms.

Step 4 *Installing the Posts* (see also Page 22)
Notes:
a). The following method of embedding posts is for posts treated for inground use or hardwood posts Durability Class 1 (see Page 8).

b). Do not trim the bottom ends of treated posts as this may expose untreated heartwood.

Ensure the minimum requirement of concrete is placed beneath the bottom of all post holes. Use stiff concrete throughout. Stretch string lines through to align the outer sides of posts. Install the posts ramming stiff concrete all round. Ensure the posts are plumb on both sides and in alignment with the string lines (see fig 4).

Apply braces both ways as in fig 5. When installing the bearers it is best to leave the braces attached while making the housings, so ensure the brace positions won't obstruct the work later.

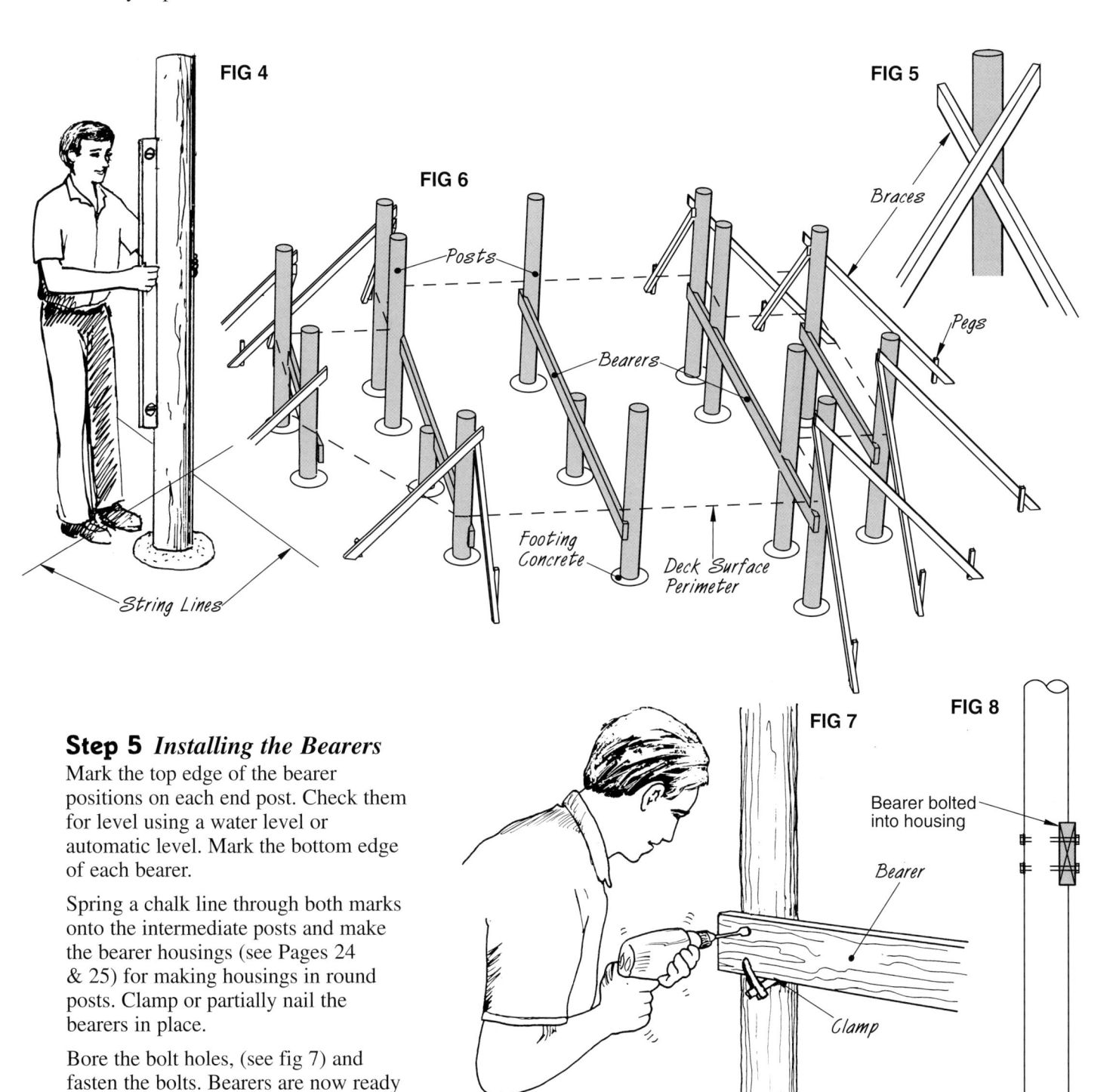

Step 5 *Installing the Bearers*
Mark the top edge of the bearer positions on each end post. Check them for level using a water level or automatic level. Mark the bottom edge of each bearer.

Spring a chalk line through both marks onto the intermediate posts and make the bearer housings (see Pages 24 & 25) for making housings in round posts. Clamp or partially nail the bearers in place.

Bore the bolt holes, (see fig 7) and fasten the bolts. Bearers are now ready for laying joists.

Cont.

Step 6 *Installing the Joists*

Mark each joist position on the end bearers and stretch a chalk line through to transfer these positions onto the intermediate bearers. Space them according to plans. If the last spaces are shorter than the rest, it doesn't matter. Alternatively, equalise the last two spaces. Lay the outer joists first keeping all bows uppermost.

Fasten them according to plans or use framing anchors or 75x3.75mm gal. nails skew driven.

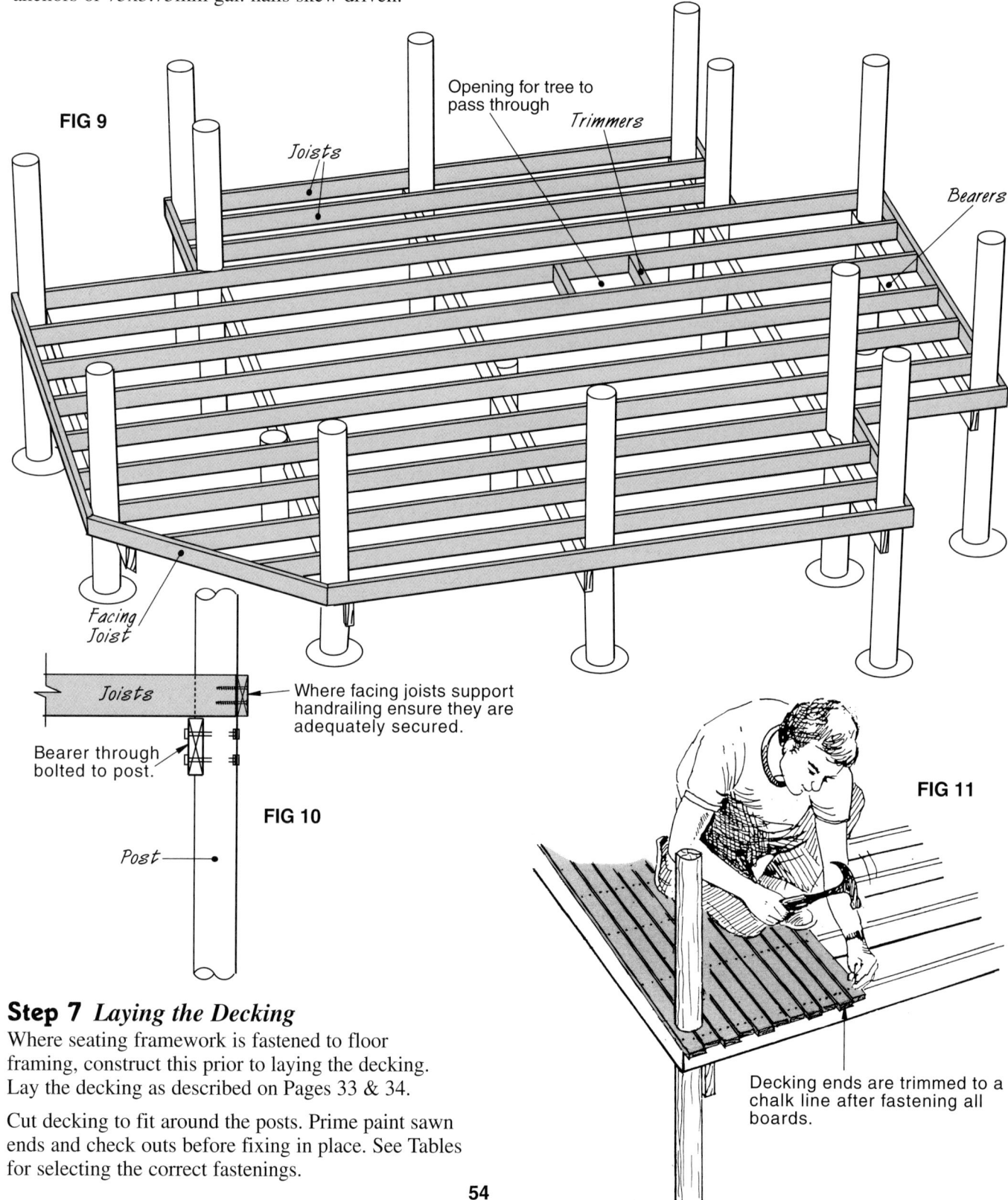

Use flat heads for softwood. Keep joist ends in a straight line by either a string line or allow them to extend past their alignment and trim them to a chalk line after all joists are laid. Attach any facing joists to joist ends.

FIG 9

Opening for tree to pass through
Joists
Trimmers
Bearers
Facing Joist

FIG 10

Joists
Where facing joists support handrailing ensure they are adequately secured.
Bearer through bolted to post.
Post

FIG 11

Decking ends are trimmed to a chalk line after fastening all boards.

Step 7 *Laying the Decking*

Where seating framework is fastened to floor framing, construct this prior to laying the decking. Lay the decking as described on Pages 33 & 34.

Cut decking to fit around the posts. Prime paint sawn ends and check outs before fixing in place. See Tables for selecting the correct fastenings.

Cont.

Step 8 *Constructing the Handrailing*
Where the main deck posts extend through the deck to support handrailing as in fig 12, spring a chalk line around the perimeter posts to represent the top edge of the top handrail. Cut and bolt or screw fasten the top rail in position.

Cut and install the handrail battens. For enclosed battened handrails as in fig 14, establish the angle required (the angle illustrated is 45°). Commence with a full length batten rather than the shortened ones at ends. Allow all ends to extend past their trimmed alignment and trim them later to a chalk line. Fig 14 is finished to this stage ready for the handrail capping to be attached (see fig 13). Without this handrail capping the batten ends will deteriorate.

Step 9 *Constructing the Seating*
Commence by fastening the ledger to the posts and to a chalk line. Cut the seating sprockets to length and shape and fasten to the ledger. Cut the braces to length and shape and fasten in place, at the same time maintain the sprockets level.

Finally, attach the seating timbers. End to end and corner joins can be mitred or butt joined.

Note: Handrail timbers laid on the flat as in fig 13 will perform better if the top surface has a slope.

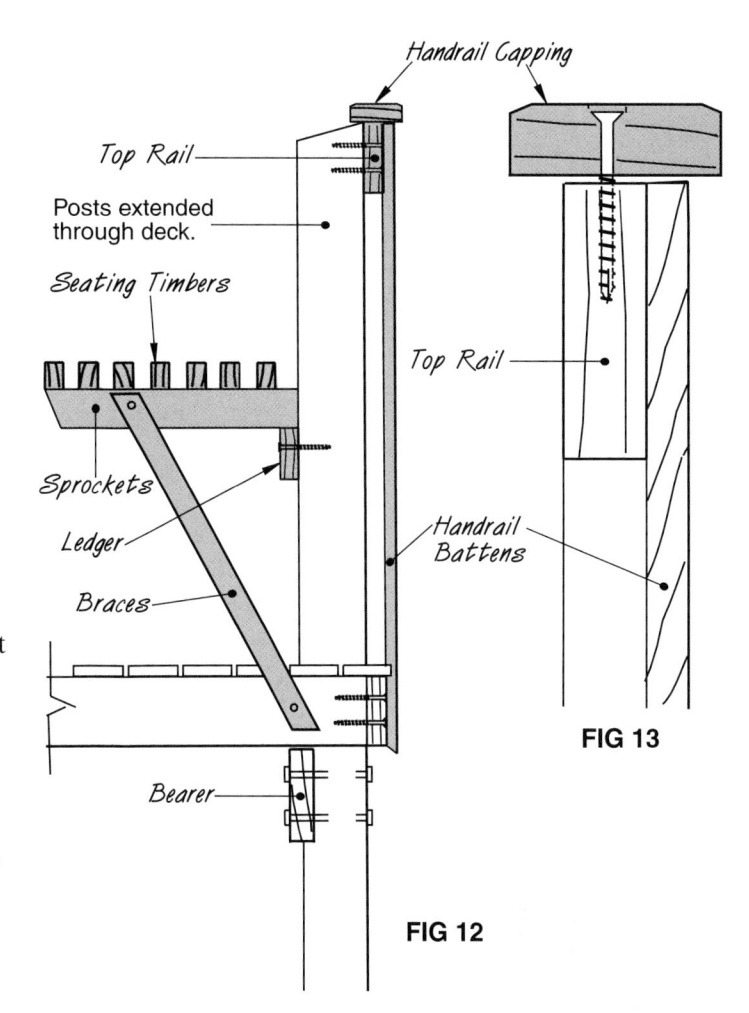

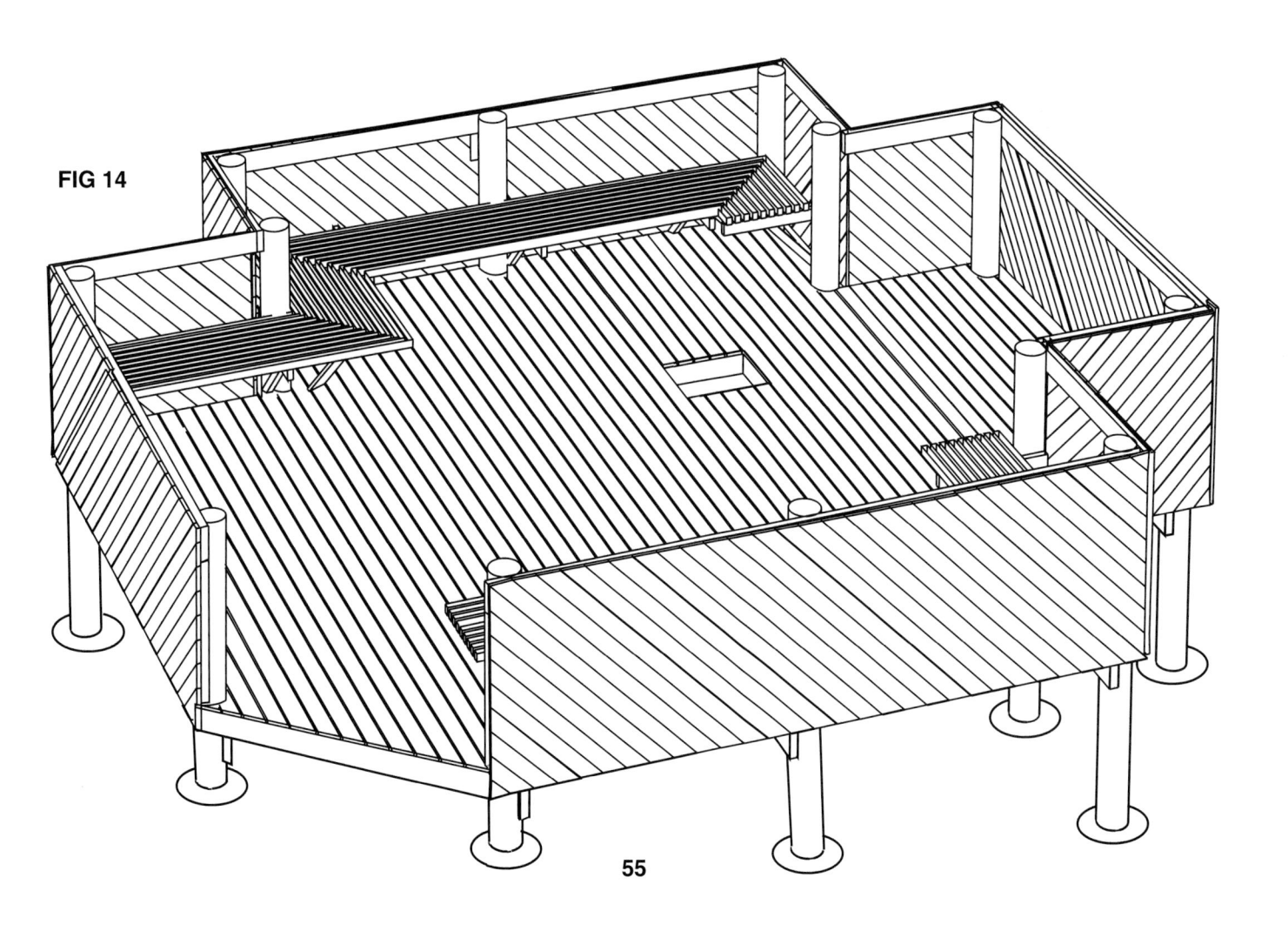

FIG 12

FIG 13

FIG 14

5 Designing Pergolas

The pergola can when thoughtfully designed, serve a number of practical purposes. The structures initial purpose may be to simply provide shade for a deck or patio. Where this is the case, it is advisable to ensure the method of attachment to the house will enable the rafters to receive cladding should you desire this in future.

The shade pergola is an ideal method for cooling a hot window and room. Where maximum shade is desirable but without cladding, attach battens close together or apply 75x35mm or 100x35mm battens on edge as illustrated. Shade cloth will also permit ventilation and rain penetration for plants.

Flowering or fruiting vines can also provide shade. In cold climates plant deciduous vines to enable sun penetration in winter. Vines and vegetation can deteriorate timbers, so use the harder hardwood species.

The Cladded Pergola

The cladded pergola will enable greater use of a deck or patio especially if wind protection is also provided. These outdoor covered areas truly become an extension of the house living areas. On a small house, even a small deck or patio with a cladded pergola will greatly improve the situation.
Where head height is restricted underneath the outer beam support, the rafters can be attached to the face of the beams (as above) with joist hangers.

Colour can greatly influence the atmosphere and feel of a relaxation area. Experiment with different colour schemes. Don't feel constrained to apply the traditional or commonly mixed pergola and deck colours. Carry out a test application at one end if you aren't confident of your choice. But only purchase a small quantity for testing.

Choosing a Cladding

A variety of roof cladding materials can be applied. Some design problems should be considered, where the pergola shelters a window, light penetration may be necessary to avoid a dark room interior.
This presents the additional problem that should direct sunlight penetrate, will its accompanying heat be desirable.

The only solution is to request translucent claddings with the highest heat deflection qualities.
Translucent claddings have a shorter life span than Colorbond metal however the heavier guage or thickness the longer its life will be.

Pergola Proportions

Proportion is just as important a rule when designing a pergola as it is for any other architectural application. Few Designers seem to realise this. Timber calculation tables may permit 90x90mm posts and 90x35mm rafters resting on a 140x45mm beam but will the whole structure look spindly and underproportioned in comparison to its overall size and the adjoining house style. It is often necessary to increase the sectional size of members to maintain good proportions.

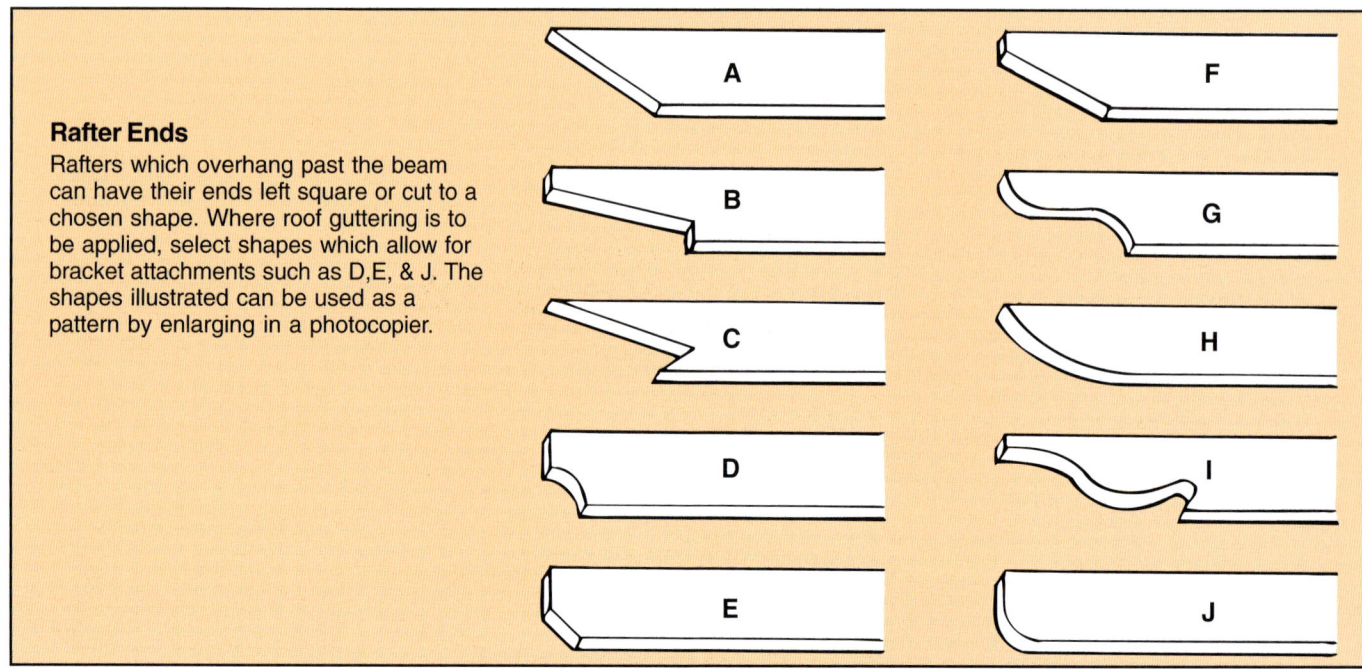

Rafter Ends
Rafters which overhang past the beam can have their ends left square or cut to a chosen shape. Where roof guttering is to be applied, select shapes which allow for bracket attachments such as D, E, & J. The shapes illustrated can be used as a pattern by enlarging in a photocopier.

Pergola Entertainment Areas

These larger pergolas can be planned to have cladded portions for rain and sun protection with other portions exposed to admit direct Winter sunshine or to allow fruiting or flowering vines to penetrate. Many folk enclose these areas with insect screens. They make an ideal sleeping space on hot Summer nights. After screening, some folk permit a few parrots to freely intermingle as well. This can be a unique experience for guests especially when the birds become accustomed to the environment.

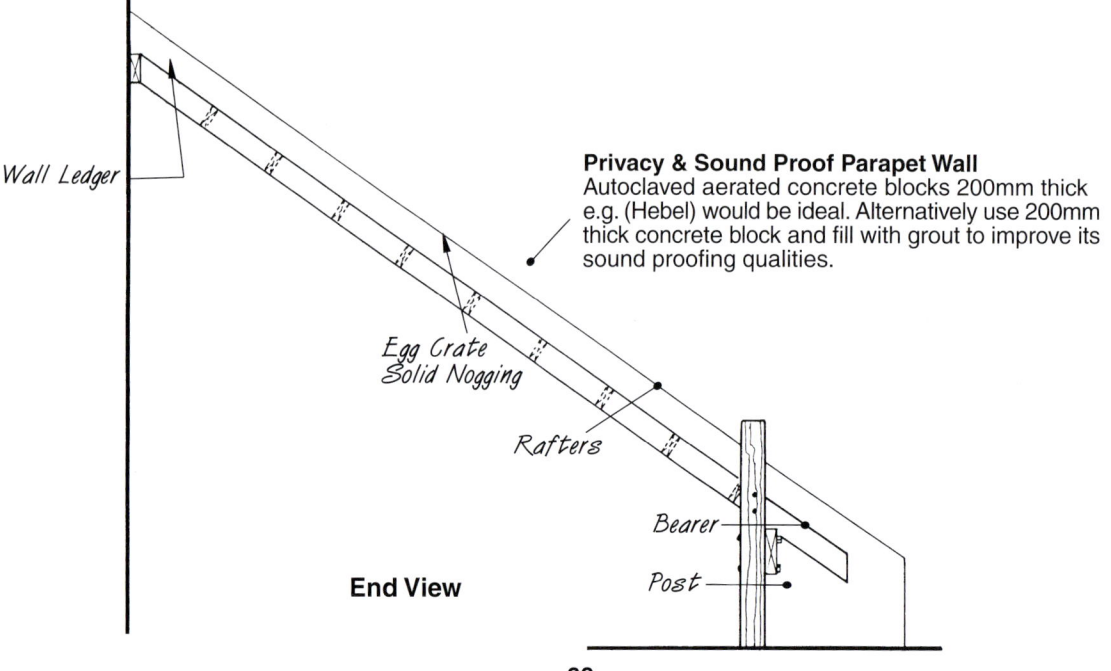

Cont.

Privacy & Sound Proof Parapet Wall
Autoclaved aerated concrete blocks 200mm thick e.g. (Hebel) would be ideal. Alternatively use 200mm thick concrete block and fill with grout to improve its sound proofing qualities.

- Wall Ledger
- Egg Crate Solid Nogging
- Rafters
- Bearer
- Post

End View

Cont.

Steep pitched gables in combination with flat or low pitched roofs will often produce a pleasing effect. The roof could remain with the typical egg crate effect or it could be clad for all weather use.

Multiple gables of the right pitch can also generate a satisfactory arrangement. This one is clad with smooth surfaced Hardiflex Fibre Cement sheets. The internal intersections require a fall for water to drain off.

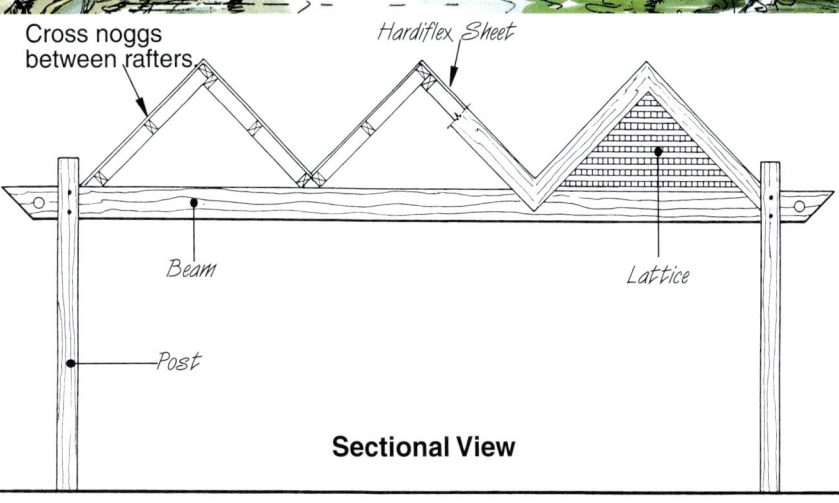

Cross noggs between rafters

Hardiflex Sheet

Beam

Lattice

Post

Sectional View

Cont.

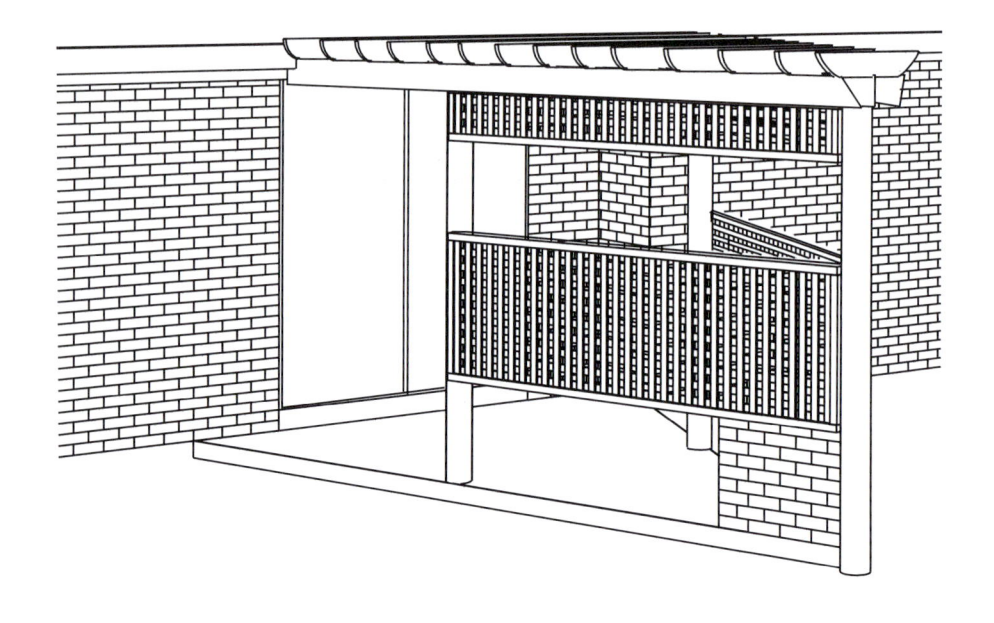

This triangular design which includes a BBQ will suit the all wood approach or a combination of materials such as smooth painted fibre cement columns with flat painted fibre cement lattice. Fibre cement columns will be concrete grout filled with the anchor bolt for the beams embedded in the grout.
The attachment of the beam to the house is not critical because the posts will carry most of the structural support.

Canal Site Pergolas

Canal frontages are relaxation areas where pergolas can offer the necessary shade element.

Design factors include:

a). area requirement for entertainment, BBQ'ing or just relaxing.

b). degree of weather (sun, wind) protection.

Consider enclosing one or two sides with screens of lattice, planking, etc or even heavy duty adjustable blinds.

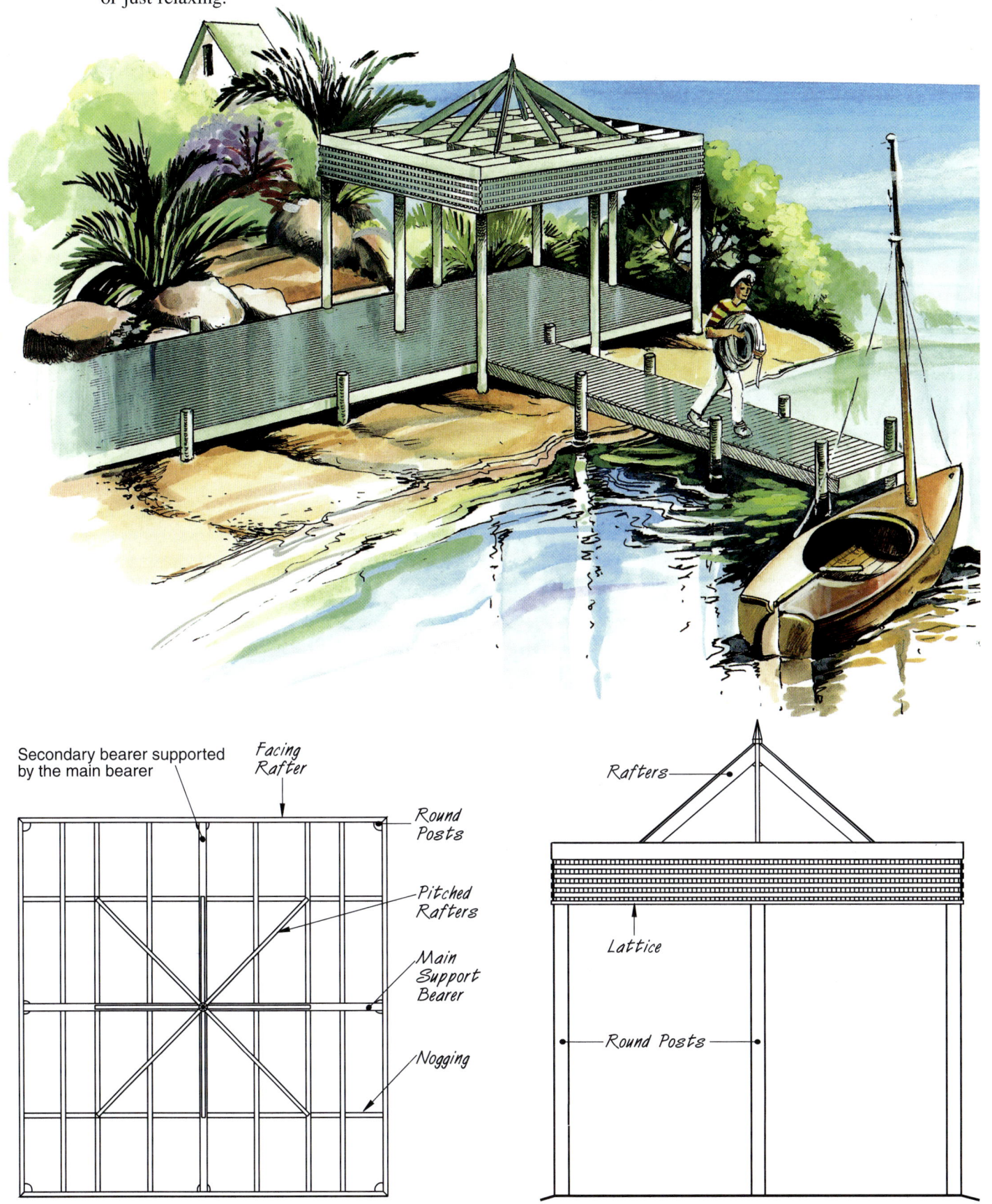

ROOF PLAN

- Secondary bearer supported by the main bearer
- Facing Rafter
- Round Posts
- Pitched Rafters
- Main Support Bearer
- Nogging

SIDE ELEVATION

- Rafters
- Lattice
- Round Posts

Pergola Covered Walkways

POST DETAIL

Rafter
Beam
Joist at each post.
Post
Gal. Post Support
Footing according to plans.

These can be open to admit rain and sun to grow flowering or fruiting creepers over the roof area or be enclosed to provide rain protection between (for example) a garage and the house. When designing, take care that the pergola is in keeping with the existing architectural design of the house. To ensure this, the roof pitch and cladding type will be the major design considerations.

Pergolas in Profile

Pergola & Carport Combined
This design enables economical dual use of posts.

Tables for this cantilevered design are not provided in this manual.

Pool Pergolas
Consideration may be necessary to permit some direct sunlight penetration. Apply coatings that will tolerate occasional splashings of chlorinated or salt pool water whichever is used.

An Adjustable Pergola
These are an ideal method of controlling direct sunlight. They can be constructed in approx. 1800mm lengths using lightweight timbers such as Western Red Cedar.

Adjustable Pergola — Pivot point — Adjust to any angle.

Handrailing omitted for illustration purposes.

6 Pergola Construction

Pergola Construction with or without Roof Cladding

Pergolas are frequently constructed initially as a semi shade area with shade cloth or battens only over the top surface, then at a later date the roof is clad with either iron, acrylic, fibreglass or other sheet material, to make the area a little more weatherproof.

Footings designed for pergolas without roof cladding are usually inadequate should cladding be attached later. This is not referring to the state of the subsoil but rather the increased uplift exerted on the structure in high winds. These winds are also prevalent in storms in non-cyclonic localities.

With this knowledge it is advisable to select footing designs for pergolas which will be capable of resisting these uplift pressures should the pergola roof be clad in future.

Attaching Roof Cladded Pergolas to the Fascia Board

This point of construction is the most vulnerable.

Proper attention should be paid to the adequacy of the fascia board to rafter connection and the existing house rafter to wall connection to withstand the additional uplift pressures applied by a covered pergola in a storm or high wind (see Pages 69-71 for recommendations).

Common Rafter Supporting Methods

The two common methods of supporting rafters are illustrated in figs 1 & 2.

In fig 1, the rafters rest on top of the beam and may also extend past the beam.

In fig 2, the rafters are supported against the inside face of the beam and are usually secured by joist hangers.

The Beam Location

The beam can extend outside the pergola raftered area as in fig 3 or remain flush with the last rafters as in figs 1 & 2.

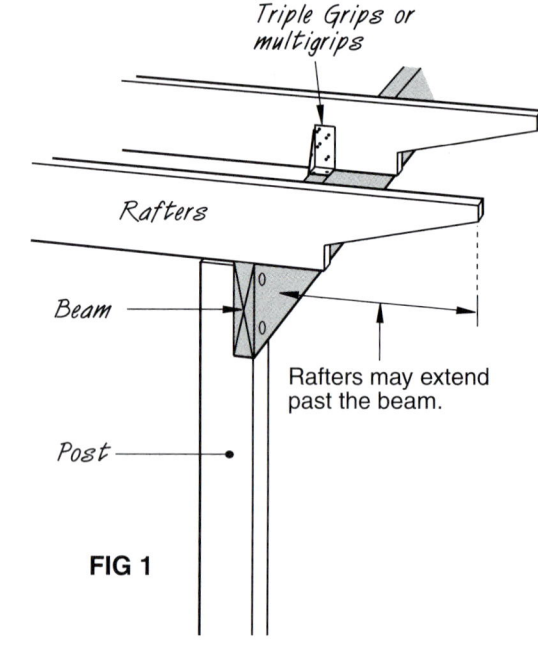

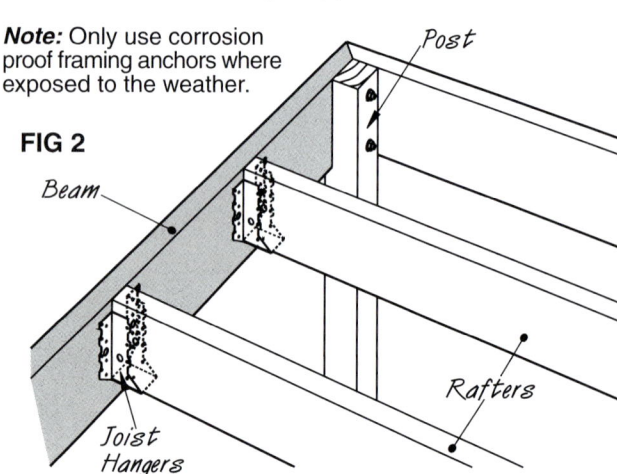

FIG 1

Note: Only use corrosion proof framing anchors where exposed to the weather.

FIG 2

Rafters supported against the inside face of the beam. Use s.s. hangers for exposed pergola rafters.

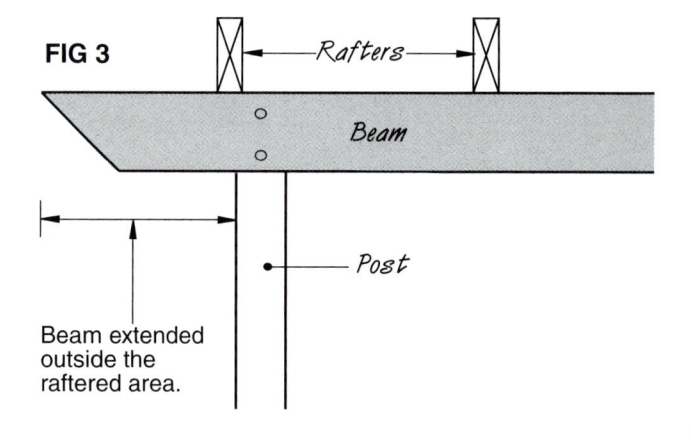

FIG 3

Beam extended outside the raftered area.

Prepare a Plan

To obtain the correct quantities of materials, it is essential to draw a plan in plan view and at least one side view as below.

How to Prepare a Plan

DRAWING THE FLOOR PLAN
Decide at the beginning the following:
- **a).** Whether to clad the roof or not (it is advisable to design the footings and method of attachment to the house, to accept roof cladding should a future need require it).
- **b).** How to attach the rafters to the house, (see Pages 69 to 71).
- **c).** Which post footing and post anchoring method to adopt.

Step 1 Draw a horizontal line representing the house wall or fascia board (see fig 2).

Step 2 Decide on the pergola depth (distance out from the house), its length and whether the supporting beam will be located underneath the rafters or along the ends of the rafters as in figs 1 & 2 Page 66. Draw the beam in position (obtain its cross section size from the Tables).

Step 3 Draw the post positions and then each rafter position (obtain the rafters cross sectional size and spacings from Tables). See tables for post sizes. Indicate all the member sizes and their spacings.

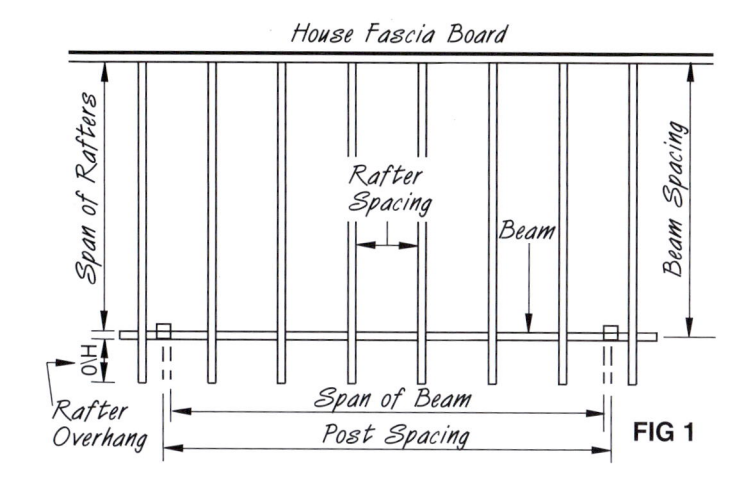

Note: See fig 1 for explanation of spans and spacings.

DRAWING THE SIDE VIEW

Step 1 Commence by drawing the vertical house wall or fascia board as in fig 3.

Step 2 Draw the rafter as in fig 3. If cladding is to be applied, allow a slope of 2 deg. min. or accord. to Roof Cladding Manufacturers requirements.

Step 3 Draw the post and beam in position see also Page 68 for further information on jointing methods.

EXAMPLE PERGOLA PLAN

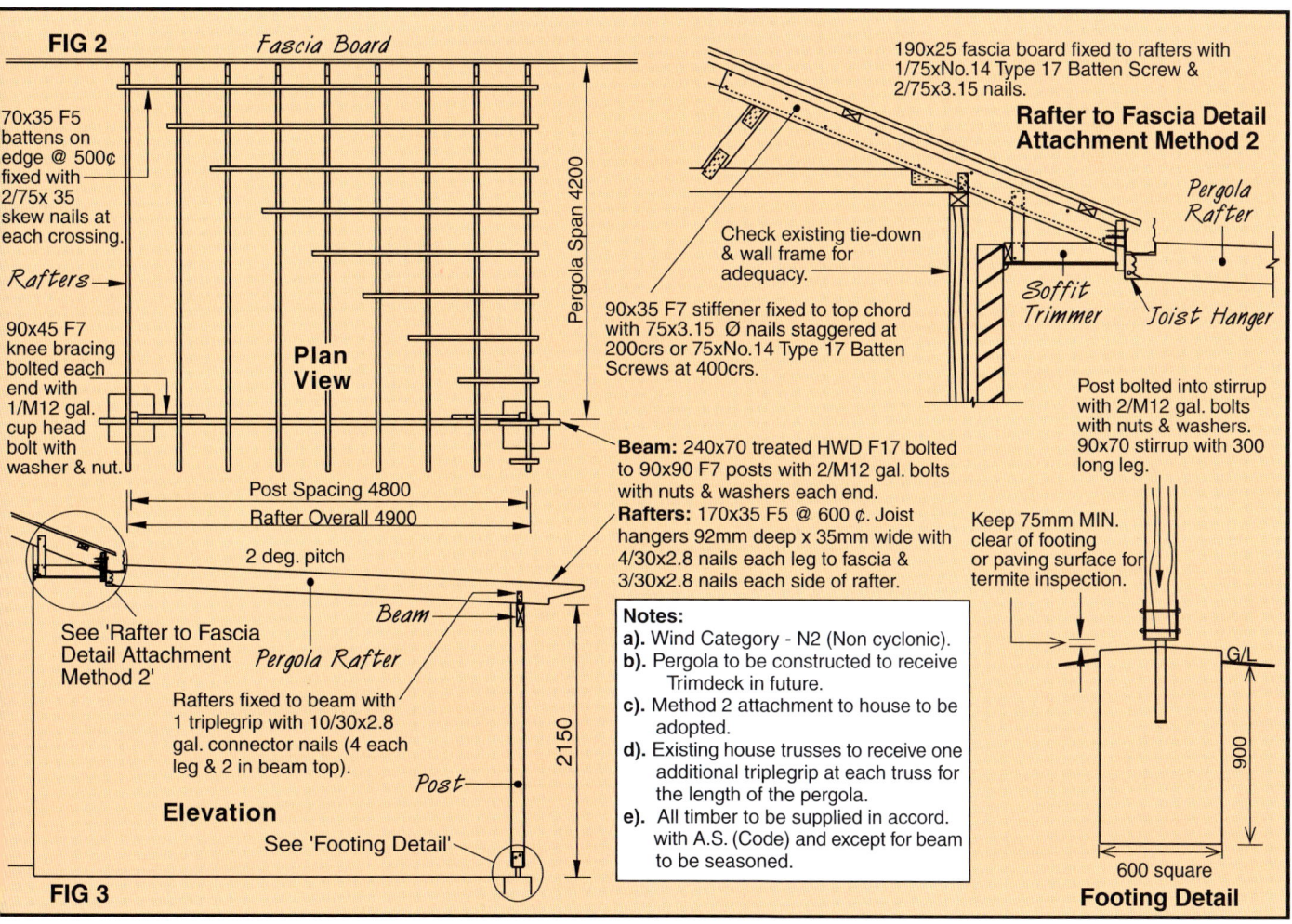

FIG 2 — Plan View

- 70x35 F5 battens on edge @ 500¢ fixed with 2/75x 35 skew nails at each crossing.
- Rafters
- 90x45 F7 knee bracing bolted each end with 1/M12 gal. cup head bolt with washer & nut.
- Post Spacing 4800
- Rafter Overall 4900
- Pergola Span 4200
- 2 deg. pitch

Elevation (FIG 3)
- See 'Rafter to Fascia Detail Attachment Method 2'
- Pergola Rafter
- Rafters fixed to beam with 1 triplegrip with 10/30x2.8 gal. connector nails (4 each leg & 2 in beam top).
- Beam
- Post
- 2150
- See 'Footing Detail'

Rafter to Fascia Detail Attachment Method 2
- 190x25 fascia board fixed to rafters with 1/75xNo.14 Type 17 Batten Screw & 2/75x3.15 nails.
- Check existing tie-down & wall frame for adequacy.
- 90x35 F7 stiffener fixed to top chord with 75x3.15 Ø nails staggered at 200crs or 75xNo.14 Type 17 Batten Screws at 400crs.
- Pergola Rafter
- Soffit Trimmer
- Joist Hanger

Beam: 240x70 treated HWD F17 bolted to 90x90 F7 posts with 2/M12 gal. bolts with nuts & washers each end.

Rafters: 170x35 F5 @ 600 ¢. Joist hangers 92mm deep x 35mm wide with 4/30x2.8 nails each leg to fascia & 3/30x2.8 nails each side of rafter.

Notes:
- a). Wind Category - N2 (Non cyclonic).
- b). Pergola to be constructed to receive Trimdeck in future.
- c). Method 2 attachment to house to be adopted.
- d). Existing house trusses to receive one additional triplegrip at each truss for the length of the pergola.
- e). All timber to be supplied in accord. with A.S. (Code) and except for beam to be seasoned.

Footing Detail
- Post bolted into stirrup with 2/M12 gal. bolts with nuts & washers. 90x70 stirrup with 300 long leg.
- Keep 75mm MIN. clear of footing or paving surface for termite inspection.
- 600 square
- 900
- G/L

FIG 1
- Span of Rafters, Rafter Spacing, Beam, Beam Spacing
- House Fascia Board
- Rafter Overhang, Span of Beam, Post Spacing

Pergola Posts or Columns

(read Pages 21 to 23 for further details)

Post Types

Pergola posts can be constructed using any one of the materials and methods illustrated for decks on Pages 21 to 23. However square timber supported by stirrups or high wind post supports are most commonly applied (see figs 1 & 2).

In non-cyclonic localities where the Local Authority permits choice between high wind post anchors and stirrups, consider which one is least likely to corrode. Stirrups with the pipe support can hold moisture which can commence corrosion. To help prevent this, fill the pipe with polystyrene pressure pak foam.

Post Position

Posts can be positioned flush with the end of the beam or set back for appearance and to reduce the beam span to enable the use of a smaller sectional size beam.

Post Footings

(For pergolas with roof cladding see 'Pergola Construction With or Without Roof Cladding' on Page 66).

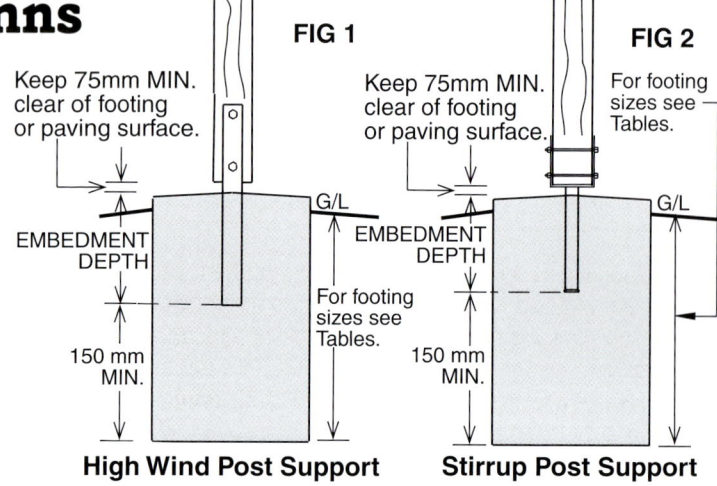

FIG 1 — High Wind Post Support
Keep 75mm MIN. clear of footing or paving surface.
EMBEDMENT DEPTH
150 mm MIN.
For footing sizes see Tables.

FIG 2 — Stirrup Post Support
Keep 75mm MIN. clear of footing or paving surface.
EMBEDMENT DEPTH
150 mm MIN.
For footing sizes see Tables.

Post footings should be taken down to depths required in approved plans or tables and down to firm subsoils. All post foundation bottoms should bear in similar substrata. Ensure the tops of footings slope away from the posts or anchors.

Post & Footing Sectional Sizes

Select 'Post and Footing Sectional Sizes' from Ch.8.

> **Hint:**
> Tamp the concrete well around posts or steel post anchors to remove any honey combing.

Beam-to-Post Connection

The beam can be fully or partially housed into the posts as in figs 3 & 4, in which case the housings should not be deeper than two-thirds of the post thickness (see fig 5). Bolt beams to posts with 2/12mm gal. round head bolts.

FIG 3 — Beam partially housed into post.
FIG 4 — Beam fully housed into post.
FIG 5 — Not less than one-third of the post thickness 'D'. Beam Housing, Round Head Bolts, Pergola Post, 'D'.

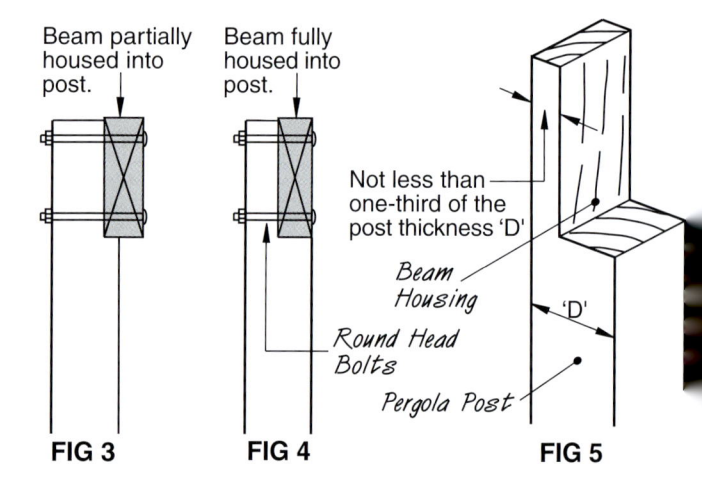

Rafter-to-Beam Connections

Rafters are attached to beams with either multigrips when beams are underneath as in fig 6 or with joist hangers when mounted on the face of beams as in fig 7.

Note: Only use corrosion proof framing anchors, bolts and nails. Where exposed, use stainless steel.

FIG 6 — Beams Underneath Rafters
Multigrips, Rafter

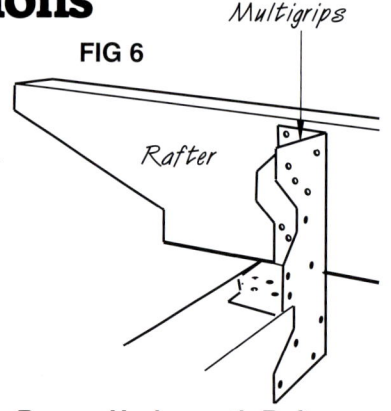

FIG 7 — Rafters Mounted on Face of Beams
Beam, Joist Hangers, Rafter, Joist

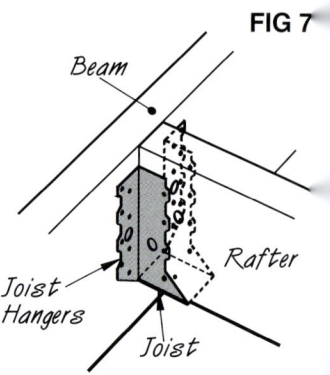

68

Attaching Pergolas to the House

The method of attachment of covered (roof cladded) pergolas or carports to the house is extremely important in a storm or high wind. This includes non cyclonic localities.

The covered pergola or carport attached to an existing fascia board will, in a storm, place additional pressures on the fascia board fastenings and the house rafter to wall connections. If these connections have not been designed to accept the additional uplift pressures of a covered pergola or carport, damage can occur not only to the pergola or carport but also to the house.

Steps You Can Take

If the eaves of a new house are to be designed and built in readiness for a future pergola the additional strengthening necessary can more easily be applied at the time. However, where the pergola is an afterthought, some strengthening may be necessary before commencing construction. Table 3 will indicate which method of attachment is appropriate.

Where to Begin

a). Check in which wind category your house is built. If in doubt, enquire at Local Authority Building Inspections Office.

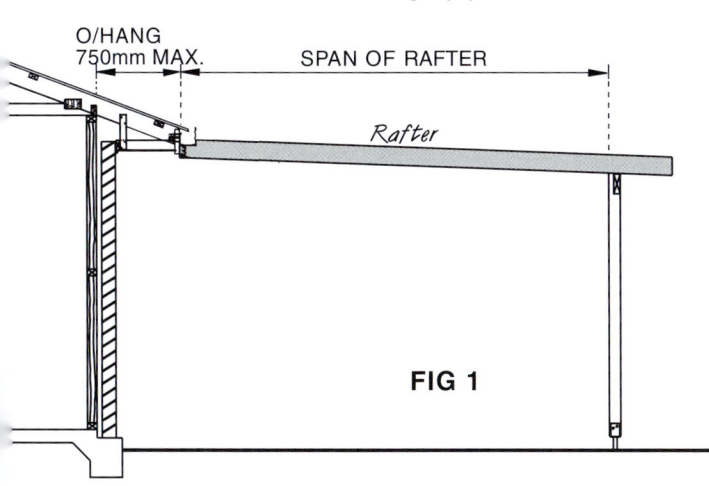

b). Check your existing house rafter or truss sizes spacings and their 'F' grade strength.

c). Check whether the fascia board is metal or timber, if timber, how thick is it?

d). Determine how much of the rafter or truss ends are accessible in order to receive additional fastenings as in figs 2 or 3. This will probably mean you may need to lift one or two lower roof tiles or roofing sheets to make an inspection.

e). Check what fastenings have been applied to secure the existing house rafters or trusses to the wall top plate. If these fastenings are inadequate you may need to attach additional triple grips or even a cyclone strap. Table 2 below provides the additional uplift force which will be applied to the existing rafters/trusses. This will determine how much (if any) additional tie down will be necessary. Seek advice from a local Designer or Engineer.

With the above information, follow Table 3 to establish which attachment method to apply. If uncertain, seek professional advice.

FIG 1

TABLE 2 ADDITIONAL UPLIFT FORCE APPLIED TO EXISTING RAFTERS OR TRUSSES

WIND SPEED m/s	ADDITIONAL UPLIFT (kN) FOR PERGOLA OR CARPORT RAFTER SPANS (m) of:-				
	2.4	2.7	3.0	3.6	4.2
N1-N3	0.8	0.9	1.0	1.2	1.3
C1	1.2	1.4	1.5	1.8	2.2

TABLE 3 PERGOLAS/CARPORTS METHODS OF ATTACHMENT SELECTION CHART

WIND CATE-GORY	ROOF TYPE	HOUSE RAFTER/TRUSS SPACING (mm)	GRADE	RAFTER/TRUSS MIN. SIZE mm	METHOD OF ATTACHMENT PERGOLA/CARPORT RAFTER SPAN (m)				
					2.4	2.7	3.0	3.6	4.2
N2	TILE	600	F5	90 X 35	1 2 3 4	1 2 3 4	-- 2 3 4	-- 2 3 4	-- 2 3 4
			F8		1 2 3 4	1 2 3 4	1 2 3 4	1 2 3 4	-- 2 3 4
	SHEET	900	F5		-- 2 3 4	-- 2 3 4	-- 2 3 4	-- -- 3 4	-- -- 3 4
			F8		1 2 3 4	-- 2 3 4	-- 2 3 4	-- -- 3 4	-- -- 3 4
N3 Non Cycl. to C1 Cycl.	TILE	600	F5		-- 2 3 4	-- 2 3 4	-- 2 3 4	-- 2 3 4	-- -- 3 4
			F8		1 2 3 4	-- 2 3 4	-- 2 3 4	-- 2 3 4	-- -- 3 4
	SHEET	900	F5		-- 2 3 4	-- -- 3 4	-- -- 3 4	-- -- 3 4	-- -- 3 4
			F8		-- 2 3 4	-- 2 3 4	-- -- 3 4	-- -- 3 4	-- -- 3 4

IMPORTANT NOTES:

a). A (--) means NOT ACCEPTABLE.
b). The adequacy of the existing house wall frame must be checked to ensure it can carry the extra dead load of the attachment.
c). Maximum pergola or carport rafter spacing is 900mm.
d). The minimum size of timber fascia boards for attaching pergolas/carports is 190 x 19mm finished.
e). The maximum overhang of existing rafters or trusses must not exceed 750mm from outside of top plate to end of rafters or trusses (see fig 1).
f). The maximum mass of roof sheeting, battens, shadecloth etc applied to the attachment permitted in the table and designs is 10kg/m^2.
g). Pressure co-efficient. Maximum pressure co-efficient assumed on the attachment is Cp = 1.2 (A.S. Code).

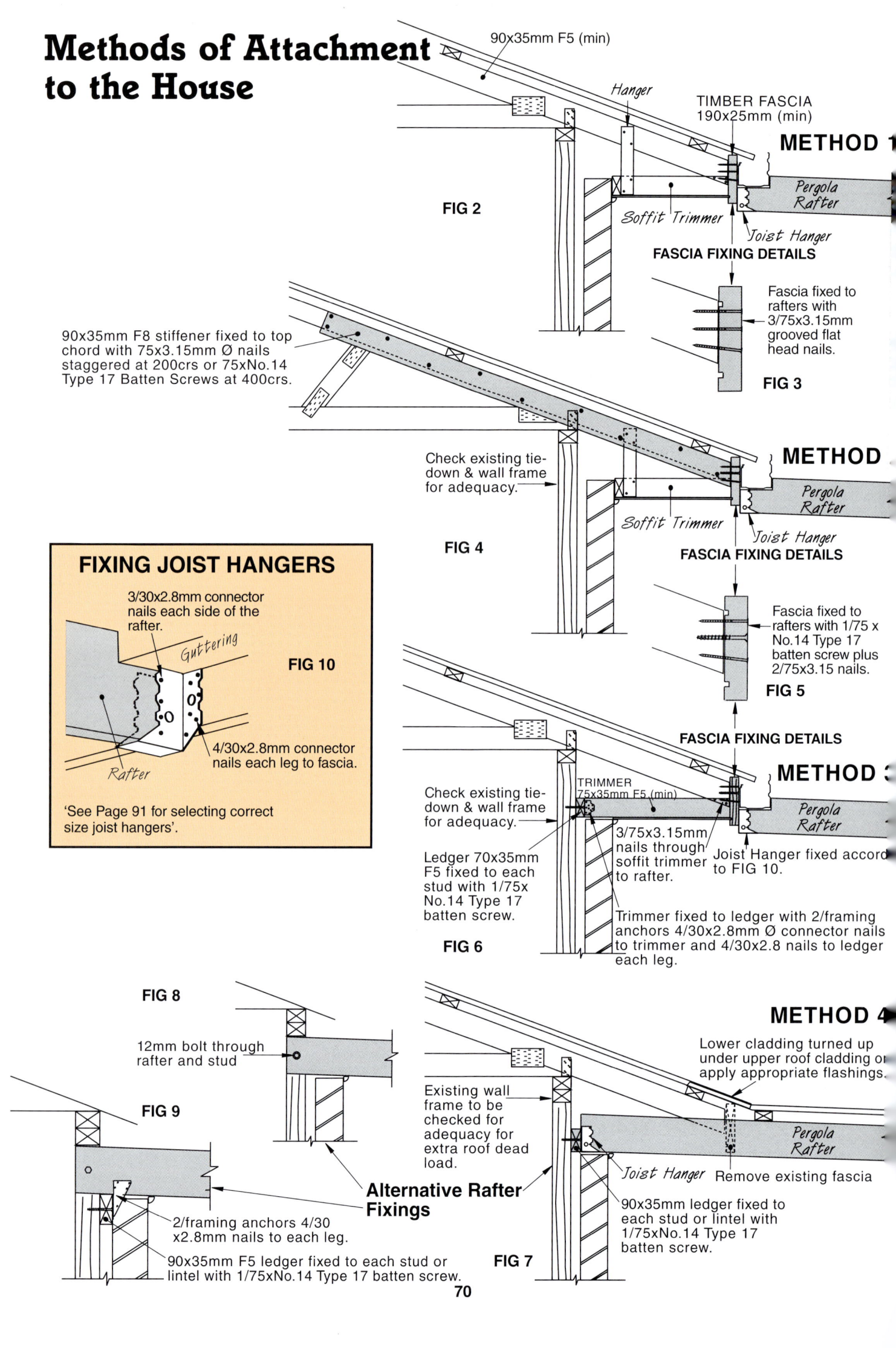

Methods of Attachment to the House

90x35mm F5 (min)

Hanger

TIMBER FASCIA 190x25mm (min)

METHOD 1

Pergola Rafter

Soffit Trimmer

Joist Hanger

FASCIA FIXING DETAILS

FIG 2

Fascia fixed to rafters with 3/75x3.15mm grooved flat head nails.

FIG 3

90x35mm F8 stiffener fixed to top chord with 75x3.15mm Ø nails staggered at 200crs or 75xNo.14 Type 17 Batten Screws at 400crs.

Check existing tie-down & wall frame for adequacy.

METHOD 2

Pergola Rafter

Soffit Trimmer

Joist Hanger

FASCIA FIXING DETAILS

FIG 4

Fascia fixed to rafters with 1/75 x No.14 Type 17 batten screw plus 2/75x3.15 nails.

FIG 5

FIXING JOIST HANGERS

3/30x2.8mm connector nails each side of the rafter.

Guttering

FIG 10

Rafter

4/30x2.8mm connector nails each leg to fascia.

'See Page 91 for selecting correct size joist hangers'.

FASCIA FIXING DETAILS

METHOD 3

TRIMMER 75x35mm F5 (min)

Pergola Rafter

Check existing tie-down & wall frame for adequacy.

3/75x3.15mm nails through soffit trimmer to rafter.

Joist Hanger fixed according to FIG 10.

Ledger 70x35mm F5 fixed to each stud with 1/75x No.14 Type 17 batten screw.

Trimmer fixed to ledger with 2/framing anchors 4/30x2.8mm Ø connector nails to trimmer and 4/30x2.8 nails to ledger each leg.

FIG 6

FIG 8

12mm bolt through rafter and stud

FIG 9

2/framing anchors 4/30 x2.8mm nails to each leg.

90x35mm F5 ledger fixed to each stud or lintel with 1/75xNo.14 Type 17 batten screw.

Alternative Rafter Fixings

Existing wall frame to be checked for adequacy for extra roof dead load.

METHOD 4

Lower cladding turned up under upper roof cladding or apply appropriate flashings.

Pergola Rafter

Joist Hanger

Remove existing fascia

90x35mm ledger fixed to each stud or lintel with 1/75xNo.14 Type 17 batten screw.

FIG 7

70

Metal Fascia Boards

Methods 1, 2 & 3 may also be applied to metal fascia boards provided the fascia is structurally stiffened as in fig 11.

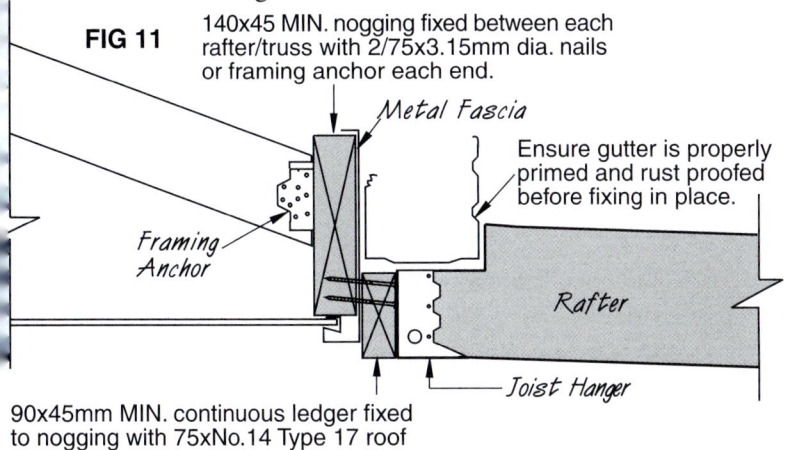

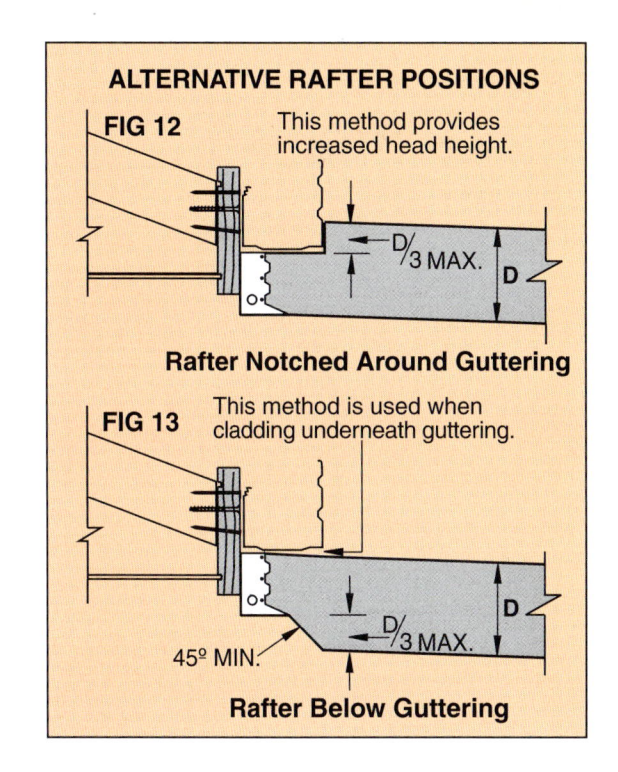

FIG 11 140x45 MIN. nogging fixed between each rafter/truss with 2/75x3.15mm dia. nails or framing anchor each end.

Metal Fascia

Ensure gutter is properly primed and rust proofed before fixing in place.

Framing Anchor

Rafter

Joist Hanger

90x45mm MIN. continuous ledger fixed to nogging with 75xNo.14 Type 17 roof batten screws at 600mm centres.

ALTERNATIVE RAFTER POSITIONS

FIG 12 This method provides increased head height.

D/3 MAX. D

Rafter Notched Around Guttering

FIG 13 This method is used when cladding underneath guttering.

45° MIN. D/3 MAX. D

Rafter Below Guttering

Steps to Attaching Rafters to Fascia Boards

Step 1 Mark along the fascia board the station for each rafter.

Step 2 Attach the joist hangers, fastening one side only at this stage.

Step 3 Erect the bearer supporting the outer ends of the rafters. Mark along the bearer the rafter positions. Install the rafters into the joist hangers and drive all remaining nails in the joist hangers.

Bracing Pergolas
Where to Apply Bracing

All pergolas should be braced unless the posts and footings have been designed as cantilevered posts.

For pergolas attached to the house, a pair of opposing knee braces should be applied parallel to the house wall as in figs 1 & 2.

For freestanding pergolas (unattached to another structure) a pair of opposing knee braces should be applied in both directions on every corner.

Braces can be applied to the outside or inside faces of the posts and beams.

Note: Knee braces do stiffen the structure however they cannot be relied upon to prevent damage to the structure in high winds. For this purpose conventional bracing is necessary. Consult the 'A.S.Timber Framing Manual'.

How to Apply Bracing

Apply 90 x 35mm F5 knee braces for short braces. Increase the thickness for longer ones. When the bearer is flush with the back or front faces of the posts, the braces can be simply face mounted and bolted each end as in figs 1 & 2.

However, when using a 70mm or thicker bearer, it

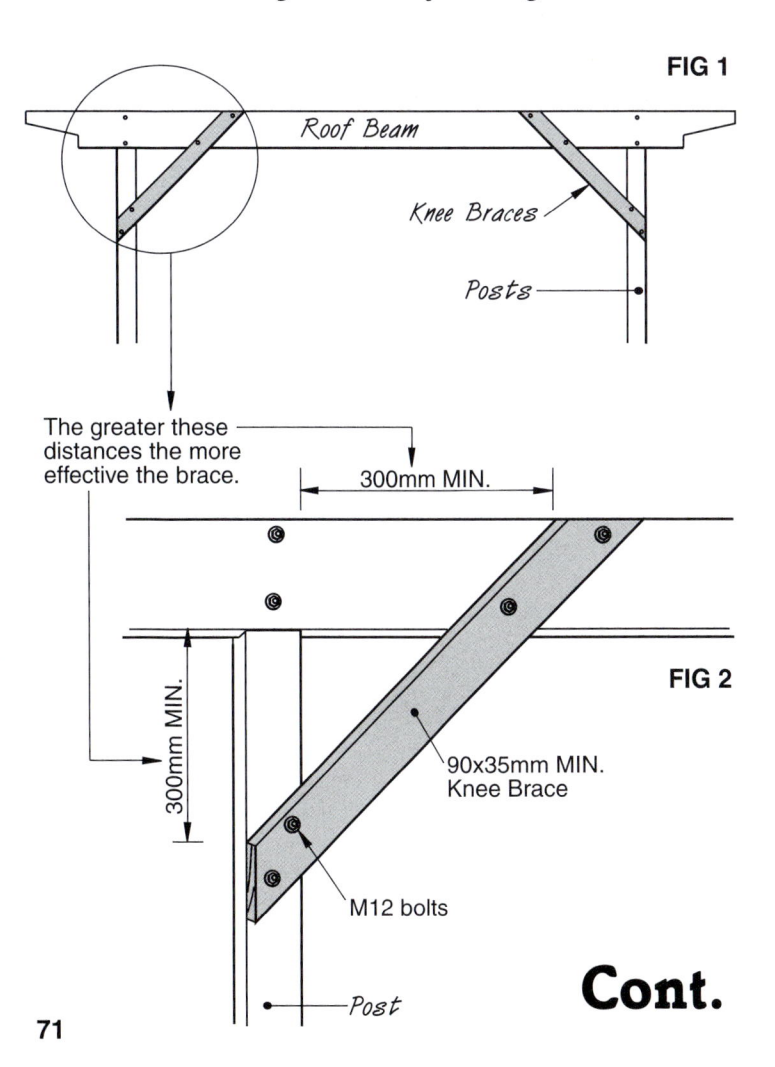

FIG 1 Roof Beam / Knee Braces / Posts

The greater these distances the more effective the brace.

300mm MIN.

300mm MIN.

90x35mm MIN. Knee Brace

M12 bolts

Post

FIG 2

Cont.

may not be flush with either the front or back of the post as in figs 3 & 4.

In this situation, the knee brace can be face bolted to the bearer with its bottom end housed into the post. The face of the brace should be planned to be flush with the post. Fasten the bottom end with a 75 x 3.75mm ring shank nail or 75mm Type 17 gal. or corrosion resistant screw. Then, apply a gal. nail plate across the joint with 4 gal. connector nails each side of the joint as in fig 4.

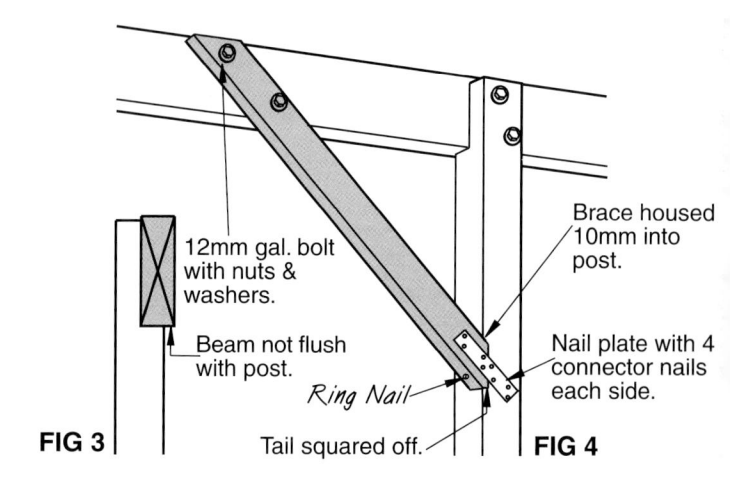

When to Apply Bracing

The bearer should be bolted to the posts and it is best to attach the two end rafters to hold the structure steady then install the bracing. Bolt one end of one brace temporarily. Brace the structure into plumb alignment with a temporary brace then attach the other end of the permanent brace. The opposite brace can also be attached.

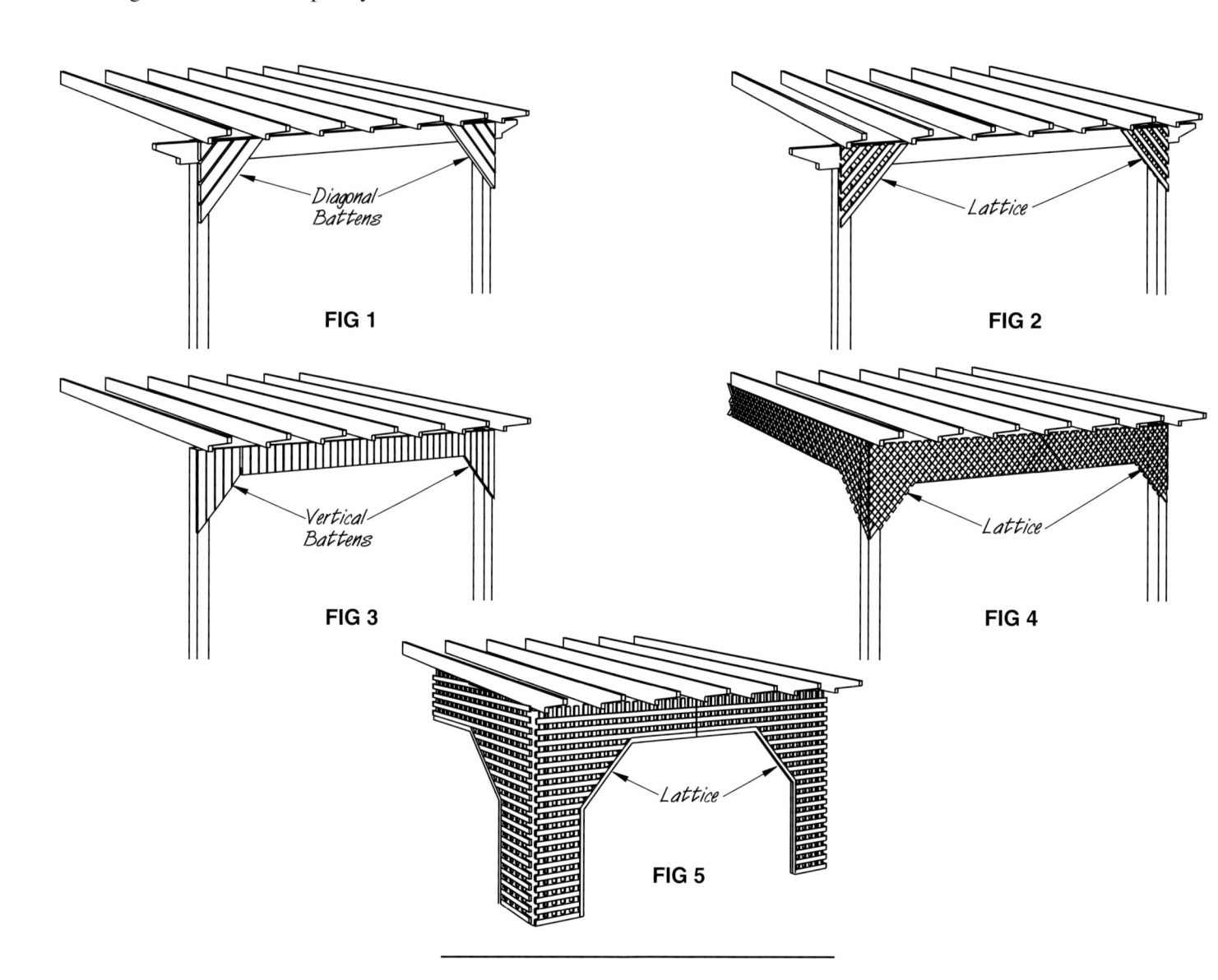

FIG 3 — 12mm gal. bolt with nuts & washers. Beam not flush with post.

FIG 4 — Brace housed 10mm into post. Nail plate with 4 connector nails each side. Ring Nail. Tail squared off.

FIG 1 — Diagonal Battens

FIG 2 — Lattice

FIG 3 — Vertical Battens

FIG 4 — Lattice

FIG 5 — Lattice

Pergola Roof Battening to Receive Cladding

Battens Sizes & Spacings
See Tables to select batten sizes and spacings. Read the cladding manufacturers' requirements in conjunction with the battening table.

Batten Fastenings
See the 'A.S. Timber Framing Manual' to select correct fastenings.

How to Build a Pergola   7

Check with your Local Authority if a permit is required.

The typical design illustrated and described here is one attached to the house fascia board.

For further details on attaching pergolas to the fascia board or house wall see Pages 69-71.

Note: Although many pergolas are initially without roof cladding, at a later date many folk choose to clad the roof with metal, fibreglass, or acrylic sheet. Footings designed to anchor pergolas with roof cladding will generally be larger than those without so it is advisable to design footings to receive roof claddings should the need arise.

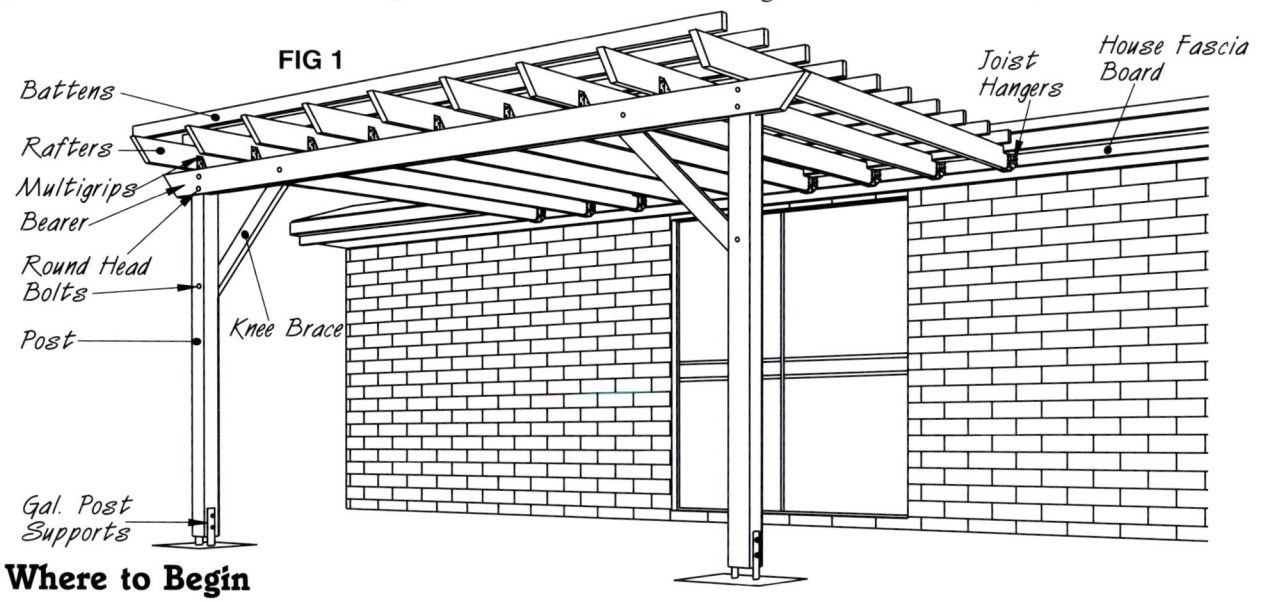

FIG 1

Labels: Battens, Rafters, Multigrips, Bearer, Round Head Bolts, Post, Knee Brace, Gal. Post Supports, Joist Hangers, House Fascia Board

Where to Begin

Step 1 *Prepare a Plan*
Prepare a layout plan and sectional view to establish lengths and quantities of materials *(see 'Example Plan' Page 67).*

EXAMPLE MATERIAL LIST
(See also Page 9)

Footings:
Concrete	1 cubic metre

Timber:
Posts	90x90	F8 treated H5	& Seasoned	2 @ 2.4
Beam	170x45	F8 treated H3	& Seasoned	1 @ 3.6
Rafters	145x35	F8 treated H3	& Seasoned	9 @ 3.0
Battens	70x35	F8 treated H3	& Seasoned	10 @ 4.2
Bracing	90x45	F8 treated H3	& Seasoned	1 @ 1.8

Hardware:
Post Supports	2/High wind gal.
Round Head Bolts	12/100mmx12mm gal.(with nuts & washers)
Triple Grips	9/(with 30x2.8mm gal. connector nails)
Joist Hangers	9/(with 30x2.8mm gal. connector nails)

Step 2 *Setting Out the Site*
Mark on the fascia board the outside face of each end rafter.

From these points drop a plumb bob down to ground pegs and drive a nail indicating these points (see fig 2). Then, drive two further temporary pegs to indicate the two outer corners where the outside of the two end rafters will intersect with the beam (see fig 3). Square this area approx. at this stage.

Remember ends of rafters and beams can extend past these points as illustrated in fig 1.

To enable easier accurate squaring and positioning of the pergola posts, drive 90 x 35mm profile pegs about 600mm outside of the two corner pegs as in fig 3 with nails to indicate the outside faces of the posts.

Stretch string lines between these nails and square this area accurately by taking diagonal measurements between the line intersections, adjust the outer two nails together until both diagonal measurements correspond. On larger more complex pergolas construct profile hurdles as in fig 4 Page 47.

Re-position the original outer corner pegs to indicate the centre of each post footing. If the posts are set back from the outer face of the end rafters, adjust centre of footing peg accordingly.

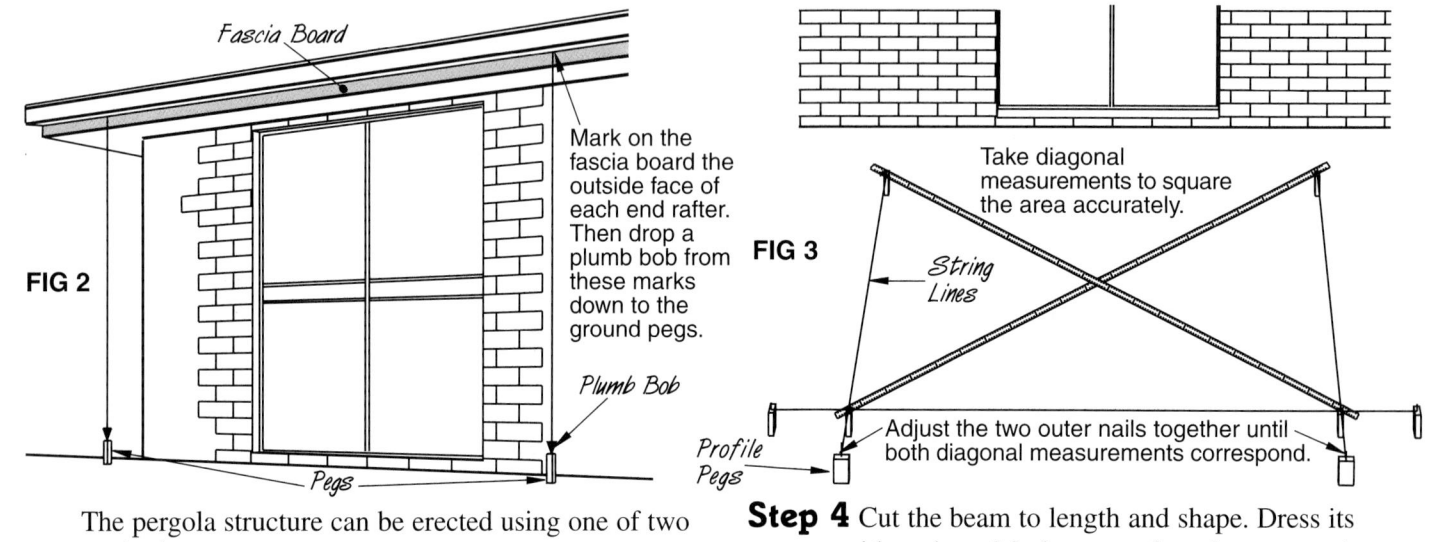

FIG 2

- Fascia Board
- Mark on the fascia board the outside face of each end rafter. Then drop a plumb bob from these marks down to the ground pegs.
- Plumb Bob
- Pegs

FIG 3

- Take diagonal measurements to square the area accurately.
- String Lines
- Profile Pegs
- Adjust the two outer nails together until both diagonal measurements correspond.

The pergola structure can be erected using one of two methods:

Method A. The permanent posts are braced plumb either into stirrups or directly into concrete at the commencement and the structure built directly on them after the concrete hardens, or;

Method B. The pergola is constructed on temporary posts and the permanent posts are installed later. Many Tradespersons prefer this method as no time is lost waiting for the concrete to harden before commencing and it is easier to establish post lengths and housings after the beam is in place.

Method B - Using Temporary Posts

Step 1 String lines are stretched through at ground level for aligning the outside face of the beam and the outside post position mark on the beam.

Step 2 Erect and brace plumb temporary posts skew nailed to 50mm thick timber sole plates embedded into the ground. Keep the posts well clear of the permanent post hole positions (see figs 5 & 6).

Step 3 Level a line onto the posts as in fig 4, then measuring down from this line mark the underside of the beam height. Attach 100x50x400mm long cleats up to the line to support the beam, fasten them with 4/100mm flat head nails (see figs 5 & 6). Use a dolly to avoid loosening the braces. Fasten the lower ends of the braces after attaching the cleats to avoid vibrating the posts out of alignment.

Step 4 Cut the beam to length and shape. Dress its corners with a plane. Mark on one face the proposed permanent post positions. When erected, the outer sides of the post positions should line up with the alignment string lines.

Step 5 Raise the beam into position on the cleats and align the face and post position marks with the string lines then clamp or nail to the temporary posts (see figs 5 & 6).

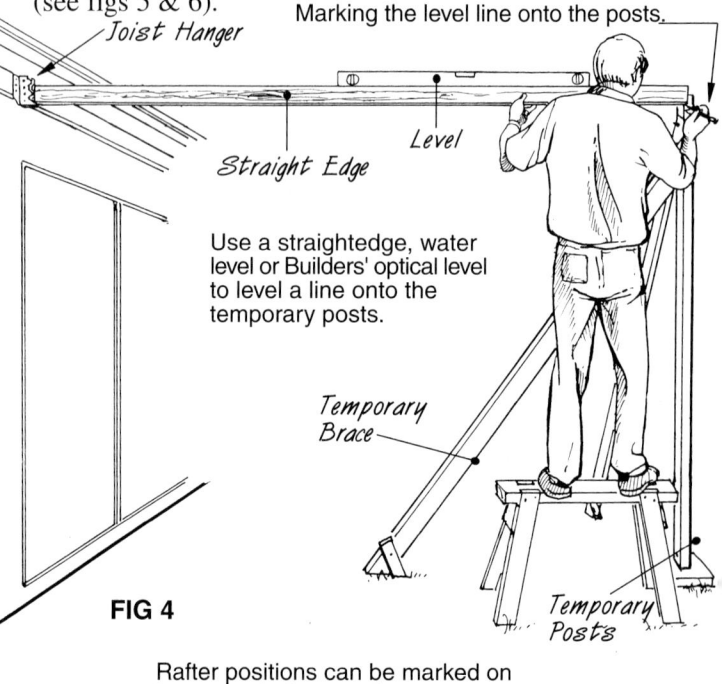

- Joist Hanger
- Marking the level line onto the posts.
- Straight Edge
- Level
- Use a straightedge, water level or Builders' optical level to level a line onto the temporary posts.
- Temporary Brace
- Temporary Posts

FIG 4

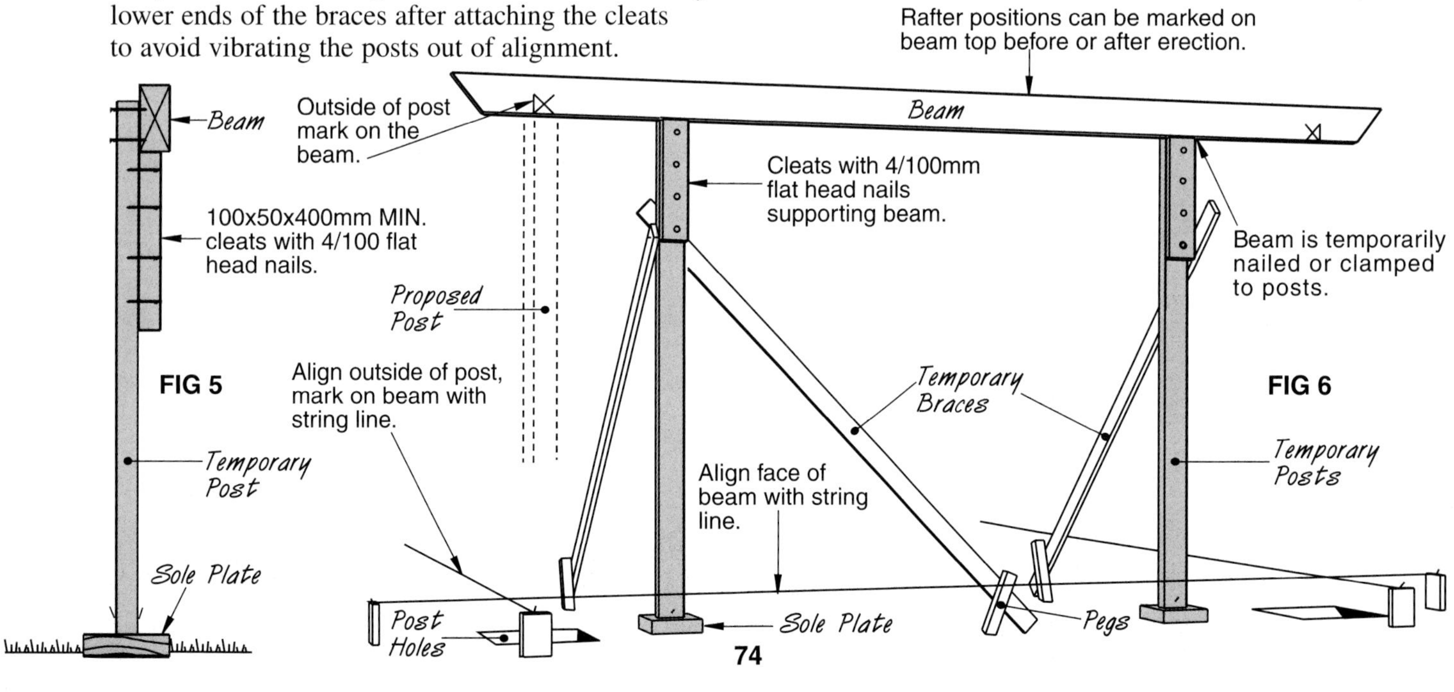

FIG 5

- Beam
- Outside of post mark on the beam.
- 100x50x400mm MIN. cleats with 4/100 flat head nails.
- Proposed Post
- Align outside of post, mark on beam with string line.
- Temporary Post
- Sole Plate
- Post Holes

FIG 6

- Rafter positions can be marked on beam top before or after erection.
- Beam
- Cleats with 4/100mm flat head nails supporting beam.
- Beam is temporarily nailed or clamped to posts.
- Temporary Braces
- Align face of beam with string line.
- Sole Plate
- Pegs
- Temporary Posts

Step 6 *Erecting the Rafters*

Important:
Check that the house fascia board is adequately fastened to the house rafters. See Pages 69-71 for methods of attaching pergolas to fascia boards.

Mark the rafter positions along the fascia board and along the beam top. Attach joist hanger brackets to fascia positions (see fig 7). Leave one side of each hanger loose. Cut rafters to length and shape see Page 58 for shape selection. When shaping the ends be sure the rounds or bows are planned to be uppermost. Dress all corners with a plane and prime paint the rafters and beam before erecting the rafters. Install the rafters keeping the bows uppermost. Secure them in the joist hangers and fasten the remaining nails in the hangers. Secure the rafters to the beam with multigrips (see fig 8).

Step 7 *Roof Battening & Cladding*
If roof battening, cladding or shade cloth is required, these can be applied now. Attach battens and cladding with the fastenings and spacings recommended by the manufacturer.

Step 8 *Installing the Permanent Posts*
Cut the permanent posts to length and make the necessary top end check out housings to receive the beam (see fig 9). Whilst these are still on the saw stools, bolt the stirrups or high wind post supports to their lower ends.

For embedding posts directly into footings see Page 22.

Excavate the post holes to the required depth. Install the posts in the holes and then bolt them to the beam with 2/10mm gal. round head bolts when roof cladding is not to be used or 2/12mm when roof cladding is to be applied. Pour and ram stiff concrete to each hole and plumb the posts both ways.

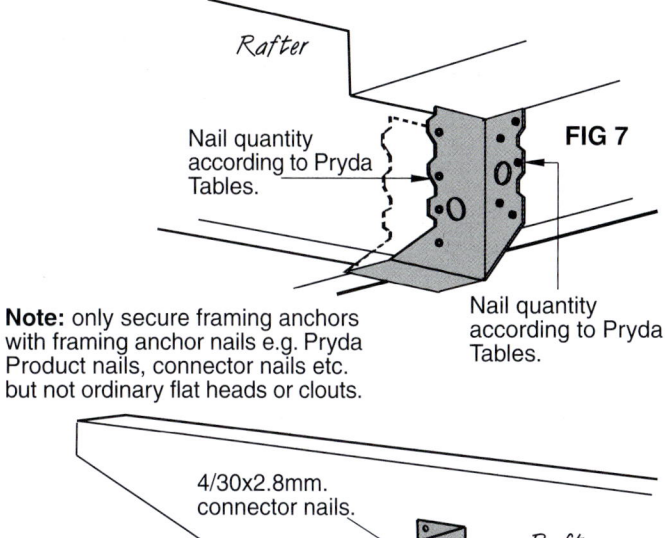

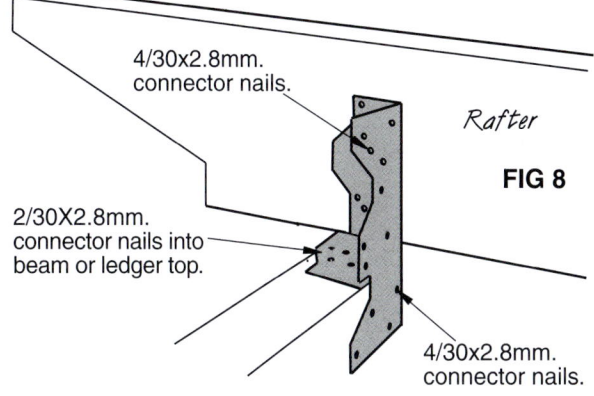

Note: only secure framing anchors with framing anchor nails e.g. Pryda Product nails, connector nails etc. but not ordinary flat heads or clouts.

Ensure the concrete is sloping away from stirrups or posts so that water cannot pond around them. The post bottoms should be a minimum of 75mm above the finished deck or patio surface for termite inspection accord. to the 'BCA'. After 24 hours, the temporary posts can be removed.

Step 6 *Applying Bracing*
Where the posts have not been designed as cantilever or bracing posts, knee braces should be applied (see Pages 71 & 72). Cut the braces to length and shape and fasten in position.

Step 7 *Painting*
Finally paint or stain with the desired coatings.

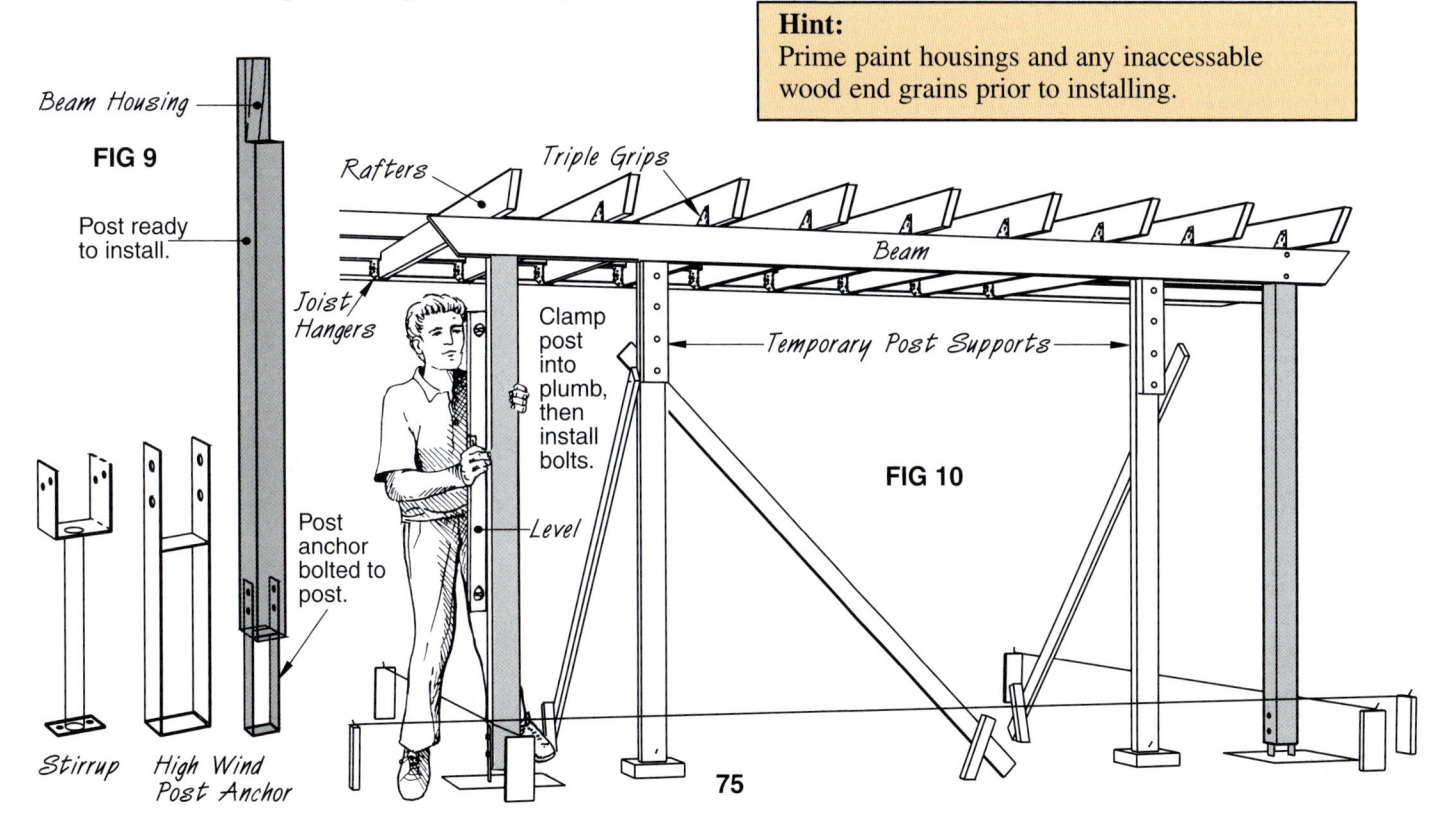

Hint:
Prime paint housings and any inaccessable wood end grains prior to installing.

Painting or Staining Deck & Pergola Timbers

The Problems
All timbers exposed to the weather should have some form of surface coating to prevent deterioration caused by either weathering or fungi. Evidence of deterioration can be surface discoloration and minor cracking to the more serious problems of rot and distortion (warping etc) and large cracks.

Rot is caused by fungal attack while discoloration, cracks and distortion are caused by direct exposure to the weather (weathering).

The Solutions
Rot is prevented firstly by the use of the correct 'H' level treatment in softwoods and Durability classification of hardwoods, thorough preservative coating and sealing of housings and sawn ends and proper continued maintenance of coated surfaces.

Weathering damage is prevented by properly maintained surface coatings.

Which Coatings to Use
For practical purposes **stains** or **paint** are recommended.

While **Water Repellent Preservatives** should be applied initially, their frequency of maintenance (as a surface coating) usually makes them an impractical alternative. (Times between recoating is usually six to eighteen months).

Stains
These are in popular use and enable the retention of the natural timber texture. However, they will require recoatings more frequently than paint approx. six months to five years depending on the situation but most likely 6 months to three years. Foot trafficable areas probably twelve to eighteen months.

In their favour is that they don't peel, crack or blister and recoating is relatively easy with only minimal surface preparation required.

Stains will perform better if the timber is pre-treated with water repellent preservatives but check beforehand that the preservative will be compatible with the chosen stain.

Paint
Paints come especially formulated for deck and pergola timbers and are mainly water based. They are available in a variety of timber colours. However, they are opaque in that they conceal the natural timber texture. This has one advantage in that the timber is totally protected from the damaging UV rays.

The main advantage of these coatings is their long life. Non trafficable areas should not require repainting for five to six years. Trafficable surfaces such as decking may require recoating every twelve months to restore the fresh appearance although the paint membrane may not be damaged.

Important Notes:
a). Re-paint before the paint membrane becomes damaged to prevent water penetration.
b). Acrylic coated decking should be left to cure and harden for seven days before walking on.

Re-paint times will also depend on weather and salt exposure (seaside localities) and also on the extent of shrinkage that may occur in the timber.

Decking laid in an unseasoned state will cause damage to the surface coating as the timber dries out.

Note: It is always advisable to pay a little extra and purchase seasoned decking.

Hints:

a). **Never** use Polyurethane or Estapol on decks and pergola timbers.

b). Always read the Manufacturers instructions on the container for surface preparation, application and re-coating.

c). Prime paint or stain joist tops before laying decking and prime paint or stain decking timber on all four sides thoroughly before laying.

d). Before coating treated timber, ensure any water and solvents have dried out and that any powdery surface deposits are washed off with a hose and scrubbing brush.

e). Only use specially formulated decking stains or paints not ordinary house paints.

Deck & Pergola Tables

8

Deck & Pergola Post Footing Sizes

Pergolas should always be designed to be capable of receiving roof cladding even if cladding is not required at present. This is mainly because the footing size requirement for Pergolas without cladding will almost certainly be inadequate. Roof cladding will greatly increase uplift forces in storms and high winds sufficient to uplift inadequate footings and/or the posts out of the ground.

How to Find the Area Supported by Each Post for Tables 4, 5, 6 or 7

Multiply 'Dimension A' in fig 1 x 'Dimension S' in fig 2.

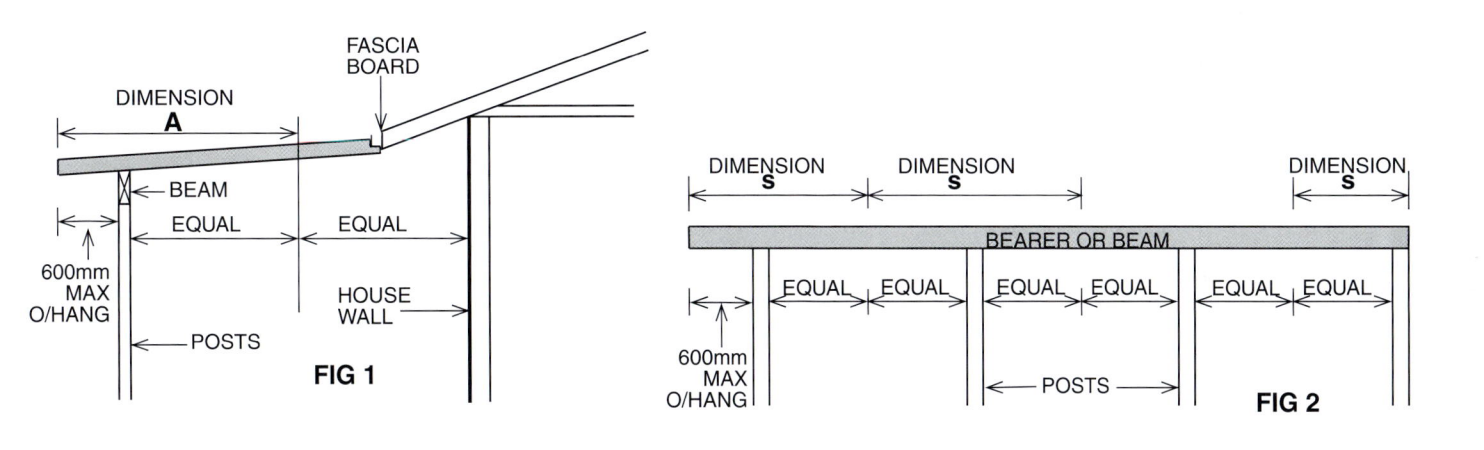

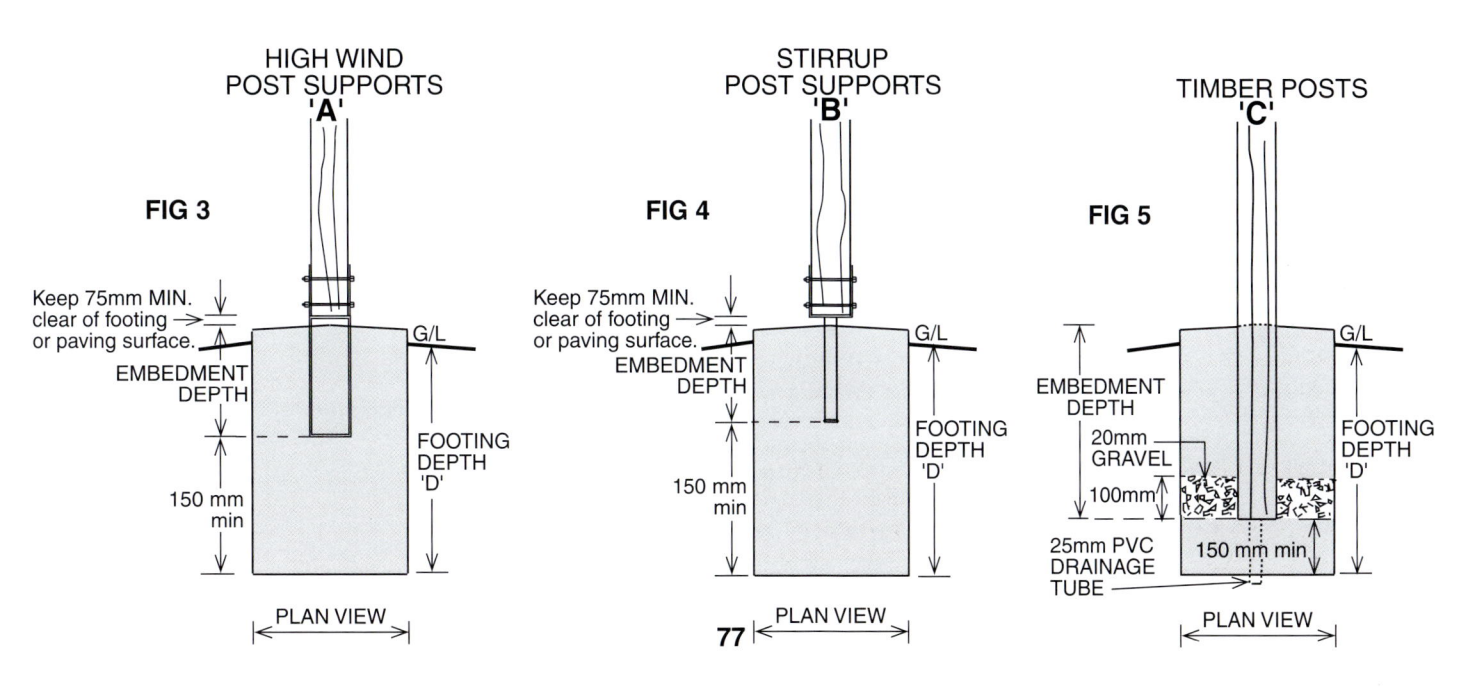

FIG 1

FIG 2

FIG 3 — HIGH WIND POST SUPPORTS 'A'

FIG 4 — STIRRUP POST SUPPORTS 'B'

FIG 5 — TIMBER POSTS 'C'

77

Cont.
Post/Stirrup Footing Sizes

TABLE 4 — POST FOOTING SIZES
For Braced Decks & Pergolas in N1 (Non Cyclonic) to C1 (Cyclonic) Categories

SOIL BEARING PRESSURE 150kPa			IMPORTANT NOTES:
AREA SUPPORTED BY EACH POST	MINIMUM FOOTING SIZE PLAN VIEW	MIN. FOOTING DEPTH D	
5 sq. m	300x300mm	650mm	
10 sq. m	600x600mm		
15 sq. m	600x600mm		
20 sq. m	750x750mm		

IMPORTANT NOTES:
a). Footing sizes are only suitable for Decks up to 3.6m above ground and Pergolas up to 2.7m above ground or above Decks.
b). Footing sizes are suitable for Pergolas with or without roof cladding.
c). Minimum soil bearing pressure 150kPa includes Rock, med dense to dense sand or gravel, moderately reactive to stiff clay. If in doubt, consult a local Building Inspector. For subsoils with less bearing pressure than 150kPa refer to AS (Code) or a local Geotechnical Engineer.

TABLE 5 — POST FOOTING SIZES
For Cantlivered Posts (unbraced) Decks or Pergolas in N1 (Non Cyclonic) to C1 (Cyclonic) Categories

SOIL BEARING PRESSURE 150kPa		
AREA SUPPORTED BY EACH POST	MINIMUM FOOTING SIZE PLAN VIEW	MIN. FOOTING DEPTH D
5 sq. m	300x300mm 300 dia. 450x450mm 450 dia.	900mm 900mm 600mm 600mm
10 sq. m	450 dia. 600x600mm	900mm 600mm
15 sq. m	600x600mm 600 dia.	900mm 900mm
20 sq. m	600x600mm 600 dia.	900mm 900mm

IMPORTANT NOTES:
a). Footing sizes are only suitable for Deck or Pergola posts up to 2.1m above ground to underside of bearer.
b). Footing sizes are suitable for Pergolas with or without roof cladding.
c). Footings should be taken through fill and bearing depth of footing in underlying soil should be used as Minimum Depth D.
d). For footings taken through fill, maximum column height should be measured from base of fill.
e). Minimum soil bearing pressure 150kPa includes Rock, med dense to dense sand or gravel, moderately reactive to stiff clay. If in doubt, consult a local Building Inspector. For subsoils with less bearing pressure than 150kPa refer to AS (Code) or a local Geotechnical Engineer.

TABLE 6 — POST FOOTING SIZES
For Braced Pergolas Only in N1 (Non Cyclonic) to C1 (Cyclonic) Categories

SOIL BEARING PRESSURE 150kPa		
AREA SUPPORTED BY EACH POST	MINIMUM FOOTING SIZE PLAN VIEW	MIN. FOOTING DEPTH D
5 sq. m	300x300mm	450mm
10 sq. m	300x300mm	450mm
15 sq. m	450x450mm	450mm
20 sq. m	450x450mm 600x600mm	600mm 450mm

IMPORTANT NOTES:
a). Footing sizes are only suitable for Decks or Pergola posts up to 3.6m above ground and Pergolas up to 2.7m above ground or above Decks.
b). Footing sizes are suitable for Pergolas with or without roof cladding.
c). Minimum soil bearing pressure 150kPa includes Rock, med dense to dense sand or gravel, moderately reactive to stiff clay. If in doubt, consult a local Building Inspector. For subsoils with less bearing pressure than 150kPa refer to AS (Code) or a local Geotechnical Engineer.

Post Sizes for Decks & Pergolas

Note: See Page 8 for further information on timber species, treatments and 'F' ratings.

Maximum Heights
Maximum heights for decks are taken from above ground level and for pergolas, above ground level or above a deck surface.

How to Find the Area Supported by Each Post for Table 7
Multiply 'Dimension A' in fig 1 x 'Dimension S' in fig 2 on Page 77.

TABLE 7 POSTS — For Decks & Pergolas in N1 (Non Cyclonic) to C2 (Cyclonic) Categories

STRESS GRADE/SPECIES	POST SIZE (mm)	MAX. POST HEIGHT (m) FOR AREA SUPPORTED 6 sq.m	MAX. POST HEIGHT (m) FOR AREA SUPPORTED 12 sq.m
F5 (UNSEASONED SOFTWOOD)	75x75	1600	NS
	75x100	1900	1000
	90x90	2400	1400
	100x100	3000	2000
	125x125	4700	3300
	150x150	4800	4800
F8 (SEASONED SOFTWOOD) MILLED OR ROUND	70x70	1900	1100
	90x90	3200	2200
	120x120	4800	4000
F11 (UNSEASONED HARDWOOD)	75x75	2200	1500
	75x100	2500	1800
	90x90	3200	2200
	100x100	3900	2700
	125x125	4800	4300
	150x150	4800	4800

IMPORTANT NOTES:

a). Where undressed sizes for F7/F8 are proposed, use the next largest undressed size (e.g. a listing of 90x90mm is increased to 100x100mm etc).

b). For other stress grades or for design considerations not allowed for in this table (refer to A.S. National Framing Code).

Deck Bearer Sizes N1 (NonCyclonic) to C1 (Cyclonic)

How to Select Bearer Sizes from Tables
Decide which timber species to use and its *stress grade* 'F' number for the first column (enquire at suppliers for the stress grades available, see also Page 8).

Obtain the *load width* for the second column from fig 1. Then decide whether to use single or continuous spanning bearers.

Continuous spans are when the bearer will have intermediate support. Where a requirement is for two bearers i.e. 2/150 x 50mm, the bearers are constructed as in figs 4 & 5 Page 24.

Note: Do not cripple continuous bearers otherwise consider them as simply supported (Single Span) bearers.

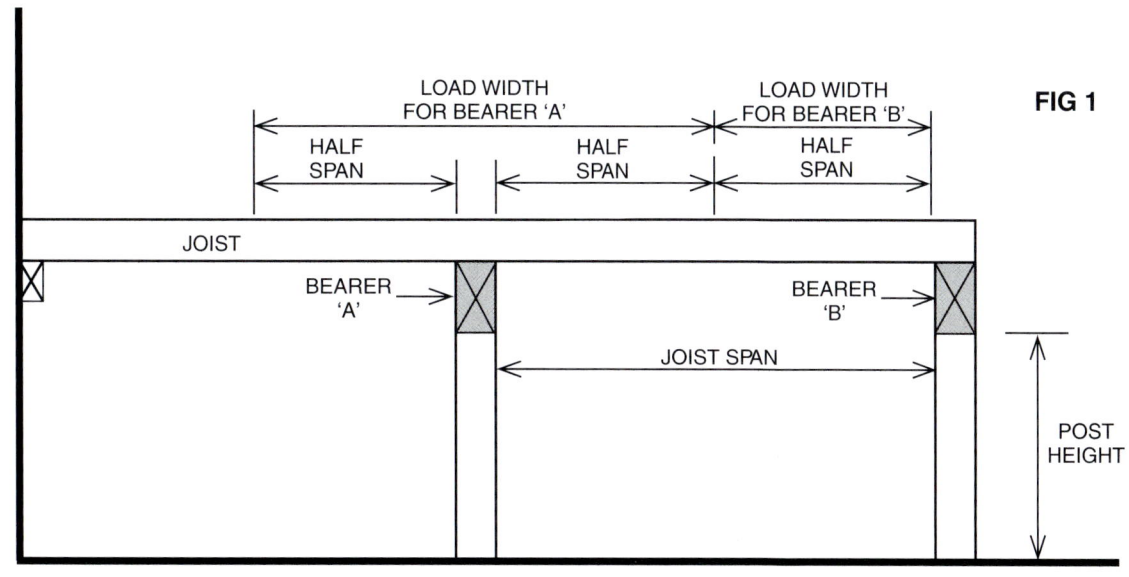

FIG 1

Continued

Cont.
TABLE 8 BEARERS (Single Span)
For Decks in N1 (Non Cyclonic) to C1 (Cyclonic) Categories

STRESS GRADE	LOAD WIDTH (refer notes)	1200	1800	2100	2400	2700	3000
F5 Unseasoned	1800	125x75 / 150x50 / ----	150x100 / 175x75 / 225x50	175x100 / 2/175X150 / 250X50	200x100 / 225x75 / 275x50	225x100 / 275x75 / ----	2/225x50 / 250x100 / ----
	2400	125x100 / 150x75 / 175x50	175x100 / 200x75 / 2/175x50	200x100 / 225x75 / 275x50	2/225x50 / 250x100 / 275x75	2/250x50 / 275x100 / ----	2/275x50 / ---- / ----
	3000	150x75 / 200x50 / ----	2/175x50 / 200x100 / 275x50	225x100 / 275x75 / ----	2/250x50 / 275x100 / ----	2/275x50 / ---- / ----	---- / ---- / ----
	3600	150x100 / 175x75 / 200x50	2/200x50 / 225x100 / 250x75	2/225x50 / 250x100 / ----	2/275x50 / ---- / ----	---- / ---- / ----	---- / ---- / ----
F7* (See Note B) Seasoned	1800	2/190x45 / ----	2/140x45 / ----	2/170x35 / ----	2/170x45 / 2/190x35	2/190x45 / ----	2/240x35 / ----
	2400	2/120x35 / ----	2/170x35 / ----	2/170x45 / ----	2/240x35 / ----	2/240x45 / ----	2/290x35 / ----
	3000	2/120x45 / 2/140x35	2/170x45 / 2/190x35	2/190x45 / 2/240x35	2/240x45 / ----	2/290x35 / ----	2/290x45 / ----
	3600	2/120x45 / 2/140x35	2/190x45 / ----	2/240x35 / ----	2/240x45 / 2/290x35	2/290x45 / ----	---- / ----
F8* (See Note B) Seasoned	1800	2/90x35 / ----	2/120x45 / 2/140x35	2/140x45 / ----	2/170x35 / ----	2/170x45 / ----	2/190x45 / ----
	2400	2/90x45 / 2/120x35	2/140x45 / 2/170x35	2/170x45 / 2/190x35	2/190x45 / ----	2/240x35 / ----	2/240x45 / ----
	3000	2/120x35 / ----	2/170x35 / ----	2/170x45 / ----	2/240x35 / ----	2/240x45 / ----	2/290x35 / ----
	3600	2/120x45 / 2/140x35	2/170x45 / 2/190x35	2/190x45 / 2/240x35	---- / ----	2/240x45 / 2/290x35	2/290x45 / ----
F11 Unseasoned	1800	100x50 / ---- / ----	2/100x50 / 125x75 / 150x50	2/125x50 / 175x50 / ----	150x75 / 200x50 / ----	2/150x50 / 175x75 / 225x50	2/175x50 / 200x75 / ----
	2400	2/100x50 / 100x75 / ----	150x75 / 175x50 / ----	2/125x50 / 200x50 / ----	2/150x50 / 175x75 / 225x50	2/175x50 / 200x75 / 250x50	225x75 / 275x50 / ----
	3000	2/100x50 / 100x75 / 125x50	2/125x50 / 150x75 / 175x50	2/150x50 / 175x75 / 225x50	200x75 / 250x50 / ----	2/175x50 / 225x75 / 275x50	2/200x50 / 250x75 / 300x50
	3600	2/100x50 / 125x75 / 150x50	175x75 / 200x50 / ----	2/150x50 / 200x75 / 225x50	2/175x50 / 225x75 / 275x50	2/200x50 / 250x75 / 300x50	2/225x50 / 275x75 / ----
F14 Unseasoned	1800	100x50 / ---- / ----	2/100x50 / ---- / ----	125x75 / 150x50 / ----	2/125x50 / 150x75 / 175x50	2/150x50 / 175x75 / 200x50	225x50 / ---- / ----
	2400	100x50 / ---- / ----	125x75 / 150x50	2/125x50 / 150x75 / 175x50	2/150x50 / 175x75 / 200x50	200x75 / 225x50 / ----	2/175x50 / 250x50 / ----
	3000	2/100x50 / 100x75 / 125x50	2/125x50 / 150x75 / 175x50	175x75 / 200x50 / ----	2/150x50 / 200x75 / 225x50	2/175x50 / 225x75 / 250x50	2/200x50 / 275x50 / ----
	3600	2/100x50 / 125x50 / ----	2/125x50 / 150x75 / 175x50	2/150x50 / 175x75 / 200x50	2/175x50 / 200x75 / 225x50	225x75 / 275x50 / ----	2/200x50 / 250x75 / 300x50
F17 Unseasoned	1800	100x50 / ---- / ----	2/100x50 / 100x75 / 125x50	125x75 / 150x50 / ----	2/125x50 / ---- / ----	150x75 / 175x50	2/150x50 / 175x75 / 200x50
	2400	100x50 / ---- / ----	2/100x50 / 125x75 / 150x50	2/125x50 / ---- / ----	150x75 / 175x50 / ----	2/150x50 / 175x75 / 200x50	2/175x50 / 225x50 / ----
	3000	100x50 / ---- / ----	125x75 / 150x50 / ----	2/125x50 / 150x75 / 175x50	2/150x50 / 175x75 / 200x50	200x75 / 225x50 / -----	2/175x50 / 250x50 / ----
	3600	2/100x50 / 100x75 / 125x50	2/125x50 / 150x75 / 175x50	175x75 / 200x50 / ----	2/150x50 / 225x50 / ----	2/175x50 / 200x75 / ----	2/200x50 / 225x75 / 275x50

IMPORTANT NOTES:
a). Bearers are not to carry roof loads (i.e. Roof/Pergola supports continued through to ground).
b). Where undressed sizes for F7/F8 are proposed, use the next largest undressed size (e.g. a listing of 120x70mm is increased to 125x75mm etc).
c). For other stress grades or for larger spans (refer to A.S. National Timber Framing Code).
d). Where two bearers are listed e.g. 2/125x50 - these are applied on either side of the post or spaced apart, not laminated together, (see Page 24).
e). For joists which are to support tiles use the next larger depth bearer.

Cont.
TABLE 8 BEARERS (Continuous Span)

For Decks in N1 (Non Cyclonic) to C1 (Cyclonic) Categories

STRESS GRADE	LOAD WIDTH (refer notes)	SIZE OF BEARERS (mm) FOR BEARER SPAN (m) CONTINUOUS SPAN					
		1200	1800	2100	2400	2700	3000
F5 Unseasoned	1800	125x75 150x50 ----	150x100 175x75 225x50	175x100 2/175x50 250x50	200x100 2/200x50 275x50	225x100 275x75 ----	2/225x50 250x100 ----
	2400	125x100 150x75 175x50	175x100 200x75 2/175x50	200x100 225x75 275x50	2/225x50 250x100 275x75	2/250x50 275x100 ----	2/275x50 ---- ----
	3000	150x75 200x50 ----	2/175x50 200x100 275x50	225x100 275x75 ----	2/250x50 275x100 ----	2/275x50 ---- ----	---- ---- ----
	3600	150x100 175x75 200x50	2/200x50 225x100 250x75	2/225x50 250x100 ----	2/275x50 ---- ----	---- ---- ----	---- ---- ----
F7* (See Note B) Seasoned	1800	2/190x45 ----	2/140x45 ----	2/170x35 ----	2/170x45 2/190x35	2/190x45 ----	2/240x35 ----
	2400	2/120x35 ----	2/170x35 ----	2/170x45 ----	2/240x35 ----	2/240x45 ----	2/290x35 ----
	3000	2/120x45 2/140x35	2/170x45 2/190x35	2/190x45 2/240x35	2/240x45 ----	2/290x35 ----	2/290x45 ----
	3600	2/120x45 2/140x35	2/190x45 ----	2/240x35 ----	2/240x45 2/290x35	2/290x45 ----	---- ----
F8* (See Note B) Seasoned	1800	2/90x35 ----	2/120x45 2/140x35	2/140x45 ----	2/170x35 ----	2/170x45 ----	2/190x45 ----
	2400	2/90x45 2/120x35	2/140x45 2/170x35	2/170x45 2/190x35	2/190x45 ----	2/240x35 ----	2/240x45 ----
	3000	2/120x35 ----	2/170x35 ----	2/170x45 ----	2/240x35 ----	2/240x45 ----	2/290x35 ----
	3600	2/120x45 2/140x35	2/170x45 2/190x35	2/190x45 2/240x35	---- ----	2/240x45 2/290x35	2/290x45 ----
F11 Unseasoned	1800	100x50 ---- ----	2/100x50 125x75 150x50	175x50 ---- ----	2/125x50 150x75 200x50	2/150x50 175x75 225x50	200x75 ---- ----
	2400	2/100x50 100x75 125x50	150x75 175x50 ----	2/125x50 200x50 ----	2/150x50 175x75 225x50	200x75 250x50 ----	2/175x50 225x75 275x50
	3000	2/100x50 100x75 125x50	2/125x50 150x75 175x50	2/150x50 175x75 225x50	200x75 250x50 ----	2/175x50 225x75 275x50	2/200x50 250x75 300x50
	3600	2/100x50 125x75 150x50	175x75 200x50 ----	2/150x50 200x75 225x50	2/175x50 225x75 275x50	2/200x50 250x75 300x50	2/225x50 275x75 ----
F14 Unseasoned	1800	100x50 ---- ----	---- ---- ----	2/100x50 125x75 150x50	2/125x50 150x75 175x50	175x75 200x75 ----	2/150x50 225x50 ----
	2400	100x50 ---- ----	2/100x50 125x75 150x50	2/125x50 150x75 175x50	175x75 200x50 ----	2/150x50 200x75 225x50	2/175x50 250x50 ----
	3000	2/100x50 100x75 125x50	2/125x50 150x75 175x50	175x75 200x50 ----	2/150x50 200x75 250x50	2/175x50 225x75 250x50	2/200x50 275x50 ----
	3600	2/100x50 125x50 ----	2/125x50 150x75 200x50	2/150x50 175x75 225x50	2/175x50 200x75 250x50	225x75 275x50 ----	2/200x50 250x75 300x50
F17 Unseasoned	1800	100x50 ---- ----	100x75 125x50 ----	2/100x50 125x75 150x50	---- ---- ----	2/125x50 150x75 175x50	200x50 ---- ----
	2400	100x50 ---- ----	2/100x50 125x75 150x50	---- ---- ----	2/125x50 150x75 175x50	175x75 200x50 ----	2/150x50 225x50 ----
	3000	100x50 ---- ----	2/100x50 125x75 150x50	2/125x50 150x75 175x50	175x75 200x50 ----	2/150x50 200x75 225x50	2/175x50 250x50 ----
	3600	2/100x50 100x75 125x50	2/125x50 150x75 175x50	175x75 200x50 ----	2/150x50 225x50 ----	2/175x50 200x75 250x50	225x75 275x50 ----

IMPORTANT NOTES: a). Bearers are not to carry roof loads (i.e. Roof/Pergola supports continued through to ground).
b). Where undressed sizes for F7/F8 are proposed, use the next largest undressed size (e.g. a listing of 120x70mm is increased to 125x75mm etc).
c). For other stress grades or for larger spans refer to AS, 'National Timber Framing Code'.
d). Where two bearers are listed e.g. 2/125x50 - these are applied on either side of the post or spaced apart, not laminated together, (see Page 24).
e). For joists which are to support tiles use the next larger depth bearer.

Deck Joists (*Note:* See Page 8 for further information on Timber Species, Treatments & 'F' Ratings)

How to Select Joists From Tables 9
Decide which timber species to use and its *stress grade* 'F' rating from the first column.

Decide on whether to use single or continuous spanning joists (continous spanning joists are those which have intermediate bearer support).

TABLES 9 JOISTS — For Decks in N1 (Non Cycl.) through to C2 (Cycl.)

JOIST SPACINGS MAX.: 450mm for Treated Softwood or Cypress & 500mm for Hardwood Decking

UNSEASONED F5

Size D&B (mm)	Single Span	Continuous Span
100x38	1000	1300
100x50	1400	1700
125x38	1700	1900
125x50	2200	2200
150x38	2300	2300
150x50	2600	2600
175x38	2700	2700
175x50	3000	3000
200x38	3100	3100
200x50	3500	3500
225x38	3400	3400
225x50	3900	3900
250x38	3800	3800
250x50	4300	4300
275x38	4200	4200
275x50	4800	4800

UNSEASONED F7

Size D&B (mm)	Single Span	Continuous Span
100x50	NS	1900
125x38	2100	2100
125x50	2400	2400
150x38	2600	2600
150x50	2900	2900
175x38	3000	3000
175x50	3400	3400
200x38	3400	3400
200x50	3900	3900
225x38	3800	3800
225x50	4300	4400
250x38	4300	4300
250x50	4600	4800
275x38	4600	4700
275x50	5000	5300

SEASONED F7

Size D&B (mm)	Single Span	Continuous Span
90x35	1000	1300
90x45	1300	1700
120x35	1900	2000
120x45	2300	2300
140x35	2300	2300
140x45	2600	2600
170x35	2800	2800
170x45	3200	3200
190x35	3100	3100
190x45	3600	3600
240x35	4000	4000
240x45	4500	4500
290x45	5200	5400

SEASONED F8

Size D&B (mm)	Single Span	Continuous Span
90x35	1300	1700
90x45	1700	1900
120x35	2200	2200
120x45	2500	2500
140x35	2600	2600
140x45	2900	2900
170x35	3100	3100
170x45	3500	3600
190x35	3500	3500
190x45	3900	4000
240x35	4400	4400
240x45	4700	5000
290x45	5400	6000

UNSEASONED F11

Size D&B (mm)	Single Span	Continuous Span
75x38	1100	1300
75x50	1300	1500
100x38	1800	2100
100x50	2100	2400
125x38	2400	2800
125x50	2700	3000
150x38	2900	3300
150x50	3200	3700
175x38	3400	3900
175x50	3800	4300
200x38	3900	4500
200x50	4200	4900
225x38	4300	5000
225x50	4600	5500
250x38	4700	5600
250x50	5000	6200
275x38	5000	6100
275x50	5400	6800

UNSEASONED F14

Size D&B (mm)	Single Span	Continuous Span
75x38	1200	1400
75x50	1400	1700
100x38	1900	2300
100x50	2200	2500
125x38	2600	2900
125x50	2800	3200
150x38	3100	3500
150x50	3400	3800
175x38	3600	4100
175x50	4000	4500
200x38	4100	4700
200x50	4400	5100
225x38	4500	5200
225x50	4800	5800
250x38	4800	5800
250x50	5200	6400
275x38	5200	6400
275x50	5600	7000

UNSEASONED F17

Size D&B (mm)	Single Span	Continuous Span
75x38	1300	1500
75x50	1500	1800
100x38	2100	2400
100x50	2400	2700
125x38	2700	3000
125x50	3000	3400
150x38	3200	3700
150x50	3600	4000
175x38	3800	4300
175x50	4100	4700
200x38	4200	4900
200x50	4500	5400
225x38	4600	5500
225x50	5000	6100
250x38	5000	6100
250x50	5400	6800
275x38	5400	6800
275x50	5800	7200

IMPORTANT NOTES:

a). Joists and Bearers NOT to carry roof loads (i.e. roof/pergola supports continue through to ground).

b). Where undressed sizes for F7/F8 are proposed, use the next largest undressed size (e.g. a listing of 120x45 is increased to 125x50, etc).

c). Although 35/38mm thick joists may be structurally adequate, the number of nails used at decking joins may cause splitting. Wider joists 45/50mm are recommended.

d). For other stress grades or for larger spans, refer to AS, 'National Timber Framing Code'.

e). For joists which are to support tiles use the next larger depth joist or reduce the spacing to 300mm.

Note: Tables are based on a deck mass of 20kg/m^2.

Decking (Deck Flooring) & Fastenings

TABLE 10 DECKING — ALLOWABLE SPANS & FASTENINGS

SPECIES	MINIMUM GRADE	THICKNESS (mm)	MAX. JOIST SPACING (mm)	NAIL FIXING	SCREW FIXING
HARDWOOD	STANDARD GRADE (AS 2796)	19	500	50x2.8 Gal. Bullet Head	
		25	650	65x2.8 Gal. Bullet Head	
CYPRESS	STANDARD GRADE (AS 1810)	21	450	50x2.8 Gal. Bullet Head	
TREATED SOFTWOOD	STANDARD GRADE (AS 1782)	22	450	50x2.8 Galv. Flat Head	8g x 10 x 57mm gal. chipboard screws

IMPORTANT NOTES:

a). When nailing into treated softwood joists, use deformed ring shank nails.

b). Drill holes if necessary at 80% of nail diameter.

c). When nail or screw fixing, use two fasteners per joist.

d). Nails should penetrate the receiving member by ten times the nail's diameter into side grain. Screws should penetrate the receiving member 35-38mm min.

Stair Stringer & Tread Sizes

FIG 1

FIG 2

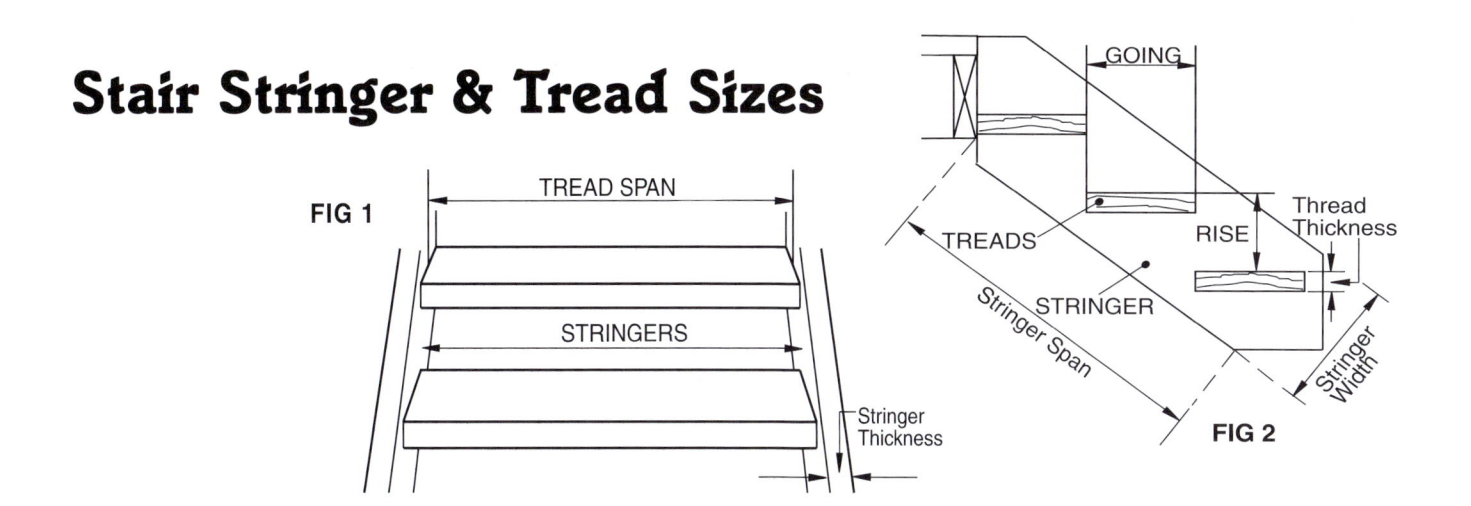

TABLE 11 STAIR STRINGER SIZES

STRINGER SPAN	TREAD SPAN	UNSEASONED — Min. Stringer thickness = 50mm, Max housing depth = 15mm						SEASONED — Min. Stringer thickness = 50mm, Max housing depth = 15mm					
		F5	F7	F8	F11	F14	F17	F5 or MGP10	F7	F8 or MGP12	F11	F14	F17	F22
UP TO 3600mm	900	225	225	225	225	225	225	220	220	220	220	220	220	220
	1000	250	225	225	225	225	225	240	220	220	220	220	220	220
	1100	250	225	225	225	225	225	240	220	220	220	220	220	220
	1200	250	225	225	225	225	225	240	240	220	220	220	220	220
	1300	250	225	225	225	225	225	----	240	240	220	220	220	220
	1400	275	250	250	225	225	225	----	240	240	220	220	220	220
	1500	275	250	250	250	225	225	----	----	240	240	220	220	220
3600mm TO 4300mm	900	275	250	250	225	225	225	----	240	240	220	220	220	220
	1000	275	275	250	250	225	225	----	----	240	240	220	220	220
	1100	275	275	250	250	250	225	----	----	----	240	240	220	220
	1200	300	275	275	250	250	225	----	----	----	240	240	220	220
	1300	300	300	275	275	250	250	----	----	----	----	240	240	220
	1400	300	300	275	275	250	250	----	----	----	----	----	240	220
	1500	----	300	300	275	275	250	----	----	----	----	----	240	220

TABLE 12 STAIR TREAD THICKNESS

For Stairs Without Risers — Minimum Tread Width 240mm

TREAD SPAN	UNSEASONED						SEASONED						
	F5	F7	F8	F11	F14	F17	F5 or MGP10	F7	F8 or MGP12	F11	F14	F17	F22
900	50	50	50	38	38	38	45	45	35	35	35	35	35
1000	50	50	50	50	50	38	45	45	45	45	35	35	35
1100	50	50	50	50	50	50	70	45	45	45	45	45	35
1200	75	50	50	50	50	50	70	70	70	45	45	45	45
1300	----	75	75	75	50	50	70	70	70	70	45	45	45
1400	----	75	75	75	75	50	70	70	70	70	70	70	45
1500	----	75	75	75	75	75	70	70	70	70	70	70	70

Handrail Design (For domestic single dwelling applications only).

Railings, balustrades, members and connections must conform to the Australian Standards 1170.1.

Loads Required to Resist

The Australian Standard requires railings, balustrades, members and connectors all together and which provide structural support to be able to resist the factored limit state load of 0.9kN/m inward, outward and downward at any point.

It also requires internal handrails and balusters to resist factored horizontal or vertical loads of 0.53kN/m for all areas within or servicing one dwelling including stairs and landings but *not* external balconies.

For external balconies in domestic and other residential buildings, infill, including balusters should be capable of resisting 0.75kN/m in any direction.

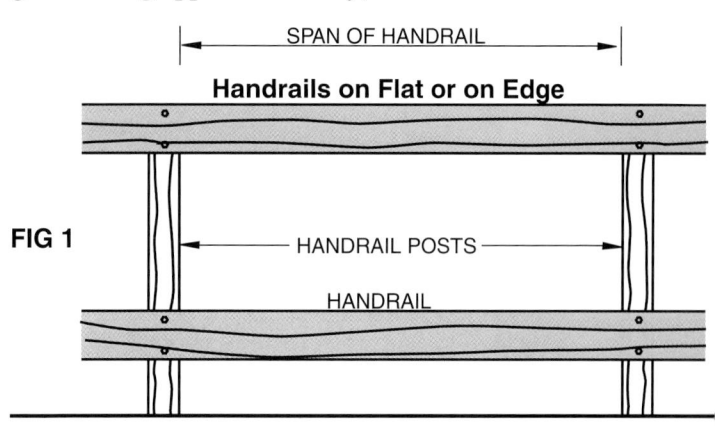

FIG 1 — Handrails on Flat or on Edge — SPAN OF HANDRAIL, HANDRAIL POSTS, HANDRAIL

Note: For safety reasons building by-laws require the spacing between handrail members not to exceed 125mm unless the handrail is to be fully enclosed.

Handrail Sizes & Spans

Establish handrail sizes and spans from Table 13.

Important: Read notes on Page 85 before selecting rail sizes.

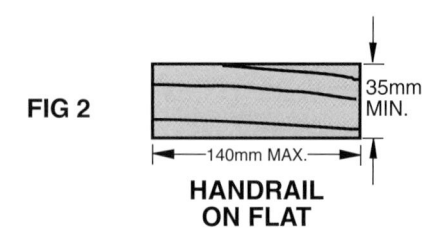

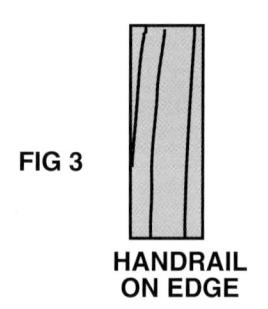

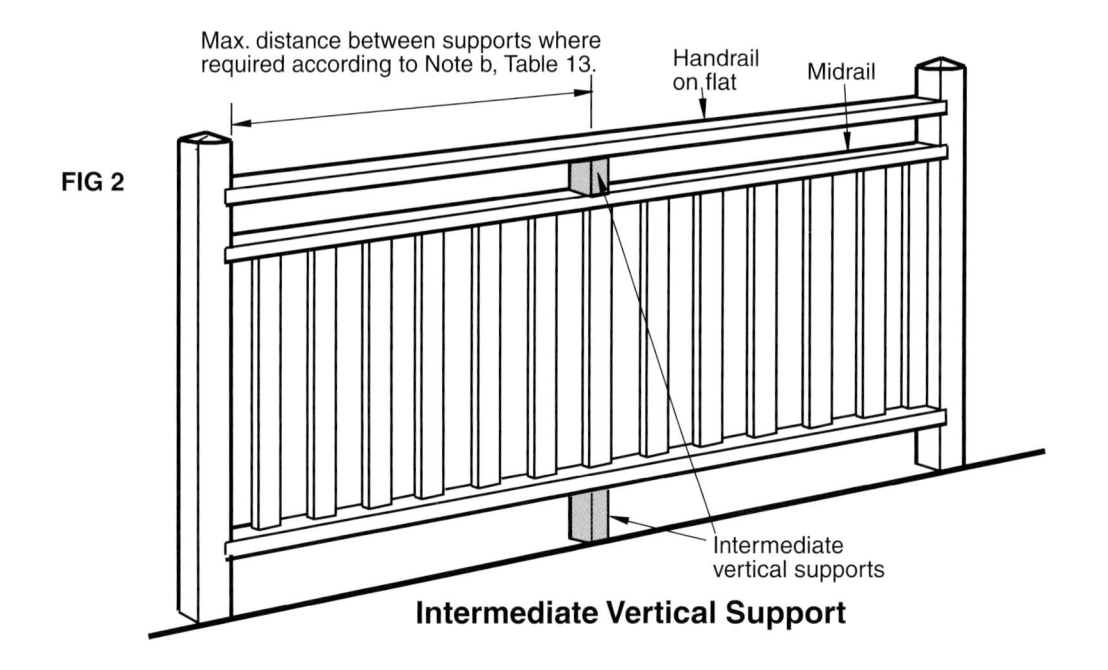

FIG 2 — HANDRAIL ON FLAT — 35mm MIN., 140mm MAX.

FIG 3 — HANDRAIL ON EDGE

FIG 2 — Intermediate Vertical Support

Max. distance between supports where required according to Note b, Table 13.

Handrail on flat — Midrail — Intermediate vertical supports

84

Cont.

TABLE 13 HANDRAILS

| Timber | Size & Description | Maximum Span of Handrail (mm) ||||
| | | Within or exclusively servicing one Dwelling (excluding external balconies) || Other areas in Residential Buildings (including external balconies) ||
		No Intermediate Vertical Supports (1)	With Intermediate Vertical Supports (2)	No Intermediate Vertical Supports (1)	With Intermediate Vertical Supports (2)
Hardwood	65 x 65 (profiled)	3000	3000	3000	3000
	42 x 65 (profiled)	2200	2700	2200	2700
	42 x 85 (profiled)	2400	3400	2400	3400
	35 x 70	2100	3000	2100	3000
	35 x 90	2200	3600	2200	3600
	35 x 120	2400	3600	2400	3600
	45 x 70	2500	3200	2500	3200
	45 x 90	2700	3600	2700	3600
	45 x 120	2900	3600	2900	3600
	70 x 70	3500	3500	3500	3500
	70 x 90	3600	3600	3600	3600
Meranti and Australian Grown Softwood	65 x 65 (profiled)	2700	2700	2200	2200
	42 x 65 (profiled)	1400	2000	1400	1800
	42 x 85 (profiled)	1800	3000	1700	2400
	35 x 70	1200	2400	1200	2000
	35 x 90	1600	3200	1600	2500
	35 x 120	2100	3600	1800	3400
	45 x 70	2000	2800	1800	2200
	45 x 90	2400	3400	2000	2900
	45 x 120	2600	3600	2400	3600
	70 x 70	3200	3200	2800	2800
	70 x 90	3400	3600	3200	3600
Softwood Imported or Unknown Origin	65 x 65 (profiled)	2400	2400	2200	2200
	42 x 65 (profiled)	1400	2000	1400	1800
	42 x 85 (profiled)	1800	2700	1700	2400
	35 x 70	1200	2400	1200	2000
	35 x 90	1600	2900	1600	2500
	35 x 120	1900	3600	1800	3400
	45 x 70	2000	2600	1800	2200
	45 x 90	2200	3100	2000	2900
	45 x 120	2300	3600	2300	3600
	70 x 70	2900	2900	2800	2800
	70 x 90	3000	3400	3000	3400

IMPORTANT NOTES:

a). Handrails with no intermediate vertical supports may be used on flat or on edge. *See figures 2 & 3, Page 84.*

b). Handrails with intermediate vertical supports should be installed on flat with intermediate vertical supports spaced not greater than the allowable spans given for the same handrail with no intermediate vertical supports. *See figures 2 and 4.*

c). Where a mid-rail (42x65mm MIN.) is within 150mm of the main handrail and is rigidly fixed to it using blocks, or balusters or dowels that pass through the mid rail and are fixed to the top rail) at least once at mid span, the allowable span of the handrail may be increased by 300mm.

d). Handrail spans have been limited to 3600mm MAX.

e). There is no negative tolerance permitted on the breadth or depth dimensions (overall outside dimensions of profiled shapes) given in the above table.

Connection Joints & Fastenings

How to Select a Handrail Connection from the Tables

Example connection:

The shaded areas in Tables 14 and 15 provide a guide to the selection of an appropriate connection for a Class 3 Building for a continous span softwood handrail with a span of 2400mm.

Step 1 From Table 14 determine the load on the handrail = 2.7kN. *See shaded area.*

Step 2 From Table 15 and Fig 1, determine a connection with the capacity to resist 2.7kN.

Step 3 Acceptable solutions determined from Table 15 are:-
Type A connection, 1/M10 bolt or;
Type B connection, 2/No 10 screws or;
Type D connection, 2/No 10 screws per leg of bracket.

TABLE 14 LOADS ON HANDRAILS

Span Type	Handrail Span (mm)	Within or exclusively servicing one dwelling (exc.external balconies)	Other areas in residential buildings (inc.external balconies)
Single Span	1800	.90	1.0
	2100	.90	1.2
	2400	.90	1.4
	2700	.90	1.5
	3000	.90	1.7
	3300	.99	1.9
	3600	1.10	2.0
Continuous Span	1800	1.1	2.0
	2100	1.3	2.4
	2400	1.4	2.7
	2700	1.6	3.0
	3000	1.8	3.4
	3300	2.0	3.7
	3600	2.2	4.1

Handrail Connection Loads (kN)

TABLE 15 CAPACITY OF HANDRAIL CONNECTIONS

Capacity of Connections (kN)

Timber	Type A No. Bolts	Bolt Size (Cuphead) M10	M12	Type B No. Screws	Screw Size (Type 17) No10	No14	Type C Screws 2/No10	2/No14	Nails 2/3.15 dia	2/3.75 dia	Type D 2/screws per leg of bracket No10	No14	Type E
Hardwood (JD2)	1	13	14	1	3.4	4.4	1.9	2.3	1.6	1.8	4.9	7.6	Refer to Manufacturers specifications
	2	26	28	2	6.8	8.8	--	--	--	--	--	--	
Softwood & Meranti (JD4)	1	8	9	1	2.0	2.6	1.1	1.3	0.9	1.0	2.8	4.3	
	2	16	18	2	4.0	5.2	--	--	--	--	--	--	

IMPORTANT NOTES:

a). For Type B connections the screw penetration into post is 38mm MIN.

b). For Type C connections the screw penetration into post is 40mm MIN and the nail penetration into post is 38mm MIN.

c). Midrails and bottom rails should be fixed with 2/3.15mm dia. skew nails MIN.

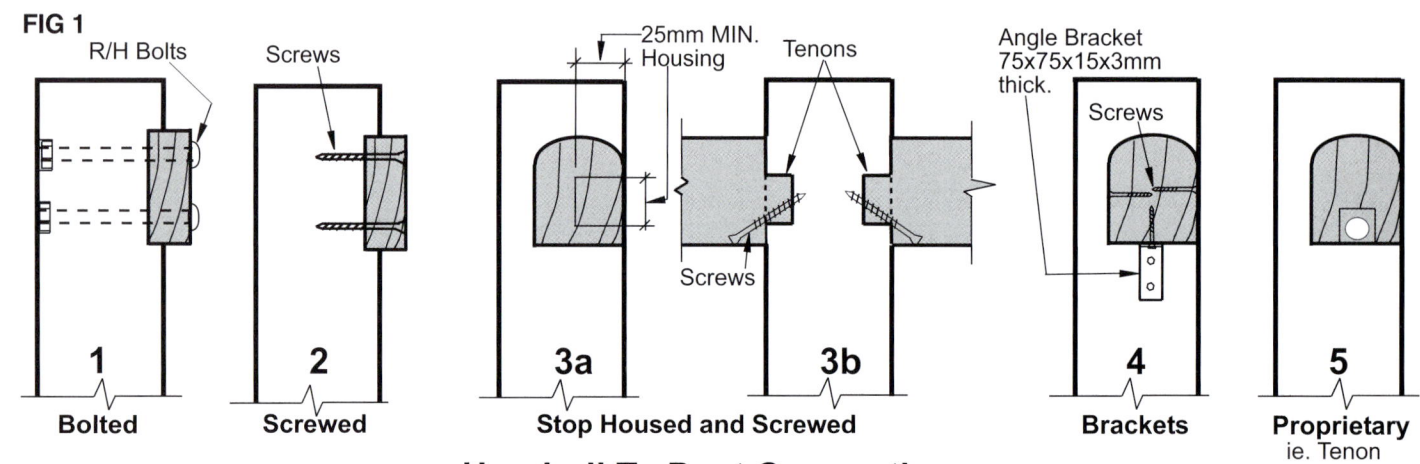

FIG 1

| 1 Bolted | 2 Screwed | 3a 3b Stop Housed and Screwed | 4 Brackets | 5 Proprietary ie. Tenon |

Handrail To Post Connections

Screw & Nail Penetration

TABLE 16 FASTENINGS FOR BALUSTERS/INFILS

Timber	Type A - Nail / Screw Penetration MIN. (mm)				Type B - Nail in Shear Penetration MIN. (mm)
	Nails		Screws		
	2 / 2.5 dia.	2 / 2.8 dia.	1 / No. 8	1 / No. 10	
Hardwood (JD2)	22	20	15	15	1 / 2.5 dia x 25 penetration
Softwood and Meranti (JD4)	53	47	15	15	2 / 2.5 dia x 25 penetration

IMPORTANT NOTES:
Where the balusters/infill are slotted into a groove or a dowel into a hole i.e. top connection in fig 1 that restrains both inward and outward forces, the above nail/screw fixing requirements are *not* applicable.

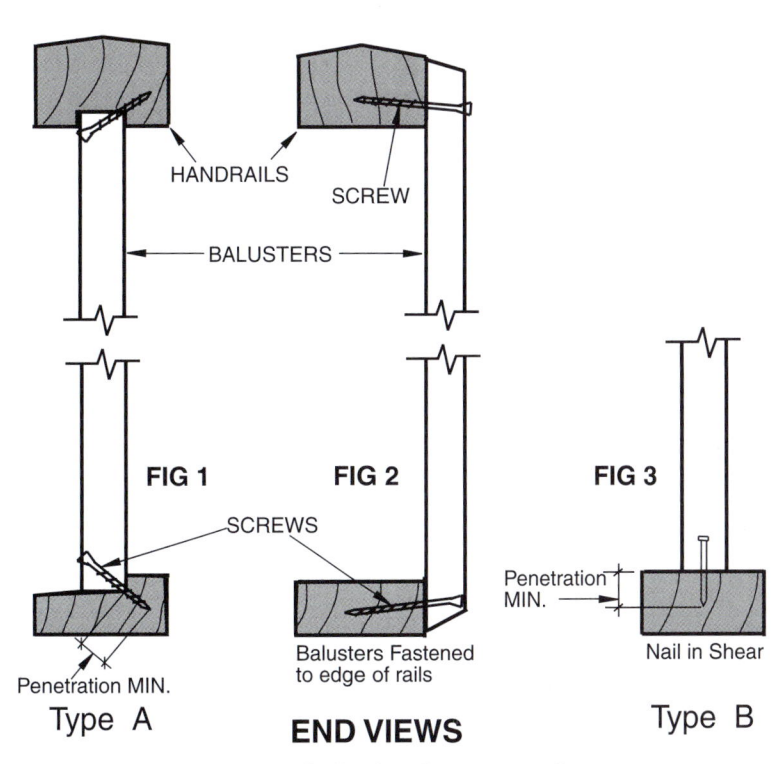

FIG 1 **FIG 2** **FIG 3**

Type A — Penetration MIN. — SCREWS — Balusters Fastened to edge of rails

Type B — Nail in Shear — Penetration MIN.

END VIEWS

Balusters & Infil Connections

Pergola Roof Beam Tables

For further information on roof beams, see Pages 66 & 68. For seasoning, see Page 8.

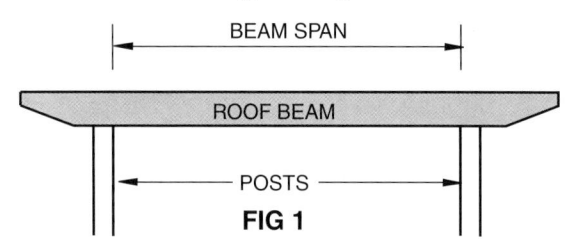

Continuous spans in tables are those which have intermediate support.

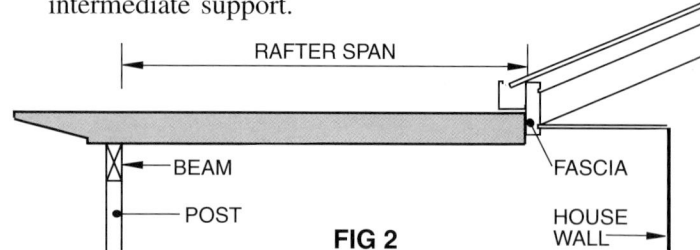

FIG 1 — BEAM SPAN, ROOF BEAM, POSTS

FIG 2 — RAFTER SPAN, BEAM, POST, FASCIA, HOUSE WALL

TABLE 17 ROOF BEAMS
For Pergolas & Carports in N1 to N2 (Non Cyclonic) Categories — Single Span (Roof Mass 10kg/m² max.) e.g. Trimdeck or Acrylic Sheet

BEAM SPAN	RAFTER SPAN		UNSEASONED F5	F7	F8	F11	F14	SEASONED F5 or MGP10	F8 or MGP12	F17
2400	2400	SINGLE	125x50 / 150x38	125x38	125x38	125x38	125x38	120x45 / 140x35	120x35	----
		CONTINUOUS	----	----	----	----	----	120x35	----	----
	3600	SINGLE	125x75 / 150x38	125x50 / 150x38	125x50 / 150x38	125x38	125x38	120x45 / 2/120x35 / 140x35	120x35	120x35
		CONTINUOUS	125x38 / 125x50	125x38	----	----	----	120x45 / 140x35	120x35	----
	4800	SINGLE	125x75 / 150x50 / 175x38	125x75 / 130x38	125x75 / 150x38	125x50 / 150x38	125x38	2/120x35 / 140x45	120x45 / 140x35	120x35
		CONTINUOUS	125x75 / 150x38	125x50 / 150x38	125x38	----	----	140x45	120x35	----
	6000	SINGLE	150x50 / 175x38	125x75 / 150x50 / 175x38	125x75 / 150x38	125x75 / 150x38	125x50 / 150x38	2/120x35 / 190x35	2/120x35 / 140x35	120x35
		CONTINUOUS	125x75 / 150x50 / 175x38	125x75 / 150x38	125x50 / 150x38	125x38	----	2/120x35 / 190x35	120x45 / 140x35	----
3000	2400	SINGLE	150x50 / 175x38	125x75 / 150x38	125x75 / 150x38	125x50 / 150x38	125x50 / 150x38	2/120x35 / 140x45	2/120x35 / 140x35	120x35
		CONTINUOUS	125x38 / 125x50	125x38	----	----	----	120x45 / 140x35	120x35	----
	3600	SINGLE	150x75 / 175x38	150x50 / 175x38	150x50 / 175x38	125x75 / 150x38	125x75 / 150x38	2/120x45 / 2/140x35	2/120x35 / 140x35	120x45
		CONTINUOUS	125x75 / 150x50 / 175x38	125x50 / 150x38	125x38	125x38	125x38	2/120x35 / 140x45	120x45 / 140x35	----
	4800	SINGLE	175x50 / 200x38	150x75 / 175x50 / 200x38	150x75 / 175x38	150x50 / 175x38	150x50 / 175x38	2/120x45 / 2/140x35 / 190x35	2/120x35 / 140x45	120x45 / 140x35
		CONTINUOUS	150x75 / 175x38	125x75 / 150x50 / 175x38	125x50 / 150x38	125x38	125x38	2/120x35 / 190x35	140x45	120x35
	6000	SINGLE	175x75 / 200x50 / 225x38	175x50 / 200x38	150x75 / 175x50 / 200x38	150x75 / 175x38	150x75 / 175x38	2/140x35 / 190x45	2/120x45 / 2/140x35 / 190x35	120x45 / 2/120x35 / 140x35
		CONTINUOUS	150x75 / 175x50 / 200x38	150x75 / 175x50 / 200x38	125x75 / 150x50 / 175x38	125x50 / 150x38	125x38	2/120x45 / 2/140x35 / 190x45	2/120x35 / 190x35	120x35
3600	2400	SINGLE	175x50 / 200x38	150x75 / 175x50 / 200x38	150x75 / 175x38	150x75 / 175x38	150x50 / 175x38	----	2/120x45	140x35
		CONTINUOUS	125x75 / 150x38	125x50 / 150x38	125x38	125x38	125x38	140x45	120x45 / 140x35	----
	3600	SINGLE	175x75 / 200x50 / 225x38	175x75 / 200x38	175x50 / 200x38	150x75 / 175x50 / 200x38	150x75 / 175x38	2/140x45 / 190x35	2/120x45 / 2/140x35	2/120x35 / 140x35
		CONTINUOUS	150x75 / 175x50 / 200x38	125x75 / 150x50 / 175x38	125x50 / 150x38	125x50 / 150x38	125x50	2/120x45 / 2/140x35 / 190x35	140x45	120x35
	4800	SINGLE	175x75 / 225x38	175x75 / 200x50 / 225x38	175x75 / 200x50 / 225x38	175x75 / 200x38	175x50 / 200x38	----	2/140x35 / 190x35	2/120x35 / 140x45 / 170x35
		CONTINUOUS	200x50 / 225x38	150x75 / 175x50 / 200x38	125x75 / 150x50 / 175x38	125x75 / 150x38	125x75 / 150x38	2/140x45	2/120x35 / 190x35	120x45 / 140x35
	6000	SINGLE	175x75 / 225x50	200x75 / 225x50	200x50 / 225x38	175x75 / 200x38 / 225x50	175x75 / 200x38	2/190x35 / 240x45	2/140x45 / 190x45	2/120x45 / 2/140x35 / 170x35
		CONTINUOUS	175x75 / 225x50	200x50 / 225x38	150x75 / 175x50 / 200x38	125x75 / 150x50 / 175x38	125x75 / 150x38	240x45	2/120x45 / 2/140x35 / 190x45	140x35

Pergola Roof Beams Cont.

TABLE 17 ROOF BEAMS — For Pergolas & Carports in N1 to N2 (Non Cyclonic) Categories — Single Span (Roof Mass 10kg/m² max.) e.g. Trimdeck or Acrylic Sheet

*BEAM SPAN	*RAFTER SPAN		UNSEASONED					SEASONED		
			F5	F7	F8	F11	F14	F5 or MGP10	F8 or MGP12	F17
4200	2400	SINGLE	200x75 / 225x38	200x50 / 225x38	175x75 / 200x38 / 225x50	175x75 / 200x38	175x50 / 200x38	2/140x45 / 190x35	2/140x35 / 190x35	2/120x35 / 140x45 / 170x35
		CONTINUOUS	150x50 / 175x38	150x50 / 175x38	125x75 / 150x38	125x75 / 150x38	125x50 / 150x38	2/120x35 / 190x35	140x45	120x35
	3600	SINGLE	225x75 / 250x50	200x75 / 225x50	200x75 / 225x38	200x50 / 225x38	175x75 / 200x50 / 225x38	2/190x35	190x35	2/140x35 / 170x35
		CONTINUOUS	175x75 / 200x50 / 225x38	150x75 / 175x50 / 200x38	150x50 / 175x38	150x50 / 175x38	125x75 / 150x38	2/140x45	2/120x35 / 190x35	120x45 / 140x35
	4800	SINGLE	225x75 / 250x50	225x75 / 250x50	200x75 / 225x50	200x75 / 225x50	200x75 / 225x38	2/190x35 / 240x45	190x45 / 2/190x35	2/140x45 / 170x45 / 2/170x45
		CONTINUOUS	175x75 / 225x50	175x75 / 225x38	150x75 / 175x50 / 200x38	150x75 / 175x38	150x50 / 175x38	240x45	2/120x45 / 2/140x35 / 190x45	2/120x35 / 140x45
	6000	SINGLE	250x75 / 275x50	225x75 / 250x50	225x75 / 250x50	225x75 / 250x50	200x75 / 225x50	2/190x45	2/190x35	2/140x45 / 2/170x35 / 190x35
		CONTINUOUS	200x75 / 250x50	175x75 / 225x50	175x75 / 200x50 / 225x38	150x75 / 175x50 / 200x38	150x75 / 175x38	2/190x45	2/140x45	2/120x35 / 170x35
4800	2400	SINGLE	250x50 / 275x50	225x75 / 250x50	225x75 / 250x50	225x50 / 250x75	200x75 / 225x38 / 250x50	2/190x35 / 240x45	190x45 / 2/190x35	2/140x45 / 170x45 / 2/170x35
		CONTINUOUS	175x75 / 200x38	175x50 / 200x38	150x75 / 175x50 / 200x38	150x75 / 175x38	150x75 / 175x38	2/140x35 / 190x45	2/120x35 / 190x35	120x45 / 2/120x35 / 140x35
	3600	SINGLE	250x75 / 275x50	250x75 / 275x50	225x75 / 250x50	225x75 / 250x50	225x75 / 250x50	2/190x45 / 240x45	2/190x35 / 240x45	2/170x35 / 190x45
		CONTINUOUS	200x75 / 225x50	175x75 / 200x50 / 225x38	175x75 / 200x38	175x75 / 200x38	175x50 / 200x38	2/190x35 / 240x45	2/140x35 / 190x45	2/120x35 / 140x45 / 170x35
	4800	SINGLE	275x75 / 300x50	275x75 / 300x50	250x75 / 275x50	250x75 / 275x50	225x75 / 250x50	2/240x35	2/190x45 / 240x45	2/170x45 / 2/190x35 / 240x45
		CONTINUOUS	200x75 / 250x50	200x75 / 225x50	175x75 / 200x50 / 225x38	175x75 / 200x50 / 225x38	175x75 / 200x38	2/190x35	2/140x45 / 2/190x35 / 240x45	2/120x45 / 2/140x35 / 170x35
	6000	SINGLE	300x75	275x75 / 300x50	275x75 / 300x50	250x75 / 275x50	250x75 / 275x50	2/240x35	240x45 / 2/240x35	2/170x45 / 240x45
		CONTINUOUS	225x75 / 275x50	200x75 / 250x50	200x75 / 225x50	200x75 / 225x38	175x75 / 200x50 / 225x38	2/190x45 / 2/240x35	2/190x35 / 240x45	2/140x35 / 170x45

TABLE 18 ROOF BEAMS — For Pergolas & Carports in N3 (Non Cyclonic) to C1 (Cyclonic) Categories — Single Span (Roof Mass 10kg/m² max.) e.g. Trimdeck or Acrylic Sheet

*BEAM SPAN	*RAFTER SPAN		UNSEASONED					SEASONED		
			F5	F7	F8	F11	F14	F5 or MGP12	F8 or MGP12	F17
2400	2400	SINGLE	125x50 / 150x38	125x38	125x38	125x38	125x38	140x35	120x35	----
		CONTINUOUS	125x50 / 150x38	125x38	125x38	----	----	120x45 / 140x35	120x35	----
	3600	SINGLE	125x75 / 150x50 / 175x38	125x75 / 150x38	125x50 / 150x38	125x38	125x38	2/120x35 / 190x35	140x35	120x35
		CONTINUOUS	125x75 / 150x50 / 175x38	125x50 / 150x38	125x50 / 150x38	125x38	----	2/120x35 / 190x35	120x45 / 140x35	----
	4800	SINGLE	150x75 / 175x50 / 200x38	125x75 / 150x50 / 175x38	125x75 / 150x50 / 175x38	125x50 / 150x38	125x38	2/120x45 / 2/140x35 / 190x45	2/120x35 / 140x45	120x35
		CONTINUOUS	150x75 / 175x50 / 200x38	125x75 / 150x50 / 175x38	125x75 / 150x50 / 150x38	125x38	125x38	2/120x45 / 2/140x35 / 190x35	2/120x35 / 140x45	120x35
	6000	SINGLE	175x75 / 200x50 / 225x38	150x75 / 175x50 / 200x38	125x75 / 150x50 / 175x38	125x75 / 150x38	125x50 / 150x38	2/140x45	2/120x35 / 190x35	120x45 / 140x35
		CONTINUOUS	150x75 / 200x50 / 225x38	150x75 / 175x50 / 200x38	125x75 / 150x50 / 175x38	125x50 / 150x38	125x40 / 150x38	2/140x35 / 190x45	2/120x35 / 190x35	120x35

*see figs 5 & 6 Page 88.

TABLE 19 ROOF BEAMS

For Pergolas & Carports in N3 (Non Cyclonic) to C1 (Cyclonic) Categories — Single Span (Roof Mass 10kg/m² max.) e.g. Trimdeck or Acrylic Sheet

*BEAM SPAN	*RAFTER SPAN		UNSEASONED F5	F7	F8	F11	F14	SEASONED F5 or MGP10	F8 or MGP12	F17
3000	2400	SINGLE	150x50 / 175x38	125x75 / 150x38	125x75 / 150x38	125x50 / 150x38	125x50 / 150x38	2/120x35 / 190x35	2/120x35 / 140x35	120x35 / ----
		CONTINUOUS	125x75 / 150x50 / 175x38	125x50 / 150x38 / ----	125x50 / 150x38 / ----	125x38 / ----	125x38 / ----	2/120x35 / 190x35	120x45 / 140x35	----
	3600	SINGLE	150x75 / 175x50 / 200x38	150x75 / 175x50 / 200x38	150x50 / 175x38 / ----	125x75 / 150x38 / ----	125x75 / 150x38 / ----	2/120x45 / 2/140x35 / 190x45	2/120x35 / 190x35 / ----	120x45 / ----
		CONTINUOUS	150x75 / 175x50 / 200x38	125x75 / 175x38 / ----	125x75 / 150x50 / 175x38	125x50 / 150x38 / ----	125x38 / ----	2/120x45 / 2/140x35 / 190x45	2/120x35 / 190x35 / ----	120x35 / ----
	4800	SINGLE	175x75 / 200x50 / ----	150x75 / 200x50 / 225x38	150x75 / 175x50 / 200x38	150x50 / 175x38 / ----	150x50 / 175x38 / ----	2/140x45 / 240x45 / ----	2/120x45 / 2/140x35 / 190x35	120x45 / 140x35 / ----
		CONTINUOUS	175x75 / 200x50 / 225x38	150x75 / 175x50 / 200x38	150x75 / 175x50 / 200x38	125x75 / 150x38 / ----	125x50 / 150x38 / ----	2/140x45 / 240x45 / ----	2/120x45 / 2/140x35 / 190x35	120x45 / 140x35 / ----
	6000	SINGLE	200x75 / 225x50 / ----	175x75 / 200x50 / ----	150x75 / 200x50 / 225x38	150x75 / 175x38 / ----	150x75 / 175x38 / ----	2/190x35 / 240x45 / ----	2/140x45 / 190x45 / ----	2/120x35 / 140x45 / 170x35
		CONTINUOUS	200x75 / 225x50 / ----	175x75 / 200x50 / 225x38	150x75 / 175x50 / 200x38	125x75 / 150x50 / 175x38	125x75 / 150x50 / 175x38	2/190x35 / 240x45 / ----	2/120x45 / 2/140x35 / 190x45	140x45 / 170x35 / ----
3600	2400	SINGLE	175x50 / 200x38 / ----	150x75 / 175x50 / 200x38	150x75 / 175x38 / ----	150x75 / 175x38 / ----	150x50 / 175x38 / ----	190x45 / ----	2/120x45 / ----	140x35 / ----
		CONTINUOUS	150x75 / 175x50 / 200x38	125x75 / 150x50 / 175x38	125x75 / 150x50 / ----	125x50 / ----	125x38 / ----	2/120x45 / 2/140x35 / 190x45	140x45 / ----	120x35 / ----
	3600	SINGLE	175x75 / 225x50 / ----	175x75 / 200x50 / 225x38	175x50 / 200x38 / ----	150x75 / 175x50 / 200x38	150x75 / 175x38 / ----	2/140x45 / 240x45 / ----	2/120x45 / 2/140x35 / 190x45	2/120x35 / 140x35 / ----
		CONTINUOUS	175x75 / 225x50 / ----	150x75 / 200x50 / 225x38	150x75 / 175x50 / 200x38	125x75 / 150x50 / 175x38	150x38 / ----	2/140x45 / 240x45 / ----	2/120x45 / 2/140x35 / 190x45	120x45 / 140x35 / ----
	4800	SINGLE	200x75 / 250x50 / ----	175x75 / 225x50 / ----	175x75 / 200x50 / 225x38	175x75 / 200x38 / ----	175x50 / 200x38 / ----	2/190x35 / ----	2/140x45 / ----	2/120x35 / 140x45 / 170x35
		CONTINUOUS	200x75 / 250x50 / ----	175x75 / 225x50 / ----	175x75 / 200x50 / 225x38	175x50 / 200x38 / ----	125x75 / 150x50 / 175x38	2/190x35 / ----	2/140x45 / ----	140x45 / 170x35 / ----
	6000	SINGLE	225x75 / 275x50 / ----	200x75 / 250x50 / ----	200x75 / 225x50 / ----	175x75 / 200x50 / 225x38	175x75 / 200x38 / ----	2/190x45 / ----	2/190x35 / 240x45 / ----	2/120x45 / 2/140x35 / 170x45
		CONTINUOUS	225x75 / 275x50 / ----	200x75 / 250x50 / ----	175x75 / 225x50 / ----	150x75 / 175x50 / 200x38	150x75 / 175x50 / 200x38	2/190x45 / ----	240x45 / ----	2/120x35 / 170x45 / 190x35
4200	2400	SINGLE	200x75 / 225x38 / ----	200x50 / 225x38 / ----	175x75 / 200x38 / 225x50	175x75 / 200x38 / ----	175x50 / 200x38 / ----	2/140x45 / ----	2/140x35 / 190x35 / ----	2/120x35 / 140x45 / 170x35
		CONTINUOUS	175x75 / 200x50 / 225x38	150x75 / 175x50 / 200x38	175x38 / ----	125x75 / 150x38 / ----	125x50 / 150x38 / ----	2/140x45 / ----	2/120x35 / 190x35 / ----	120x45 / 140x35 / ----
	3600	SINGLE	225x75 / 250x50 / ----	200x75 / 225x50 / ----	200x75 / 225x38 / ----	200x50 / 225x38 / ----	175x75 / 200x50 / 225x38	2/190x35 / ----	----	2/140x35 / 170x35 / ----
		CONTINUOUS	200x75 / 250x50 / ----	175x75 / 225x50 / ----	175x75 / 200x50 / 225x38	150x75 / 175x50 / 200x38	125x75 / 150x50 / 175x38	2/190x35 / ----	2/140x45 / ----	140x45 / 170x35 / ----
	4800	SINGLE	225x75 / 275x50 / ----	225x75 / 250x50 / ----	200x75 / 225x50 / ----	200x75 / 225x50 / ----	200x75 / 225x38 / ----	2/190x45 / 2/240x35 / ----	2/190x35 / 240x45 / ----	2/140x45 / 170x45 / 2/170x35
		CONTINUOUS	225x75 / 275x50 / ----	200x75 / 250x50 / ----	200x75 / 225x50 / ----	150x75 / 200x50 / 225x38	150x75 / 175x50 / 200x38	2/190x45 / 2/240x35 / ----	2/190x35 / 240x45 / ----	2/120x35 / 170x45 / 190x35
	6000	SINGLE	250x75 / ----	225x75 / 275x50 / ----	225x75 / 250x50 / ----	225x75 / 250x50 / ----	200x75 / 225x50 / ----	2/240x35 / ----	2/190x45 / ----	2/140x45 / 2/170x35 / 190x45
		CONTINUOUS	250x75 / 300x50 / ----	225x75 / 275x50 / ----	200x75 / 250x50 / ----	175x75 / 200x50 / ----	175x75 / 200x50 / 225x38	2/240x35 / ----	2/190x35 / ----	2/120x45 / 2/140x35 / 190x45
4800	2400	SINGLE	250x50 / 275x75 / ----	225x75 / 250x50 / ----	225x75 / 250x50 / ----	225x50 / 250x75 / ----	200x75 / 225x38 / 250x50	2/190x35 / 240x45 / ----	190x45 / 2/190x35 / ----	2/140x45 / 170x45 / 2/170x35
		CONTINUOUS	200x75 / 225x50 / ----	175x75 / 200x50 / 225x38	150x75 / 175x50 / 200x38	150x75 / 175x38 / ----	150x75 / 175x38 / ----	2/190x35 / 240x45 / ----	2/120x45 / 2/140x35 / 190x45	2/120x35 / 140x45 / ----
	3600	SINGLE	250x75 / 275x50 / ----	250x75 / 275x50 / ----	225x75 / 250x50 / ----	225x75 / 250x50 / ----	225x75 / 250x50 / ----	2/190x45 / 2/240x35 / ----	2/190x45 / 240x45 / ----	2/170x35 / 190x45 / ----
		CONTINUOUS	225x75 / 275x50 / ----	200x75 / 250x50 / ----	200x75 / 225x50 / ----	175x75 / 200x50 / 225x38	175x50 / 200x38 / ----	2/190x45 / 2/240x35 / ----	2/190x35 / 240x45 / ----	2/120x35 / 170x45 / 190x35
	4800	SINGLE	275x75 / ----	275x75 / 300x50 / ----	250x75 / 275x50 / ----	250x75 / 275x50 / ----	225x75 / 250x50 / ----	2/240x45 / 2/290x35 / ----	2/190x45 / 2/240x35 / ----	2/170x45 / 2/190x35 / 240x45
		CONTINUOUS	275x75 / ----	250x75 / 275x50 / ----	225x75 / 250x50 / ----	175x75 / 225x50 / ----	175x75 / 200x50 / 225x38	2/240x45 / 2/290x35 / ----	2/190x45 / 2/240x45 / ----	2/140x45 / 2/170x35 / 190x45
	6000	SINGLE	300x75 / ----	275x75 / ----	275x75 / 300x50 / ----	250x75 / 275x50 / ----	250x75 / 275x50 / ----	2/290x35 / ----	2/240x35 / ----	2/170x45 / 2/190x35 / 240x45
		CONTINUOUS	300x75 / ----	275x75 / ----	250x75 / 275x50 / ----	200x75 / 250x50 / ----	200x75 / 225x50 / ----	2/240x45 / 2/290x35 / ----	2/240x35 / ----	2/140x45 / 2/170x35 / ----

* see figs 5 & 6 Page 88.

Pergola Rafters

Important Note: **The tables below are for Single Span (Roof Mass 10kg/m² max e.g. Trimdeck or Acrylic Sheet).**

For information on Seasoning, (see Page 8).

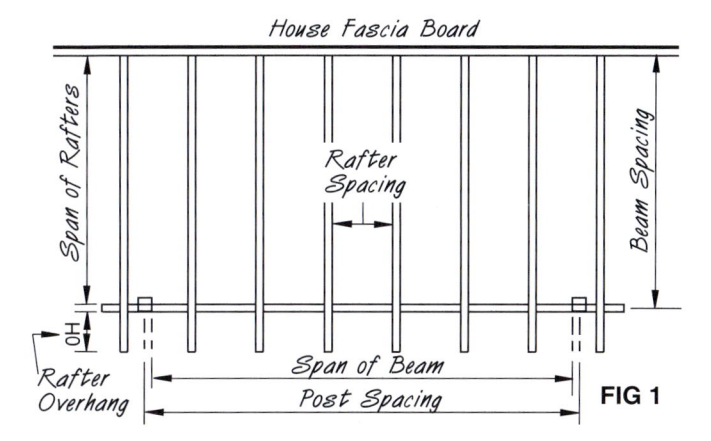

FIG 1

TABLE 20 RAFTERS (Single Span)
For Pergolas & Carports in N1 to N2 (Non Cyclonic) Categories

SPAN	SPACING	UNSEASONED F5	F7	F8	F11	F14	SEASONED F5 or MGP10	F8 or MGP12	F17
1200	600	75x50	75x38	75x38	75x38	75x38	70x45	70x35	70x35
1200	900	75x50	75x38	75x38	75x38	75x38	90x35	70x35	70x35
1200	1200	75x50	75x38	75x38	75x38	75x38	90x35	70x35	70x35
1800	600	100x38	100x38	100x38	75x50	75x50	90x35	90x35	70x45
1800	900	100x38	100x38	100x38	100x38	75x50	90x45	90x35	70x45
1800	1200	100x50	100x38	100x38	100x38	75x50	120x35	90x35	70x45
2100	600	100x50	100x38	100x38	100x38	100x38	120x35	90x35	90x35
2100	900	100x50	100x50	100x38	100x38	100x38	120x35	90x45	90x35
2100	1200	100x50	100x50	100x50	100x38	100x38	120x35	90x45	90x35
2400	600	125x38	100x50	100x50	100x38	100x38	120x35	90x45	90x35
2400	900	125x38	125x38	100x50	100x38	100x38	120x35	120x35	90x35
2400	1200	125x38	125x38	100x50	100x50	100x38	120x35	120x35	90x45
2700	600	125x38	125x38	100x50	100x50	100x38	120x35	120x35	90x45
2700	900	125x38	125x38	125x38	100x50	100x50	120x35	120x35	90x45
2700	1200	125x50	125x38	125x38	125x38	100x50	120x45	120x35	90x45
3000	600	125x38	125x38	125x38	100x50	100x50	120x35	120x35	90x45
3000	900	125x50	125x38	125x38	125x38	100x50	120x45	120x35	120x35
3000	1200	150x38	125x50	125x38	125x38	125x38	120x45	120x35	120x35
3300	600	125x50	125x50	125x50	125x38	100x50	120x45	120x35	120x35
3300	900	150x38	125x50	125x50	125x38	125x38	140x35	120x45	120x35
3300	1200	150x50	150x38	150x38	125x50	125x50	140x35	120x45	120x35
3600	600	150x38	125x50	125x50	125x38	125x38	140x35	120x45	120x35
3600	900	150x50	150x38	150x38	150x38	125x50	140x35	120x45	120x35
3600	1200	175x38	150x50	150x50	150x38	150x38	140x45	140x35	120x35
3900	600	150x50	150x38	150x38	150x38	125x50	140x35	120x45	120x35
3900	900	175x38	150x50	150x50	150x38	150x38	140x45	140x35	120x35
3900	1200	175x50	175x38	175x38	150x50	150x50	170x35	140x45	120x45
4200	600	175x38	150x50	150x50	150x38	150x38	140x45	140x35	120x35
4200	900	175x50	175x38	175x38	175x38	150x50	170x35	140x35	120x45
4200	1200	200x38	175x50	175x50	175x38	175x38	170x35	140x45	120x45
4500	600	175x50	175x38	175x38	175x38	150x50	140x45	140x35	120x35
4500	900	200x38	200x38	175x50	175x38	175x38	170x35	140x45	120x45
4500	1200	200x50	200x50	200x38	175x50	175x50	170x45	170x35	140x35

Pergola Rafters Cont.

Important Note: The tables below are for Single Span (Roof Mass 10kg/m² max e.g. Trimdeck or Acrylic Sheet).

TABLE 21 RAFTERS (Single Span)
For Pergolas & Carports in N3 Non Cyclonic & C1 Cyclonic Categories

SPAN	SPACING	UNSEASONED F5	F7	F8	F11	F14	SEASONED F5	F8	F17
1200	600	75x50	75x38	75x38	75x38	75x38	70x45	70x35	70x35
1200	900	75x50	75x38	75x38	75x38	75x38	90x35	70x35	70x35
1200	1200	75x50	75x38	75x38	75x38	75x38	90x35	70x35	70x35
1800	600	100x38	100x38	100x38	75x50	75x50	90x35	90x35	70x45
1800	900	100x38	100x38	100x38	100x38	75x50	90x45	90x35	70x45
1800	1200	100x50	100x38	100x38	100x38	75x50	120x35	90x35	70x45
2100	600	100x50	100x38	100x38	100x38	100x38	120x35	90x35	90x35
2100	900	100x50	100x50	100x38	100x38	100x38	120x35	90x45	90x35
2100	1200	125x38	100x50	100x50	100x38	100x38	120x35	90x35	90x35
2400	600	125x38	100x50	100x50	100x38	100x38	120x35	90x45	90x35
2400	900	125x38	125x38	100x50	100x38	100x38	120x35	120x35	90x35
2400	1200	125x38	125x38	100x50	100x50	100x38	120x45	120x35	90x45
2700	600	125x38	125x38	100x50	100x50	100x38	120x35	120x35	90x45
2700	900	125x50	125x38	125x38	100x50	100x50	120x35	120x35	90x45
2700	1200	125x50	125x38	125x38	125x38	100x50	140x35	120x35	90x45
3000	600	125x38	125x38	125x38	100x50	100x50	120x35	120x35	90x45
3000	900	125x50	125x38	125x38	125x38	100x50	120x45	120x35	120x35
3000	1200	150x38	125x50	125x38	125x38	125x38	140x45	120x45	120x35
3300	600	125x50	125x50	125x38	125x38	100x50	120x45	120x35	120x35
3300	900	150x38	125x50	125x38	125x38	125x38	140x45	120x35	120x35
3300	1200	150x50	150x38	150x38	125x50	125x50	170x35	120x45	120x35
3600	600	150x38	125x50	125x50	125x38	125x38	140x35	120x45	120x35
3600	900	150x50	150x38	150x38	150x38	125x50	140x45	120x45	120x35
3600	1200	175x38	150x50	150x50	150x38	150x38	170x45	140x45	120x35
3900	600	150x50	150x38	150x38	150x38	125x50	140x35	120x45	120x35
3900	900	175x38	150x50	150x50	150x38	150x38	170x35	140x35	120x35
3900	1200	175x50	175x38	175x38	150x50	150x50	170x45	140x45	120x45
4200	600	175x38	150x50	150x50	150x38	150x38	140x45	140x35	120x35
4200	900	175x50	175x38	175x38	175x38	150x50	170x45	140x45	120x45
4200	1200	200x38	175x50	175x50	175x38	175x38	190x45	170x35	120x45
4500	600	175x50	175x38	175x38	175x38	150x50	140x45	140x45	120x45
4500	900	200x38	200x38	175x50	175x38	175x38	170x45	140x45	120x45
4500	1200	200x50	200x50	200x38	175x50	175x50	240x35	170x45	140x35

TABLES 22 PERGOLA ROOF BATTENS
To Receive Metal Cladding for N1 (Non Cycl.) to C1 (Cycl.) Categories

UNSEASONED F5
Batten Size DxB (mm)	Batten Spacing (mm) 600	900	1200
	Batten Span (mm)		
38x75	700	NS	NS
50x75	900	900	900

UNSEASONED F7
Batten Size DxB (mm)	600	900	1200
38x75	850	650	650
50x75	900	900	900

UNSEASONED F8
Batten Size DxB (mm)	600	900	1200
38x50	750	NS	NS
38x75	900	850	850
50x75	900	900	900

UNSEASONED F11
Batten Size DxB (mm)	Batten Spacing (mm) 600	900	1200
	Batten Span (mm)		
38x50	900	850	850
38x75	900	900	900
50x75	900	900	900

UNSEASONED F14
Batten Size DxB (mm)	600	900	1200
38x50	900	900	900
38x75	900	900	900
50x75	900	900	900

SEASONED F5
Batten Size DxB (mm)	Batten Spacing (mm) 600	900	1200
	Batten Span (mm)		
35x70	650	NS	NS
35x90	850	700	700
45x42	650	NS	NS
45x70	900	900	850
45x90	900	900	900

SEASONED F8
Batten Size DxB (mm)	Batten Spacing (mm) 600	900	1200
	Batten Span (mm)		
35x42	650	NS	NS
35x70	900	850	800
35x90	900	900	900
45x42	900	800	800
45x70	900	900	900
45x90	900	900	900

D = Depth
B = Breadth
NS = Not Suitable

Notes:
a). End Bearing Lengths=35mm
  Internal bearing lengths=35mm
b). During construction, roof battens should only be walked on at support points. Overhangs should NOT exceed 50% of actual span.
c). See the 'A.S. National Timber Framing Manual' to obtain the correct batten fastening requirements.

Pryda Post Anchor (Supports)

Note: These anchors are referred to throughout the manual as post supports and stirrups.

These post anchors are engineered to A.S. (Code).
The joints either dry welded (swaged), a superior anchor or some models are welded (standard range) see below examples. Also most of the anchors illustrated are designed to enable moisture to escape with the post supported directly on the base plate. Two raised ridges make this possible.

IMPORTANT:
To establish design capacities for these anchors to resist wind uplift loads, refer to Pryda Post Anchors Guide for the 'Engineered' or 'Standard' range available from their website - www.pryda.com.au.

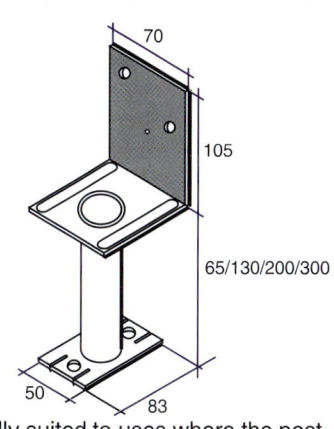

Installation Instructions

1. Use 10mm (³⁄₈") diameter galvanised bolts except for the high wind type (PSQ) which requires 12mm (½") diameter bolts. Where the bolt head or nut bears directly on the timber (half stirrup and centre fix types, a 45mm dia. by 2.5mm thick washer is required.

2. Use galvanised coach screws — 50x10mm into side grain and 75x10mm into end grain.

3. Anchors and bolts embedded into wet concrete must extend at least 75mm into the concrete to develop the uplift loads tabulated in this guide.

4. The distance from the top surface of the concrete to the underside of the post anchor saddle should *not* exceed 300mm.

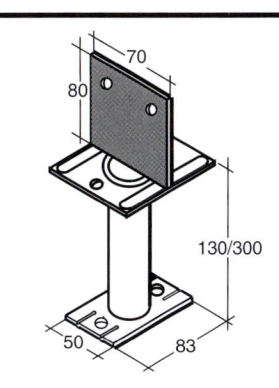

Ideally suited to uses where the post is located against a wall or step and can only be bolted from one side. Can be bolted to existing concrete or decking or embedded into concrete.
Swaged or welded available.

HALF STIRRUP POST ANCHOR (PAH or PSH)

Generally used to 'hide' the post anchor. The post is slotted at the bottom and bolted through the post and anchor, leaving only the bolt heads, nuts and washers visible. Can be bolted to existing concrete or decking or embedded into concrete.
Swaged or welded available.

CENTRE FIX POST ANCHOR (PAC or PSCF)

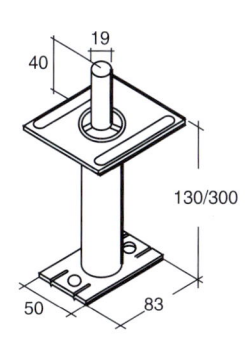

For use where the post anchor is NOT to be visible. However, due to the fixing method, it is only suitable for small spans or where no roofing is to be used. Can be bolted or embedded into concrete.

CENTRE PIN POST ANCHOR (PAP or PSCP)

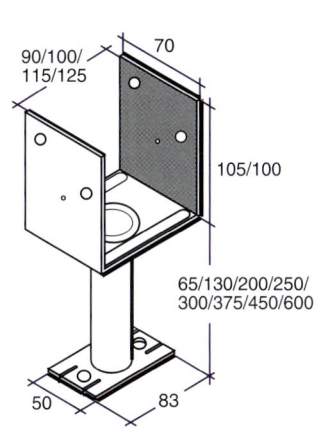

Primarily used for bolting to existing concrete. Can also be used for embedding in concrete.
Swaged or welded available.

FULL STIRRUP POST ANCHOR (PAF or PSF)

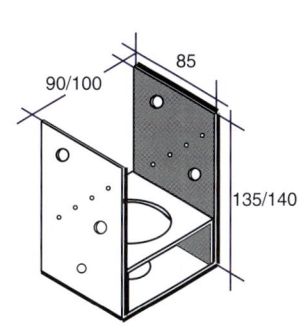

With knockout 3mm adjustable washer to facilitate adjustment after bolt holes have been drilled. Used for locating posts onto existing concrete or decking.

BOLT DOWN POST ANCHOR (PSB)

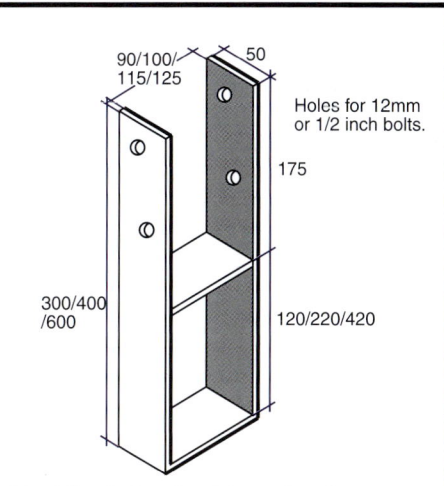

Hot Dip, Galvanised 6mm Steel. Engineered for high wind application areas including tropical regions. The 'U' shaped base is designed for maximum hold down in concrete.

HIGH WIND POST ANCHORS (PSQ)

Pryda Framing Brackets (Joist Hangers)

Note: These brackets have been referred to as 'Joist Hangers' throughout the manual.

Important:

a). The bracket thickness should be matched to the timber thickness being used.

b). These brackets should receive the type and number of nails or bolts recommended.

FIG 1 — Supporting Beam 'A', Framing Bracket or Joist Hanger, Timber Thickness, Supported Beam 'B', Depth of bracket, 36, 45, 32, 32, 32, 75 Bearing.

Note: Never use clout nails for framing brackets. Framing bracket nails are manufactured so their heads won't easily break off.

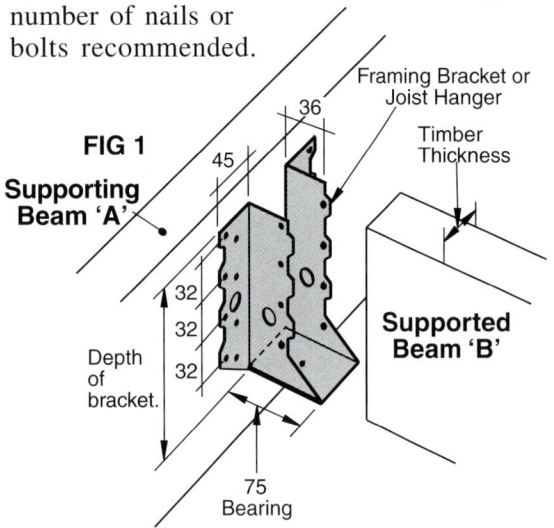

How to Select the Correct Hanger

Determine the following:

1. The **joint group** of the timber to be jointed from Table 24.

TABLE 24 TIMBER & JOINT GROUP

TIMBERS	JOINT GROUP Dry	JOINT GROUP Green
North American Oregon	JD4	J4
Radiata pine and other softwood (heart-ex.)	JD4	J4
Pine as above (heart-in)	JD5	----
Slash pine	JD3	J3
Cypress	----	J3
Ash type Hardwoods from Victoria, NSW highlands and Tasmania	JD3	J3
Non Ash type Hardwoods from Qld. & NSW	JD2	J2

Note: The moisture content of 'dry' timber must *not* exceed 15%. Where beams of different joint groups are to be joined together, apply the lower group to both.

2. Loads to be supported. Applied loads are to be calculated in accordance with appropriate standards. **Pryda roof, Pryda floor,** and **Pryda frame** software output reaction loads can be used for support bracket selection.

3. Thickness of beam, truss or joist to be supported and supporting beam thickness.

4. Fixing method: nails or bolts or both.

5. Hanger size from the 'Design Load Tables 25 and 26.

How to Install

Use only 35x3.15mm galvanised or stainless steel Pryda timber connector nails, Senco 50x2.87mm hardened, roll threaded gun nails (code:WGF21AZA) driven through the metal, *not* into the holes or M12 or ½ inch bolts as required to achieve the design load. Where bolts are used, a 50x50x3.0mm square or 55x3.0mm dia. round washer must be installed on the supporting beam on the face opposite to the bracket only.

TABLE 25 DESIGN LOADS
LIMIT STATE DESIGN — FLOOR LIVE LOAD + DEAD LOAD

HANGER CODE	FIXING IN SUPPORTING BEAM 'A'	BEAM THICKNESS	J4	J3	JD5	JD4	JD3
FB3860, FB5060	6 NAILS	35 MIN.	2.4	3.4	2.9	3.4	4.8
FB3590, FB3890 FB4590, FB5090	10 NAILS 2/M12 BOLTS	35 MIN. 35 45	3.6 3.1 4.0	5.1 4.8 6.1	4.5 3.9 5.0	5.4 5.4 6.5	7.5 6.5 6.5
FB35120, FB38120 FB45120, FB50120	12 NAILS 2/M12 BOLTS	35 MIN. 35 45	4.3 3.1 4.0	6.0 4.8 6.1	5.3 3.9 5.0	6.4 5.4 6.5	8.9 6.5 6.5
FB35140, FB38140 FB45140, FB50140	16 NAILS 2/M12 BOLTS	35 MIN. 35 45	5.4 3.1 4.0	7.7 4.8 6.1	7.0 3.9 5.0	8.4 5.4 6.5	11.8 6.5 6.5
FB35180, FB38180, FB45180, FB50180	20 NAILS 4/M12 BOLTS	35 MIN. 35 45	6.5 7.0 9.0	9.1 10.8 14.0	8.6 8.8 11.4	10.3 12.4 13.0	14.4 13.0 13.0
FB38220 FB50220 FB45220	26 NAILS 4/M12 BOLTS	35 MIN. 35 45	8.3 6.2 7.9	11.6 9.6 12.3	11.0 7.8 10.1	13.1 10.9 13.0	18.4 13.0 13.0
FB60130	12 NAILS 2/M12 BOLT	35 MIN. 60	4.3 4.7	6.0 6.3	5.3 5.9	6.4 6.5	8.9 6.5
FB65170	18 NAILS 4/M12 BOLT	35 MIN. 65	6.0 9.9	8.4 12.9	7.8 12.4	9.3 13.0	13.1 13.0
FB70200	20 Nails 4/M12 BOLT	35 70	6.4 10.4	9.2 13.0	8.6 13.0	10.2 13.0	14.4 13.0
FB72163	18 Nails 4/M12 BOLT	35 72	6.0 10.4	8.4 13.0	7.8 13.0	9.4 13.0	13.0 13.0
FB90200	22 Nails 4/M12 BOLT	35 90	7.1 10.4	10.0 13.0	9.4 13.0	11.2 13.0	15.7 13.0
FB94152	18 Nails 4/M12 BOLT	35 70	6.0 10.4	8.4 13.0	7.8 13.0	9.3 13.0	13.1 13.0

TABLE 26 DESIGN LOADS
LIMIT STATE DESIGN — WIND LOAD − DEAD LOAD

HANGER CODE	FIXING IN SUPPORTED BEAM 'B'	BEAM THICKNESS	J4	J3	JD5	JD4	JD3
FB3860, FB5060	3 NAILS	35 MIN.	2.3	2.9	2.9	2.9	2.9
FB3590, FB3890 FB4590, FB5090	5 NAILS	35 MIN.	3.4	4.8	4.2	4.8	4.8
FB35120, FB38120 FB45120, FB50120	6 NAILS	35 MIN.	4.0	5.7	5.0	5.8	5.8
FB35140, FB38140 FB45140, FB50140	8 NAILS	35 MIN.	5.1	7.2	6.6	7.7	7.7
FB35180, FB38180 FB45180, FB50180	10 NAILS	35 MIN.	6.1	8.6	8.1	9.6	9.6
FB38220, FB45220 FB50220	13 NAILS	35 MIN.	7.8	11.0	10.4	12.4	15.0
FB60130, FB65170 FB70200, FB72163	10 NAILS	35 MIN.	3.8	5.4	5.1	6.1	8.4
FB90200	11 NAILS	35 MIN.	6.7	9.4	8.9	10.6	10.6
FB94152	9 NAILS	35 MIN.	6.0	8.3	5.8	6.9	8.7

IMPORTANT NOTES:

a). Beam A=supporting beam, Beam B=supported beam.

b). If applied loads are based on AS/NZS1170:2002, reduce design loads above by 15%.

c). Where both bolts and nails are used together, dead or live load capacity=nails capacity+bolt(s) capacity, maximum: FB70200, FB90200 - 22.6kN, all other brackets - 26.9kN.

d). These capacities apply directly for joints in houses and on secondary beams in other structures. For joints on primary beams in structures other than houses, multiply the capacity by 0.75.

94

House Builders Series

This entirely Australian manual is thoroughly researched in co-operation with the Australian timber, brick and concrete associations. It is written in Allan Staines usual easy to comprehend style.

It has literally hundreds of clear and technically accurate drawings covering each stage of construction. The text and drawings correlate well. The manual covers the carpentry aspect in detail as well as brick veneer, cavity brick and concrete block systems.

The manual provides current trade practices and hints that help bridge the gap between theory and practice. For these reasons it is an essential class room text.

This all Australian title has large scale drawings to make it easy to understand how the various stages and components fit together. The Owner Builder is shown how to plan the house to suit the chosen allotment and the most economical methods of owner building.

You will learn how to identify and correct faulty building practices, the correct trade terms to use and how to order building products.

This manual will provide you with confidence to build a typical Australian home in weatherboard, brick veneer, cavity brick or concrete block. The manual is cross referenced with 'The Australian House Building Manual' which provides further in-depth construction information.

This step by step guide is full of easy to follow instructions. An indispensible aid for teaching Apprentices, plus quick and easy to use tables and bevels for all roof pitches from 5 degrees to 75 degrees. Bevels drawn on the page ready to transfer directly to the bevel tool.
A Builder's dream.

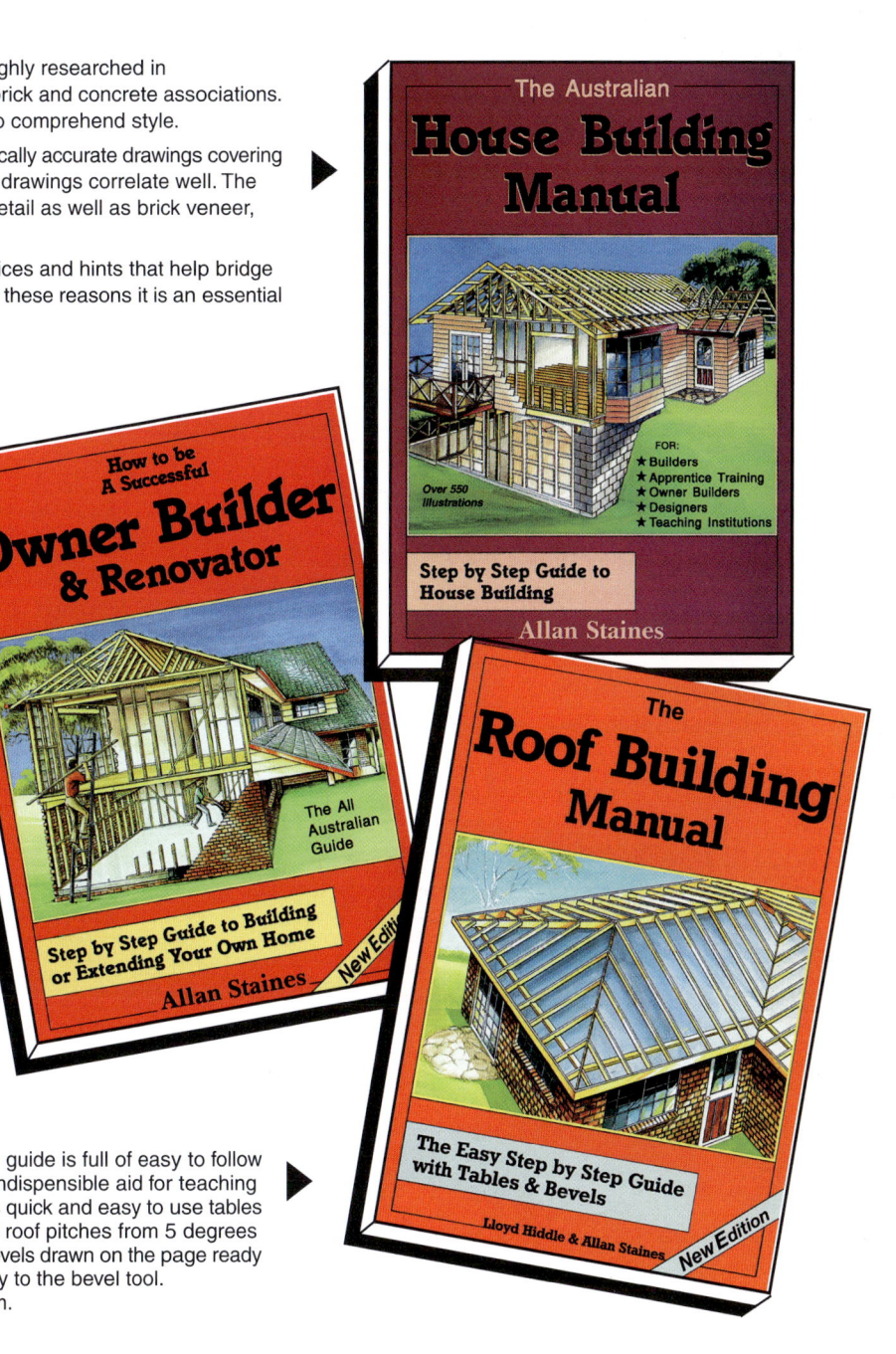

Contents of Manuals

Australian House Building Manual
Understanding:
Timber Frame Weatherboard Construction
Brick Veneer Construction
Cavity Brick Construction
Concrete Block Construction
Footing & Slab Floors
Timber Floor Framing
Timber Wall Framing
Truss Roof Construction
Plus the installation of fittings such as windows, doors, weatherboards, baths, shower recesses, mouldings and more.

How to be a Successful Owner Builder & Renovator
Understanding House Construction
Designing the House
Weatherboard Houses
Brick Veneer Houses
2 Storey Brick Veneer & Weatherboard
Split Level Houses
Double Brick
Concrete Block Masonry
Extensions & Renovations
Extending Brick Veneer Houses
Extending a Weatherboard House
Adding a Verandah or Carport
How to Supervise the Site
Raising a House
Identifying & Correcting Common Problems
Fireplace Chimney Plan

The Roof Building Manual
Roofing Basics
Roof Designs
Roofing Members & Where They Fit
Roofing Terms
The Triangle Makes it Easy
The Rafter Length
Marking Out Top Plates & Ridges
Marking Out Rafters
Cutting Out Rafters
Erecting the Roof
Miscellaneous Details
Easy to Follow Rafter Lengths, Tables & Bevels

ORDERING COUPON OVER PAGE

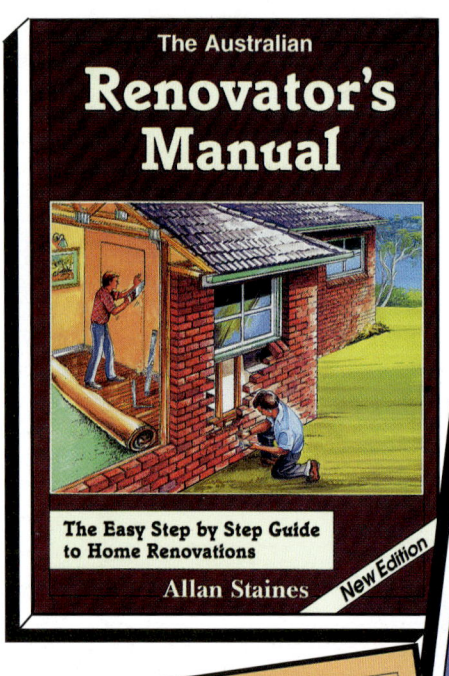

The Australian Renovator's Manual

The Easy Step by Step Guide to Home Renovations — Allan Staines

This book is specifically designed to deal with problems confronted when renovating or altering an existing dwelling. It also shows step-by-step how to accomplish popular renovation projects.

It solves problems such as rising damp, floor and wall cracking, rot in members, small kitchens and bathrooms, leaking shower recesses, and termites. It also describes how to support the roof when making openings in walls.

How to build attic rooms. Installing skylights, guttering, shelving. Replacing existing floor joists, flooring. Fixing sagging roof rafters. Installing french doors. Building carports, enclosing patios and verandahs, installing sliding patio doors, enlarging window openings. Applying Gyprock, restumping, cooling a hot house, attaching laminate and fixing laminate panelling to shower recesses. Wall and floor tiling. Painting. Gives the correct adhesives, sealants and fillers to use and much much more.

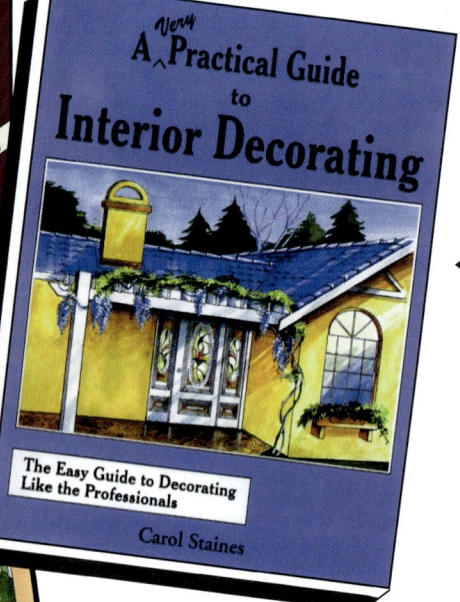

A very Practical Guide to Interior Decorating

The Easy Guide to Decorating Like the Professionals — Carol Staines

This book will teach you how to successfully decorate your home and achieve that professional decor look. Step-by-step it will show you how to avoid costly mistakes by understanding the key principles of decorating and their relevant application. It will be just like having a professional decorator on-hand to help you with much needed advice.

Chapters cover: How to discover your own decorating style, the principles of design, colour, tonal values, using neutrals, colour combinations to achieve a specific image or atmosphere. How to use pattern and texture, furniture and its placement, using decorator materials, environmentally friendly options, hands-on decorating and decorating to re-sell.

An easy to follow, well illustrated manual.

The Australian Decks & Pergolas Construction Manual

Allan Staines — 2nd Edition

This all Australian manual is packed with ideas and know how and will suit the Builder, Architect or Home DIY'er. It provides many fresh ideas in colour and easy to follow step-by-step instructions cover every procedure. From designing and drawing an acceptable plan for Councils to constructing the post supports, attaching decks or pergolas to the house, methods of handrailing and lots more. All using proper trade procedures. The easy to follow tables included have been prepared by the Timber Associations - TDA in Sydney and Timber Queensland in Brisbane. These cover footing sizes, posts, bearers, joists, deck fastening, handrailing, pergola bearers, rafters and battens. The manual is an indispensible tool in the hands of Designers and Architects.

(All Prices include GST)

Take a photocopy of this page and indicate your requirements on the order form. Books are normally return mailed within three days of receiving order.

Quantity	Title	Cost	Total	
	Decks & Pergolas Construction Manual	$22.00		*I have enclosed a cheque/money order with this coupon.*
	The Australian House Building Manual	$33.00		Name:
	Successful Owner Builder & Renovator	$27.50		Address:
	The Australian Roof Building Manual	$22.00		Phone Number:
	The Australian Renovators Manual	$27.50		Please send to:
	A Practical Guide to Interior Decorating	$22.00		Pinedale Press
Special Offer	Any Four of the above Building Books	$93.50		2 Lethbridge Court CALOUNDRA QLD 4551 Fax Number: (07) 54 919 219
	Postage & Packaging	$ 6.50		**Special Rates for Colleges.**
	Payment Enclosed			*Contact the Publisher for Reseller Prices Fax (07) 54 919 219*